None the Wiser

A Mid-Century Passage
Part One, 1932-1952

Paul Adamson

with drawings by Caroline Elkington

Judge: 'Having listened to your speech with great interest Mr. Smith, I have to confess that I find myself none the wiser.'

F. E. Smith: 'Quite so, My Lord, but I trust Your Lordship is at least better informed.'

HAYLOFT

First published 2004

Hayloft Publishing Ltd, Kirkby Stephen,
Cumbria, CA17 4DJ

tel: (017683) 42300
fax. (017683) 41568
e-mail: books@hayloft.org.uk
web: www.hayloft.org.uk

© 2004 Paul Adamson

ISBN 1 904524 25 7

A catalogue record for this book is available
from the British Library

Apart from any fair dealing for the purposes of research or private study, or criticism or review, as permitted under the Copyright, Designs & Patents Act, 1988, this publication may only be reproduced, stored or transmitted, in any form or by any means, with the prior permission in writing of the publishers, or in the case of reprographic reproduction in accordance with the terms of the licenses issued by the Copyright Licensing Agency.

Produced, printed and bound in the EU
Line drawings by Caroline Elkington

To all those former National Servicemen who served their country 1947-1962, both the willing and the unwilling. In particular memory of those who lost their lives, or were injured or were made prisoners in conflicts not of their own making.

In transit - Car Nicobar, 1951.

Acknowledgements

First and foremost I wish to thank my wife. Without her patience and understanding - and her early editing and criticism - this memoir might never have been completed. Percy Wood has been constructive and helpful in his detailed editing of the text, and hopefully he has steered me around any legal problems or libellous statements I may have made (unintentionally of course) in the course of my narrative. Eric Robson generously gave his time in reading my early manuscript and offered useful advice and encouragement. Especial thanks are due to my god-daughter, Caroline Elkington, talented artist and poet, for her line drawings that illustrate this memoir and for permission to include her poem *Hearing Things*. (When she reads this it may help in persuading her to illustrate the second volume *Still None The Wiser* the African sequel to this book.) Finally, my thanks go to the editor of the RAF Seletar Association's magazine *Searchlight* for permission to reproduce the photograph 'Jankers' in Chapter 15.

Illustrations

The author c. 1935	18
Great Aunt Sally	20
My father	30
A M Pamphlet	74
Castel Benito, Libya, April 1951.	108
On the barrack verandah, en route for the day's work	115
Chinese 'Sew-Sew'	116
The Singapore waterfront, 1951	121
Sunderland Flying Boat	127
Cathay Cinema, Singapore	133
Union Jack Club, Singapore	141
The harbour at Georgetown, Penang	143
The shoreline at Tanjong Bungah, Penang	144
The ditch where the High Commissioner, was killed	160
Selangor bandits article	163
Christmas Day menu, 1951	166
'Passive Defence' course, Fraser's Hill	170
En route to Fraser's Hill	171
Malay Police and Home Guard, Empire Day	173
Convoy assembling at Kuala Kubu Bahru	175
Armoured car escort en route to Fraser's Hill, May 1952	176
Travelling on leave	182
Travelling on duty	185
A Kubu	186
Escort detail, guarding bombs and ammo.	188
Car Nicobar en route to Ceylon	194
Author at Car Nicobar	199
Guard of Honour for visiting VIP	200
M.S. Dilwara	219
'Jankers' parade at Seletar	235
Korea, 1952	235
Suez, 1956	236

Contents

	Acknowledgments	5
	Illustrations	6
	Author's Introduction	9
1	Beginnings	16
2	Happy Days, 1932-1939	26
3	Childhood and Wartime	38
4	War and post-war School days	52
5	A Farmer's Boy	67
6	The RAF - 1950-52 - Called up and Broken Down	73
7	Picking up the Pieces	88
8	Posted!	99
9	Singapore	114
10	Seletar - Browning the Knees	125
11	North to Penang	134
12	Courses for Horses	151
13	Trains and Planes and Things	182
14	The Great Train Robbery	203
15	Homeward Bound	209
	Postscript	236
	Appendix to Book One, Notes 1-19	239

Author's Note

In writing this book it is necessary at the outset to make simultaneously a confession and a statement of intent. I confess here and now that not everything you may read in the following pages is necessarily either one hundred per cent factually true or historically correct.

Some of the events that I describe took place more than fifty years ago and also when I was a child, and I rely on childhood memory. Of the many extraordinary people that I encountered, particularly in Africa in later years, some known only briefly, many are dead. It is now impossible to recall in detail conversations or often to recall with whom or when they took place. Although I am sure that what I know to be correct is so, others who were present and who can still recall these situations will almost certainly differ in their recollections. Old friends' versions of what occurred at a particular time and place where we were present together often show up minor hiccups in my memory and gaping holes in theirs. I can also claim a legitimate excuse, common to many old West Africa hands. It is called 'Coast Memory', a debilitating condition of the brain brought about by too long an exposure to the great heat of the sun on too many hot tin roofs, too many pink gins on Saturday mornings and too many daily doses of anti-malarial pills.

In memory time telescopes and expands; total recall is both impossible and at the same time what remains is highly selective. It becomes necessary to compound one's memory with imagination. Where memory conflicts with fact then I make no excuses and indeed prefer to rely on memory. In some instances I have forgotten names, in others it is perhaps diplomatic to change them, the same with places where perhaps feelings may still be sensitive even after the passage of years. If people who may think they recognise themselves or others in situations which they prefer not to remember, or feel offended or say, 'That was not how it was,' then I apologise and assure them that no malice is intended and furthermore that I am not referring to whoever it might be thought that it could have been. Several years ago my daughter gave me a little card on which I think was printed the following: "I know that you believe you understand what you think I said, but I am not sure you realise that what you think you heard is not what I meant." Or words to that effect.

For more than thirty years I have kept a series of notebooks and disjointed and abbreviated diaries. Some of the contents are indecipherable and I have long since lost the key. As for the rest, some is of little consequence or no longer of interest, but some recall for me people, places and happenings that deserve to be remembered, if only as a piece of unimportant social history of Britain, the Far East and Africa. That about covers the confessional part of the preamble.*

My intention in writing this account is not to create a connected narrative, although there is a thread, which is myself, but to describe what it was like to be a child from a particular background in the 1930s and during the Second World War subsequently growing up and participating in the final years of the British Empire at first hand, although in a very minor role. Insignificant role playing it may have been and one was invariably powerless to influence any but the most trivial events, but I was nevertheless interested and often felt myself to be a personally involved though impotent spectator.

Times and attitudes have changed so rapidly that I and many others of my generation have been caught unawares by the pace and rapidity with which old mores and ideals are not only discarded but forgotten. G.K. Chesterton wrote in 1904: 'There is no more remarkable psychological element in history than the way in which a period can suddenly become unintelligible.' He was in fact referring to the early and mid-Victorian periods, a lapse of a mere fifty years. The key, he said, had been lost. In his own words: '...the Crystal Palace is now the temple of a forgotten creed.' In more recent times I believe the same quantum leap has taken place. The 1930s, the 1940s and the 1950s with their beliefs and attitudes which in themselves evolved so rapidly with the catalyst of the war years, are now part of L.P. Hartley's 'Foreign Land' where things were done so differently, done in a manner that is often incomprehensible to many of those born and brought up since those times. I have heard it suggested that the twentieth century did not really begin in Britain until 1940. Certainly most of the older generation responsible for my upbringing were themselves the products of an Edwardian or Victorian education

---

* Alert readers may notice that this introduction at times refers to incidents not necessarily covered in this book, which concludes in 1952. The second volume of this memoir entitled *Still None the Wiser, (1952-1967)* takes the reader to West Africa (along with the author) and will be published later.

although they were 'modern' in their own outlook and in their own time. In that respect I sit uneasily at the end of the twentieth century amid its accumulated high-tech gadgetry and rapidly changing standards and beliefs. I find myself in the situation where the world in which I still have my being is fast becoming unrecognisable. I fear that one day I shall awake to find myself not just in a strange world but on an alien planet.

So much of value has now been discarded by the present generation without their being aware that it ever existed. Our modern 'heroes' acquire fame and celebrity unhampered by achievement. Those whom the younger generations aspire to emulate are as likely to die of drug-induced vomit or suicide than of natural causes. A real hero of this country's past, the great Duke of Wellington, that great reactionary die-hard soldier and statesman to whom this country owes so much, once said: 'Progress is not always forward. Change is not necessarily always for the better,' and as Field Marshal Montgomery said when reading the lesson in church: '...and the Lord said unto Moses... and I for one, wholeheartedly agree with Him.' Is it necessarily reactionary to regret the passing of differing values abandoned in the avalanche of progress? In my later life I have frequently been accused of being reactionary in times of ever increasing rapidity of change, because of the frequency with which I have urged the need to change only those things that it is necessary to change and to leave alone those things that do not need changing. The Americans put it more succinctly: 'If it ain't broke, don't fix it!'* But then they ignore it just as we do. Continually re-inventing the wheel has always been one of mankind's failings and each generation in its turn is obsessed with the need to discard the old and to bring in the new.

The attitudes, manners, habits and patterns of thought that I write about may surprise and shock present day sensibilities. With age I have myself discarded much that I once firmly held true. History, example and experience have changed me with the passing of the years. It must also be understood that different times have different rules and that what is held wrong today was not necessarily so the day before yesterday. The immediate post-war years were a time of hope. A Brave New World was possible. Exploding populations, a damaged environment, famines, the destruction and desertification of vast areas of the globe, diminishing and

---

* A more modern version of this is more likely to be 'It it ain't bust - fiddle with it until it is!'

threatened wildlife, the rise of despotic dictators in newly independent countries, these were all in the future. Had we in 1950 realised that in the first half of the twentieth century mankind had used (and largely wasted) more of the Earth's non-renewable resources than in the whole of previous history - it would have been interpreted then as 'Progress'. Such considerations did not really affect the mind of a young man launching himself upon the world at the age of eighteen in 1950. As an earlier example of such changing attitudes I have long treasured the memory of John Newton, the pious and proselytising eighteenth century Liverpool merchant who composed the words of that ever popular hymn *How Sweet the Name of Jesus Sounds in a Believer's Ear*, as he awaited the overdue arrival of his latest shipment of slaves from Africa. I am not trying to tell my reader that things were better in the past - they were often totally and incomprehensibly different. Napoleon Bonaparte once said: 'If you want to understand a man, you have to know what was going on in the world when he was twenty years old.' This book tries to explain a small part of that distant time.

Much of what I have to write in the later period (the second part of these memoirs covering 1952-1967) concerns West Africa during the last days of colonialism. It may be about Africa but it is not necessarily about Africans, it is about Africa from a very particular and perhaps peculiar, view point, a West Africa that is now long gone together with those years when the British Empire faded into history. It is also about the early period of post-colonialism and independence that sadly and tragically in some instances preceded a descent into profligacy, despotism and economic swamp lands. It is a period almost impenetrable to the generations born and educated since that time: indeed it is just as obscure to many of my contemporaries who led more conventional lives and whose careers followed more well-worn paths.

'Old Coasters' (as seasoned West Africa hands were known) after a while rarely reminisce - except with each other - about the more outlandish episodes that made up the warp and woof of their daily lives, that is to say they talk about them only to close friends and to those acquaintances who will neither question their veracity, nor in some cases their sanity. This attitude can be summed up by the experience of a friend who left West Africa in the 1960s to work in New York. When I saw him some two years later when he briefly re-visited the Coast, I couldn't stop him talking, it was as if some overstrained pressure valve had suddenly burst. After some months in America he began to realise that he was being regarded as a liar or as an unreliable and eccentric oddball, thereby placing his career in danger. The simple reason was that when he regaled his sober-minded Wall Street business colleagues with stories of everyday life in West Africa, he was seen by others as a victim of wild and fictional hallucinations. He therefore bottled-up his past life as if it were some previous criminal experience to be hidden away. When he met any old friends it all had to come bursting out from the floodgates of memory and common experience. Poor chap, perhaps he will be able to recall some of his exploits, triumphs and disasters which may (or may not) figure in these pages.

'When dealing with Africa you can't write about the place or the people with a logical mind. You have to suspend judgement and education and see it afresh.' So in 1987 said Ben Okri, then a new Nigerian writer making a name in London. That really sums up the problem. Truth is stranger than fiction. It is also weirder, more fantastic and tortuous in construction than we can generally credit. It is often pointless, self-defeating, circuitous and amazing. On a rare occasion it may help to achieve understanding. Africa is a harsh environment, the land itself, the people, the animals, all exist in a world away from the sheltered life we lead in the West. I look backwards sometimes in amazement, sometimes touched with guilt - and with regret - but things were different more than forty years ago.

If these following pages are memoirs, as I suppose they are, then both reader and I must tread warily to avoid the traps - or perhaps it is better to acknowledge them and trigger them off with due circumspection. Two quotations will serve to illustrate the pitfalls. As the late Robert Morley wrote in *The Pleasures of Age:* 'In writing memoirs, it is not in the commercialism that the pleasure necessarily resides. That could be considered a bonus. The pleasure is in conjuring up the past - and amending it when the spirit takes one - that is so satisfying.' The second comes from George Santayana: 'A man's memory may almost become the art of his continually varying and misrepresenting his past according to his interests in the present.' There is perhaps a third reason - to put matters straight with God by revealing the Truth. 'Ah yes,' you may say, 'but surely God knows the Truth already?' 'Agreed, but not this version.' There may be quite a number of people still alive, who knew me forty and more years ago in West Africa or elsewhere, who will say, 'Why is the old bastard, saying that about X, or Y, he left out that time when he himself... etc., etc.' Well, one would say that wouldn't one? It is the author's privilege to leave out the deeply embarrassing moments, or those split seconds that one would give almost anything to retrieve, to have that second chance. There are also matters of shame and regret, that long-dead albatross that we all carry with us hung around our necks. If I choose not to reveal certain matters, that is my concern, not the reader's. All I will say as a pertinent reminder is that life is not a dress rehearsal: there are few second chances. I have changed over the years. Many things that I did do, I would that I never had. In describing events of forty years and more past, it must not be assumed that I always approve - it is just the way things were.

Finally, as the years advance, I feel that I am becoming a member of an endangered species - not quite on the basis of a condom salesman in the Vatican - but simply in becoming old. My past is so much longer than my foreseeable future. The years stretch behind, full of incident and people and places, many now blurred - names and faces half-forgotten. But at least I know they existed and happened. The future has suddenly become finite, constantly shrinking. All of us, if we survive to become old, become different people, but by some strange enchantment we find that we have inherited a young person's memories. Life has one certain outcome of which little warnings, twinges, aches, bring to mind the fragility of our existence. Life has but one entrance and ten thousand exits; we all pass through many doors in a lifetime and before that final door opens I intend to try and bring some of those early memories to life in these pages. (This paragraph contains a series of clichés - it is a cliché in itself to say that such aphorisms are the distillation of mankind's wisdom and experience through the ages - so I will let them stand.)

I therefore ask the reader to accept the following history as in essence a basically truthful account of a personal Odyssey from the days of my pre-war childhood until I finally left Africa in 1967. I shall preface my tale with the traditional disclaimer of the Ashanti story teller as he begins his tale:

'Ye 'nse se, nse se o.'*

Translation: *We do not really mean, we do not really mean (that what we are going to say is true).

** This is my story which I have related, if it be sweet, or if it be not sweet, take some elsewhere and let some come back to me.

Author's Note

When he has finished the story, he concludes:

'M'anansesem a metaoye yi, se eye de o, se ennye de o, momfa bi nko na momfa bi mmera.'**

This is simply how your average academic ethnographer-cum-anthropologist would interpret it, instead of saying literally, 'This is how it is, take it or leave it!' as the storyteller intends. I think I shall direct my tale at a slightly less elevated pitch, perhaps somewhere half-way between that of the high-toned ethnographer and that of the BBC's *Listen With Mother*: 'Are you sitting comfortably? Then I'll begin.'

I shall leave you to be the judge.

This is my story.

Note: The name 'Walter Plinge' is, I believe, a fictitious name used to pad out theatre programmes to conceal the fact that one actor may be playing several roles. To avoid giving offence to any living person, some of my characters in these reminiscences might be taken as composite caricatures, see also 'Hamish MacPlinge', 'Mimsie Borogrove', 'Fingal O'Plinge', et alia, (particularly in Africa). Corporal 'Jonah' Plinge is based on several RAF NCOs of that ilk. The incidents described are all true to the best of my recollection, compiled both from memory and my contemporary notes.

1
BEGINNINGS - A LITTLE FAMILY HISTORY

'Where shall I begin, please your Majesty?'
'Begin at the beginning,' the King said gravely,
'and go on until you come to the end: then stop.'
Lewis Carroll, *Alice in Wonderland*

I can really only go as far back as my grandparents, on both sides of the family, with any degree of certainty. It is a sad fact that by the time the average person becomes interested in his or her ancestors, usually in middle age, those elderly relatives who would have known the answers are either dead, or have forgotten what little they knew about their own antecedents - or they have become ga-ga. To trace one's heredity then becomes a major exercise in time and cost. I am interested, but more or less satisfied with what I know. So it will be left to my children, if they want to know more to dig it all up again for themselves.

It always strikes me that when one looks at a particular family tree how chancy and haphazard the whole thing is. So many marriages, so many children, so many generations, so many deaths and often in so short a time, that the task of tracing a direct line of descent through the tangle of a thicket of devious branches is an entirely subjective exercise. Female lines, male lines, eldest sons, younger daughters, inheritances, cousins emerging and re-emerging, (how often it seems that close cousins married before the saving dawn of the bicycle age), sprigs and twigs!

A glance at the pedigree of our dear old long-departed dog reveals that a total of thirty individual German short-haired pointers are named in going back a mere four generations, to take it back one more to a fifth, then adds a further thirty-two - perhaps no more than twenty years have passed. Whose canine characteristics in particular did she inherit? Give a family list of similar dimensions to a human genealogist - and what would he do? By taking it further in human terms, doubling the figure each generation and allowing four generations to a century very soon you have over a thousand progenitors in only ten generations. By the fourteenth century you could have eight million ancestors - or more properly pluralist progenitors! Your genealogist? Why, he would simply chart a single track back through those multiplying numbers via the successful, the famous, the wealthy, with excursions into diverging bloodlines here and there - in other words to winkle out the most flattering ancestry possible to please the client. But what of the black sheep, the proper bastards both illegitimate and legitimate, the barren dispossessed, the lunatics, the whores, the libertines, the fools and oafish dunces, the thieves, swindlers and murderers, let alone the fourth cousins thrice removed! Do we not have all their genes as well? By those methods, were our records accurate, could we not all claim Royal blood by now? As some might have it, does not the blood of Christ run through all our veins from Ages long past? All mankind are cousins (umpteen times removed) whether you like it or not - and when cousin marries cousin the resulting progeny are frequently less than perfect. We can take some comfort from the Chinese who sensibly allege that one cannot have a care either for ones' ancestors or for ones' descendants for more than seven generations in each direction. Depending on one's upbringing either we are each of us at the apex of a reversed pyramid (or is it a lozenge) at the dim and distant base of which are Adam and Eve - or a pair of East African ape-like creatures who have just given up walking on their knuckles. Chance rather than destiny is the more likely to have delivered us into our present predicament.

If you have followed my argument, (I agree there are apparent inconsistencies and flaws which can be simply rationalised in mathematical and geometrical terms but they also make my brain hurt so I will go no further here) you will understand why I am content to delve no deeper than those layers I have uncovered or have been led to believe existed.

My mother's family, the grand-paternal Doughtys, probably emerged from Shropshire and the Welsh Marches. My uncle Gray claimed to have traced the family back to the Battle of Bosworth Field where one worthy ancestor, Thomas, was knighted on the spot by Henry Tudor (had the battle been won by Richard Crookback we would of course have heard no more of this). Yet another Thomas Doughty, having signed on the Golden Hind as 'gentleman', was hanged by his friend Sir Francis Drake, for treason, in a well documented episode on Tierra del Fuego during the latter's global circumnavigation. In between and up to my grandfather Thomas Doughty's time they established themselves as Shropshire yeomen in and around the Severn River valley, although one branch (a

17

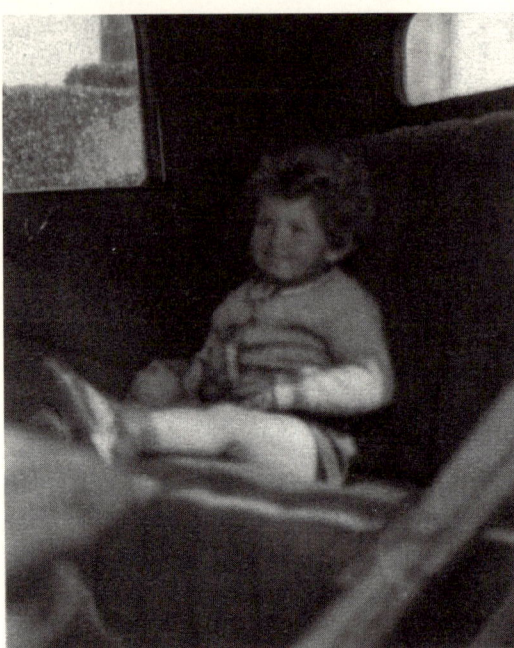
The author circa 1935, obviously well satisfied with life in general, in back seat of the Chrysler.

branch again) went broke waiting for a missing ship or two lost on passage from their West Indies plantations. My uncle Gray had much later vainly tried to establish grounds for a claim to former family lands in the West Indies.

The Severn Valley - Coalbrookdale, Ironbridge, Broseley and Jackfield - was a good place to be in on the ground floor of the Industrial Revolution spear-headed by Abraham Darby and the other iron-masters and master potters of the second half of the eighteenth century. Coalbrookdale in the eighteenth and early nineteenth centuries was leading the cutting edge of contemporary technology. The techniques of casting iron developed there were the equivalent of late twentieth century nuclear physics. Cast iron was in certain circles considered to be the Holy Grail of their modern world. In Coalbrookdale itself, cast-iron door and window frames were commonplace, kerb stones were fabricated from iron as were virtually indestructible tombstones - still to be seen in the Dale's churchyards in my childhood. I was once told that even sets of dentures and false teeth were moulded from cast iron. It is not too far-fetched to conjecture that had the valley remained in business until the 1960s the descendants of Abraham Darby would have prepared their blueprints to tender for the first moon ship to be constructed from cast iron, the rockets fuelled by the finest coke from the local furnaces.

By the end of the nineteenth century my grandfather, Thomas, born in 1863 at Jackfield, the third of fourteen children, had come to own clay pits and a successful tile works near his birthplace. He was a well known gentleman cricketer, a Mason and a county councillor (Conservative - it goes without saying). He and my grandmother lived in a large house, called The Tuckies, high above the river at Ironbridge, with their five children - including my mother, in well-heeled comfort until the advent of the First World War sowed the seeds of disaster. The men who worked the deep clay pits and the coal mines (whose dangerous and derelict shafts and drifts still honeycombed the area in my childhood) went off to war. Demand for decorative tiles slipped away as fashions changed, the pumps broke down for want of skilled men, the pits flooded and the whole industry of the area, never recovering from these setbacks, slowly declined into dereliction. Thomas Doughty died in 1939, my grandmother once showed me his passport. Her husband's occupation was shown as 'gentleman.'

Grandfather Doughty was one of fourteen children and part of an extensive family. The more prosperous of the mid-Victorians were prolific breeders with a high survival rate. There was great-uncle Jackson,* a favourite of my grandmother, who took his father's best hunter, and rode off to the Boer War with the Imperial Yeomanry. Alas, only to be killed by a Boer marksman - on a Sunday notwithstanding, when the dour, covenanting Afrikaners of the Dutch Reformed Church were reputed (incorrectly) to observe a cease-fire while they read their bibles. The horse was never returned, kept by the colonel in settlement of a debt of honour, or so it was said.

There was great-uncle Theophilus, a genuine roistering black sheep, a great favourite of my last and sole surviving aunt - no mean roisterer herself in her own time. Theophilus took off for Australia and then eventually to America either to escape his creditors or to make his fortune and was heard of no more. There were great-aunts Sally and Polly, both profoundly deaf from the age of seventeen when stricken by scarlet fever, but both sharp and wickedly witty into their old age, keen participants and acute observers of the human comedy, and swift to deliver a slap or a clout with their ear-trumpets if they thought any child was taking liberties behind their back. They were a fairly robust lot who gave and took a lot from life.

---

* In 1954 when I told my family I was departing for the Gold Coast in West Africa, my grandmother asked me to visit great-uncle Jackson's grave. She suggested that if I had a Saturday afternoon to spare I should jump on a bus and nip down to South Africa and pay my respects on her behalf.

My maternal grandmother Matilda, always known as Tillie, was born a Pritchard, also in Shropshire. At the time she married in 1898, she and two of her sisters were perforce the proprietors of a genteel girls' school, Ellesmere Ladies' College. They had been left comfortably off by their father, but their solicitor having made off with the bulk of the money from their father's estate they were obliged to turn their hands to teaching. I have a charming painting of the college depicted on a Coalport plate (what else?) of the period, along with paintings of the other houses she lived in during her long life. On the day of her marriage to my grandfather it was said that the bridegroom's employees took the horses from the shafts of their wedding carriage and drew it themselves through the streets.

My grandmother Doughty as befitted a genteel schoolmarm spoke good French, she was a talented pianist and craftswoman - she had made gloves for Queen Mary; she carved in wood, making delicate stools and tables. A late Victorian paragon, she was kind but strict, a pillar of local society and imbued with a strong sense of duty and of character.

During World War Two, already well over sixty years of age, my grandmother Doughty was instrumental in setting up the first Ironbridge Citizens' Advice Bureau. She also organised and

Great aunt Sally with her ear trumpet.

administered the local Child Welfare Clinics. To her eternal and considerable credit she was also one of the very first (self-taught) occupational therapists to help the wounded and often badly burned patients at the RAF Hospital at Cosford. For all the war years, and after, she made the difficult journey by bus and train two or more days a week from Coalbrookdale to Cosford. I very much doubt if she was paid for her work. She never spoke of the shock and pain she must have encountered in dealing with the desperately burned and mutilated men she helped. When she died in the early 1960s, in her late eighties, and was taken back to Coalbrookdale for burial in the family plot at Broseley, I was told that the roads and streets were lined with sorrowing and respectful mourners.

I don't know that my grandmother had a sense of humour, I cannot recall any sign of it. But that may be doing her an injustice. Although small in stature and in her later years stout and dumpy like Queen Victoria, with a fine aquiline nose she had an imposing presence that commanded respect. I find it a little daunting that I can sometimes see her likeness, and also that of my mother in my own daughter's features.

My father's family, although of similar social standing, had a background in solid trade and the professions, in seafaring and engineering. There was a strong Bohemian streak kept under strict rein, but which surfaced from time to time in 'art', in slightly 'raffish' and sometimes scandalous behaviour, unusual Christian names and occasional outbursts of eccentricity among my paternal uncles and aunts, perhaps the result of consanguinity, my paternal grandparents being first cousins to each other. It was said by my father and others that his maternal (my great) grandfather and grandmother did not speak to each other for more than twenty years, but communicated by notes left around their house. One must assume in the absence of better information that this situation only arose after the birth of their children.

My grandfather Alexander Adamson, who died before I was born, had been a marine engineer. Before he married he had travelled widely; my grandmother's house was sprinkled with exotic curios, spear-shaped and fretted canoe paddles from the South Pacific, strings of Chinese copper 'cash', strange sea-shells, tasselled Turkish and Indian slippers, odd little bits and pieces fascinating to a child. An old photograph album that surfaced when my last paternal aunt died contains a multitude of sepia photos of stern, bewhiskered sailors in peaked cap and brass-buttoned reefer jackets, pictures of ancient steamships, of pretty ladies with bustles and hats and parasols - some of whom look remarkably familiar. But who are they? Where were they and when? Some of the pictures have names pencilled lightly on the reverse - there is nothing more. No titles beneath the picture, nothing. All quite meaningless. All long gone to the grave.

My grandfather must have swallowed the anchor after marriage. He founded the Liverpool Refrigeration Company which specialised in its early days in marine refrigeration. His six children, four girls and two boys, were brought up in the family house at Corwen in North Wales away from the hurly-burly of Liverpool while the business prospered. From what my father Ivan (you see what I mean about unusual Christian names - their house was also named Ivanhof) told me, he enjoyed an idyllic childhood, fishing for trout and salmon in the River Dee (he was a life-long angler of great skill) and, because of being English, having to fight and forever scrapping with the local Welsh children.

My grandmother Matilda, (yet another Matilda) was a daughter of Sir Richard Wise, a Cornish engineer from the West Country - so being a first cousin of my grandfather his family roots also were probably in the south west. I know remarkably little about her in spite of the fact that I spent two or three years with her during the war. She was then a fearsome old lady, tall, beaky-nosed, with a screechy voice, smelling of lavender and mothballs. She laughed quite a lot, had eccentric and fixed ideas about most things and gave a hard time to my aunt Fairlie who looked after her, and to my father who paid most of her expenses. I loved her. Some of her quaint and irrational opinions I have had the greatest difficulty in shaking off in later life.

In her very old age she became quite batty and was a great trial to everyone close to her until her death in 1954. From the time my grandfather died in 1928 she lived in North Wales, near Betws-y-Coed, in a house built and designed by another daughter, the eldest girl Dorothy, who before her early death at the age of forty was well on her way to becoming a painter of repute. Had Dorothy lived longer and her output been greater (being her own strongest critic she burned most of her earlier work shortly before she died, my elder brother remembers helping her to do this in the old stone cottage she had as a studio up in the woods), she would have earned a more enviable reputation than she already has. Her paintings that survive are both desirable and sought after.

My father Ivan, the eldest son, was born in 1899. Brought up in

Corwen as I have already said, on completion of his secondary education he was finally conscripted into the Army in 1917. My sister says that she was told when a child, that in 1914 aged fifteen, he ran away from home to join the Army but was recovered from the clutches of the recruiting sergeant by my grandmother. Because of his technical abilities, one assumes, he became a sergeant in the newly formed Machine Gun Corps and later served as a driver/gunner in the early primitive tanks then coming into service. I know that he served in France before the end of the war, but whether or not he saw action I never knew. He would say little or nothing of his own service but would speak of other men's and of friends' experiences. My elder sister, who has a vivid imagination but whose own recollections of childhood add to my own memories, says that she heard hushed and whispered suggestions of some incident, a cruel accident when men were crushed and killed beneath his tank.

Immediately following the Great War my father resumed his studies for an engineering degree at Liverpool University. In his second or third year he was obliged, as was the practice, to undergo a basic engineer's apprenticeship, telescoped into a year. At that time the Coalbrookdale Iron Works was manufacturing castings for my grandfather Adamson's flourishing refrigeration company. I suspect, although he never said so, that my father chose the the venue because of the proximity of excellent fishing in the River Severn.

One summer's day then, while fishing above a bend of the river, further down the bank from where my father plied his rod and line someone either fell in, or swimming was in danger of drowning - the Severn being a notoriously treacherous stream. Between my father and the drowning person now vanishing downstream lay a rowing boat drawn up on the grassy bank around which sat my grandparent Doughtys enjoying a family picnic with three of their younger children, of whom my mother, then aged seventeen, (or eighteen - in later years she 'interfered' with her birth certificate) was the eldest present. On raising the alarm my father had cast aside his fishing rod. Running down the bank he swiftly commandeered both boat and my mother-to-be as crew. Setting off down stream in their role as lifeboat I suppose presaged their somewhat stormy life together. It was certainly no firm basis for a marriage. Having rescued and returned to dry land the distressed person (whose gender and identity remain a mystery - but whose presence on that fateful day was so vital to my very existence), my father rowed back up stream to return my mother once more to the bosom of her family. Reporting their task completed, for the action had taken place out of sight beyond the river bend, my father was duly quizzed and invited for tea on the following day, Sunday.

It had to be a Saturday when this dramatic first encounter occurred, for my father, socially speaking, could not have fished openly on the Sabbath, neither would my grandparents have mounted a pleasure excursion on the river. During the remainder of the week my father would have either worked or busied himself at his studies. On such simple hypotheses are scholarly researches based.

I doubt if my father had the slightest inkling at the age of twenty-one as he was then, of what risky, uncharted waters he was embarking on when he presented himself for afternoon tea on that Sunday. I have to assume that my grandparents had done some lightning checks on my father's social acceptability since the previous meeting. They must also have spoken to their daughter Marjorie to assess whether or not she found the young man who had swept her off down-river acceptable as a suitor. What happened next, either before or after tea I do not know, but my grandfather took my father aside into the study. Sitting him down, he coolly informed him that having 'compromised' his daughter by being alone with her in the rowing boat down the river, out of sight and unchaperoned for some fifteen minutes, as her parents, he and my grandmother wished to be informed immediately as to his intentions. My father, young, handsome - as a child he always appeared to me as a mix of Anthony Eden and Clark Gable - must have been rocked to his heels had he not already been seated, no doubt already stirred by my mother at the age of eighteen or nineteen who was extremely attractive. What else could he reply but that his 'intentions' were completely 'honourable'. Shortly afterwards my mother and father, on such flimsy grounds, on such short acquaintance, unsuitably young and temperamentally ill-matched, became engaged and the following year on the 16 July 1921 were married in the Parish Church of Coalbrookdale. For which fact I remain profoundly grateful to them both. They were finally divorced twenty-seven years later in 1948.

My sister says that for a few weeks before my arrival, she and my brother were sent from the family home in Wallasey, (my father was now running the business his own father had founded in Liverpool) to stay with the Doughty grandparents in Coalbrookdale. On my birthday my grandmother came to them and said, brandishing a telegram, 'You have a little brother!' My elder siblings looked at her in some astonishment and said as one, 'No! - No! There must be some mistake. We don't have a brother!' My grandmother then read out the telegram, 'Look! It says here: 'IT'S A BOY STOP MAISIE."

'There now!' said my sister, 'I said you were wrong - it's Auntie Maisie who's had the baby! Not our Mummie at all.'

I was born on the longest day of the year in 1932, the 21st June, in Wallasey, Cheshire. What else occurred at that time I have no idea. I was the youngest of my parents' three children, having an elder sister born in 1922 and a brother in 1925.

2
HAPPY DAYS - 1932-1939

Childhood is the kingdom where nobody dies.
Nobody that matters, that is.
Edna St. Vincent Millay

There is no clear recollection of the march of time in those pre-war days of childhood in Wallasey. Certain memories stand out, but unlike my sister I cannot claim to remember being born. My earliest memory is of being in my pram, while 'Jonah' (Lily Jones) - my mother's 'companion' and my nursemaid gossiped with a group of workmen leaning on their shovels at the roadside on the edge of a large hole. I gave vent to a loud, weary sigh - probably exasperated with Jonah for ceasing to propel my conveyance. The workmen burst into roars of laughter, probably interpreting my tedious sighing as an expression of sympathy for the heavy labour involved in their excavations. I remember being distinctly put out and annoyed by their laughter.

According to my mother I was a paragon of a baby, this reputation unfortunately was not substantiated in later years by either my ten year old sister or my brother, then seven. I was probably spoiled at their expense, being the youngest by several years. My mother insisted that I was potty-trained by six months and after one year I could take the top off a boiled egg single-handed. I cannot confirm either of these facts.

Jonah my nursemaid had been taken on by my mother at the age of fifteen or sixteen, from an orphanage. I have the fondest memories of her and the photographs of our pre-war family holidays at Llanbedrog in North Wales on the beach show a smiling, cheerful young woman, short in stature and clearly of generous spirit. The last time I saw Jonah was after the war, when aged fourteen, I went with my mother on a seaside summer holiday with Jonah and her own two young adopted boys. She had married in Birmingham during the war and was herself unable to have children.

Memories of these times do not come flooding back. My few recollections are both episodic and highly selective. The sun shone as it always does in childhood. Our home in Wallasey was a large house (although memory can be deceptive) with a driveway and an extensive garden - in which my constant ambition was to dig holes in the soft soil of the vegetable patch, deep and capacious enough for personal concealment. There was a roomy double garage with an inspection pit, where my father kept both his American Indian motorcycle and his two cars, the larger of the two, a Chrysler, sporting a radiator cap cast in bronze in the form of a winged Pegasus - the work of his elder sister Dorothy, the artist and painter. We must have been comfortably off for I can remember the

gardener and the Guy Fawkes' fireworks displays in the garden - during which my father discharged huge and ostentatious five-shilling rockets! As well as the cars and a motorcycle, indicative in themselves of the comfortable status enjoyed by my parents, the house had both a large refrigerator and a 'walk-in' freezer (neither being common domestic fittings in the 1930s) in which from time to time were kept huge blocks of delicious chocolate-covered mint and vanilla ice-cream, no doubt my father's 'perks' as managing director of the Liverpool Refrigeration Company. There was of course a telephone - very much an indication of status in those pre-war times.

We had neighbours who I remember well. At the top of our garden was another large house which fronted an adjacent road. Here lived the

Trelevan family, two daughters the ages of my brother and sister, the father Bert, I think must have been a business associate in some way of my father. Amy, his wife was my mother's close friend. As far as I was concerned the major attractions were Mickey, their spotted dalmatian dog and their dovecote at the back of the house from which Bert would extract pigeons' eggs for his breakfast, accompanied by slices of fresh pineapple to be consumed on summer mornings in his garden. Their own large car was equipped with long running boards and a 'dickie' seat in which I was sometimes ensconced on summer Sunday mornings when both families would drive to the 'Derby' open-air swimming pool on the Wallasey sea front. The older children would ride on the running-boards like G-men bodyguards in the films - Mickey the spotted dalmatian dog running alongside as we cruised the empty roads. This house was very badly damaged by German bombs in 1941, my father in Liverpool on business at that time, drove over in the early morning in the immediate aftermath of a heavy air raid to check their welfare. He found their house abandoned and a neighbouring house with all the occupants dead and a badly shocked and injured child lying unattended in the road outside. The Trelevan family were all safe elsewhere.

To the right of the driveway of our house, The Limes, leading to St. George's Road was the house of Maisie Lewis - the 'Auntie' May, or Maisie of the telegram announcing my birth (which my brother and sister had rejected as being too far-fetched). Maisie Lewis was a widow, a keen bridge player and another close friend of my mother. She had two sons, Teddy, the elder boy who was my godfather was a Lieutenant in the Navy, having entered via Dartmouth. By 1939 he was First Lieutenant on the destroyer *HMS Keith*, a sister ship of Mountbatten's *HMS Kelly*. When we moved to London in the year before the outbreak of war, I remember visiting his ship in dock at Chatham and being chided to doff my school cap to the quarter-deck as we boarded. *HMS Keith* was sunk at Dunkirk in 1940 after taking a German bomb down the funnel. In 1941 my godfather was on the battlecruiser *HMS Hood* when a plunging shell from the German raider *Bismarck* penetrated the main magazine. Teddy Lewis was not one of the three survivors. A few days before his death, his mother was playing bridge with two or three neighbours in her house during an air-raid. Later that same night she was killed outright when a bomb made a direct hit on the third house she had taken refuge in during the night's bombing. Neither son nor mother knew of the other's death.

Leonard, 'Auntie' May's younger son, joined the RAF and eventually served as a glider pilot and survived the war. He remained a family friend until his recent death. I can remember as no more than a babe-in-arms being carried to 'Auntie' May's bedroom while she and my mother discussed the most intimate and personal matters, May wearing pink silk cami-knickers while she brushed her hair at her dressing table. Mothers of very young children should remember that small children are often far more aware of what is going on around them than they are given credit for. Childhood is the time of life when the mind is hyper-receptive to outside images.

At the age of I suppose, four or five, I was sent to the nearby Dame School run by two sisters, the Misses Polly and Annie Perkins - presumably to be taught the Three Rs. I am sure I had already learned to read by that age. The only image remaining with me is of the lavishly equipped percussion band for the infants. My well-known defective sense of rhythm first surfaced at this period - from playing the tin drum I was relegated to the triangle, then to the tambourine, even that simple instrument proving beyond my abilities to hold a beat, I then became the band's conductor, waving the baton up, down and sideways in a strict 'One, Two, Three' sequence to my entire satisfaction.

In 1937 or 1938, I could have been no more than six at the most, when I was sent to the boarding school, which my brother Peter, then aged twelve, was already attending. Elleray School was not far away in Birkenhead. I have few memories except of being forced to eat the fat and gristle served with our meals, an ordeal previously spared me; no doubt on the worthy principle that starving millions elsewhere in the world would be grateful to receive it. Suggestions to the effect that food parcels should be made up on the spot and dispatched post-haste to the needy are never met with the respect that such simple solutions demand. I think we must have been well-treated. I certainly do not remember otherwise, and of course, having an elder brother on the spot must have been re-assuring. It was at this school that I won a cup for boxing, presumably having bludgeoned some other more puny tot into submission with my flailing fists. This was my sole sporting accomplishment for many years and I falsely based my own estimation of my physical abilities on this achievement; no doubt fostered by my brother who was indeed a boxer of some renown when he later went on to St. Paul's School.

The English, rather than the British, are a most curious nation in the manner in which the middle classes long felt it necessary to educate their children, detaching them from the bosom of the family at a tender age and placing them in the care of paid semi-professional child minders - often in cold and uncomfortable converted country houses in near primitive conditions. There can be no doubt that this enforced separation had a deep and lasting effect on the psyche of many children from which some of them may have never recovered.

In my case, going off to boarding school heralded the end of a childhood family life, for when we moved in 1938 to London, we were in the last family home I was to enjoy for many years. The outbreak of war in September of the following year split up our family as effectively as a bomb burst. It never fully re-assembled thereafter.

Before all this happened, back in Wallasey, I remember our long summer holidays as sheer bliss. My father took a house each year for the month of August at Llanbedrog, near Abersoch in North Wales. He owned a twenty-five foot fishing boat, the *Water Gypsy,* with a cuddy, an unreliable Kelvin engine and a dipping lug-sail, kept moored for most of the year at Pwllheli. In the high summer months he pursued the tope and porbeagle sharks of Cardigan Bay with relentless zeal, inspired by the only books he ever seemed to read, the true-life big-game fishing stories of Zane Grey and Mitchell Hedges. His one true love however was fishing for sea-trout, mainly at night, in the swift, dark waters of the Conway river near Betws-y-Coed where my grandmother and Aunt Fairlie lived. In

My father's passion was fishing.

1937 or 1938 he did figure in the pages of *Country Life* having landed a record sea-trout of twenty-one pounds. Other family friends joined us at Llanbedrog and I suppose my father must have attended to his business in Liverpool during the long summer weeks while we paddled and bathed and picnicked around our beach hut, fishing for prawns and shrimps for our tea in the tidal pools along the sunlit shore.

In 1938 my father's business failed in the tail-end of the Depression. The plant and machinery were sold to another major refrigeration company and my father was taken on by another former competitor as sales director based near Park Royal in Middlesex. The entire family minus Jonah, then moved to a large basement flat in De Vere Gardens, no more than a few minutes' walk from Kensington Gardens in fashionable West London. We still cannot have been too poor for my brother and I immediately became day boys at Colet Court Preparatory School in Hammersmith and this area of Kensington was definitely up-market even then. The mansion block in which we lived not only boasted a lift - which delighted me - but also a caretaker to clean the hallways and staircases, one Mrs. Bowen, who if my mother was out during the day, would make us delicious fish pies.

London, in particular Kensington Gardens, Hyde Park and the Serpentine, the Natural History and Science Museums of South Kensington, were a delight to a small boy newly rescued from his first boarding school. There were trips to the Round Pond to sail model boats and to fly kites on windy days. I didn't mind moving to London at all, this was much more fun, feeding ducks in the park and allowed to stay at home in my own bed again. There was a sense of unease abroad, of which I began to be aware, as deep trenches were being dug in Kensington Gardens and barrage balloon sites were being prepared. The grown-ups spoke in hushed tones at times, when they noticed that I was listening, they changed the subject. Gas masks were issued to civilians from Kensington Town Hall - contained in square cardboard boxes to be suspended from the shoulder by a piece of stout string. The mask itself, a pig-snouted rubber and fabric monstrosity, foul smelling and with a mica visor that misted with the moisture from one's breath within seconds, was fun.

In the meantime school continued, we made new friends and family came to visit. My great-aunt Sally came to stay from Coalbrookdale and we took her to the last Royal Tournament to be held at Olympia before war broke out. She was as delighted by the pageantry and display as I was. The horses, the guns and uniforms made us clap our hands with wild applause - she was even more pleased than I, for having been profoundly deaf since her teens, the gunfire was so ear-splitting that she could hear it even without the aid of her usual black leather ear-trumpet.

Alas, it was all to end in tears - my mother's - not mine. Behind my back plans were being made. News vendors' placards bore alarming head-lines. My parents were arguing heatedly with one another more and more frequently. My brother Peter was now at St. Paul's School and there were plans afoot to move the entire school to the Berkshire countryside. Evacuees from the East End and other cities and towns throughout the country were being sent to allegedly 'safe' rural areas. My wife-to-be then aged eight, was sent together with her two sisters and their entire school from Bermondsey to Worthing on the South Coast - in the direct line of any expected invasion. Bad news I was beginning to learn, came from the wireless, as well as simple entertainment like Henry Hall and his *Guest Night* or *In Town Tonight*. People listened in to the BBC news bulletins more frequently.

In 1936 back in Wallasey, I can remember listening with my mother and Jonah to the wireless. The announcer's voice was intoning in a cut-glass Home Counties' accent, 'The King's life is drawing peacefully to its close .....' My mother wept freely, shedding copious tears for the first time ever in my sight. 'He was a good man,' she said. I remained totally unmoved, waiting for more suitable radio fare for my young, barely-formed ears - preferably Paul Robeson singing *Ol' Man River,* whose deep bass I could join with my piping treble. The next time I saw her crying was when her father, my Doughty grandfather Thomas, died in 1939 - again this failed to move me, as he had always seemed a large and grumpy man, clad in scratchy plus-four tweeds.

I remember however that in September 1939 when I was again with her at my grandmother's house in Coalbrookdale (having left London already as 'evacuees') listening to that self-deluded and pompous prophet of appeasement, Neville Chamberlain, speaking in his distinctive and monotonous drone, '...No such assurances having been received, consequently we are at war with Germany from eleven o'clock this morning.' At last I was moved by her tears and as the air-raid sirens sounded on the stroke of the hour I began to feel that perhaps after all, my world was not as safe and secure as it had seemed up until now.

There are several landmarks that sprinkle the passage of childhood and the war. I quite clearly remember the stranding of the submarine *HMS Thetis* on her trials from the dock yards of Camell Lairds, in 1938. The drama was closely followed by our household, being played out only a few miles away off Birkenhead. At low tide part of the submarine's hull was visible, the stern projecting skywards at an angle from the water. Apart from a handful of men who escaped early on by using their Davis apparatus the entire crew and the dockyard men on board perished within a few days as their air ran out. I find it as unimaginable now as I did then at the age of six or seven that they could not be saved. The hull was exposed at low water, *Thetis* was surrounded by rescue craft and divers who appeared to be helpless apart from banging on the hull in response to the tapping noises, gradually decreasing, made by the trapped submariners inside. The *Thetis* was eventually raised, emptied of its corpses, re-named and re-equipped in time to be sunk again with all hands, by the Germans. She could not have been a happy ship.

I remember that first icy-hard winter of the war, 1939-1940, evacuated from London and living with my grandmother and great-aunt Sally at their house in Coalbrookdale. My sister, then aged seventeen and not yet volunteered for the ATS was with us, and was ostensibly in charge of the education of Iain Paton (a friend of my own age from our London school who had come with us) and myself. I remember my sister and her friend Nancy, the village policeman's daughter - with Iain and myself as chaperones, walking through the snow with the two older girls up to the hill above Buildwas and the River Severn, taking 'comforts' to the lonely Lance-Bombardier, one 'Tommy' Thomas, who manned the single Lewis gun, with its one drum of forty-seven .303 rounds, inside a sandbagged emplacement - from where he bravely and single-handedly ensured the safety from air attack of the power station in the valley below.

Again, later in 1940 when invasion appeared imminent, I remember Churchill's speeches on the wireless. In North Wales my other grandmother listened to the Prime Minister's exhortations to the citizens 'to resist the Hun' - encouraging those so feeble as she felt herself to be - 'at least to take one with you!' At this my grandmother prepared jars of ground-up glass with which to poison the food of the Hun when they took over and forced her to cook for them. This was in case they were not already repelled by the open pots of pepper she kept behind each door, ready to throw into their eyes as the invaders burst in. In the interests of safety my Aunt Fairlie eventually persuaded her to remove the powdered glass from the kitchen, and by early 1942 - as wartime shortages began to bite, the jars of pepper went back to re-reinforce the fast dwindling contents of the store cupboard as the dangers of invasion receded.

The night of 15 November 1940 heard the air-raid sirens wailing throughout the Midlands. During eleven hours of continuous bombardment by the Luftwaffe, 30,000 incendiaries and 500 tons of high explosive fell on Coventry. In Coalbrookdale, as the sirens sounded I suppose at first my grandmother and great-aunt feared a raid on the iron-works and the factories in the valley. Iain and I were woken up by his mother, who was visiting, and brought downstairs, past the framed engravings on the wall that I have always remembered - that of the seated and severely solemn-visaged Doctor Samuel Johnson awaiting an audience with Lord Chesterfield - and that masterpiece of nineteenth century Afghan propaganda, *The Remnants of an Army* (by Lady Butler, 1879 - one doubts that she could actually have been in the pay of Afghanistan). This picture depicted the sole survivor of the British retreat from Kabul in 1844, the English Dr. Brydon approaching the fort at Jellalabad, his head thrown back as he slumps on his exhausted pony, his broken sword dangling from his hand by its wrist knot. Iain and I were wrapped in blankets and popped underneath the dining room table for safety. After a while, in spite of the sound of occasional aircraft overhead in the darkness and the beams of distant searchlights when we went outside, it was obvious we were not the target. As the night wore on, the skies to the south-east grew brighter and redder - as if with a false dawn, as Coventry blazed and burned in silence some forty or fifty miles distant. Our local 'All Clear' did not sound until long after grey daylight came. It must have been about this period that my family home, the flat in Kensington, was wrecked by a bomb and rendered uninhabitable. Fortunately no-one was home at the time and the surviving furniture was put into storage for the duration.

My sister had already volunteered for the ATS and was a driver with an AA gun battery in London all during the Blitz. Iain and I attended the local school, which was not considered a great success by our parents. My grandmother and great-aunt Sally also found us a handful once my sister had left. We played too many tricks on them. I remember Iain and I discovered that we could vacate the upstairs lavatory, through the open sash window and, shinning down the drainpipe to the garden, would leave the door mysteriously locked behind us. As mysteriously, the door would magically unlock itself as we climbed up again several hours later. In early 1941 we were both packed off to boarding school in North Wales where Dulwich College Preparatory School - after some wanderings in Kent and elsewhere - had finally settled into their wartime quarters at the Royal Oak Hotel in Betws-y-Coed, conveniently close to my other grandmother's house.

Aged eleven I was back in London for part of the school's summer holidays in September 1943. It was safe enough by then as there were only occasional sneak raids from the Luftwaffe and the V1s and V2 rockets were still several months in the future. Iain and I were in a Regent Street cinema at a matinee - probably on free press tickets with which Iain's journalist father was liberally furnished. The film we were watching has long since escaped me. During the afternoon an ill-written notice was flashed on to the screen announcing the surrender of all Italian forces and the collapse of the pro-Axis Italian government. The cinema audience went wild, cheering, singing and shouting. The film was abandoned - I think most of us thought the war was now virtually over, instead of realising that it was only a 'blip' in the progress of the conflict that still had nearly two years to run before completing its course.

D-Day was another major milestone; June 1944, back at school in Betws, the whole school listened to the wireless broadcasts over our Tannoy system. Monsieur Meyrat, who was Swiss, who taught us French and German and 'Mademoiselle' Melita, the headmaster's secretary, a remarkable German refugee, tearfully pointed out on the wall maps where the landings had been made. Within a week or so Miss Herbertson, another teacher, received a heavily censored letter from her brother who had been dropped by parachute during the night of 5 June 1944 - she read out his account of the initial battles to the assembled pupils. We were thrilled to learn that the Allied paratroops had identified each other in the dark, on the ground, not by secret password, but with the little metallic tin 'clickers' that we all knew from the contents of our Christmas crackers.

We were still at school in Betws-y-Coed when VE Day arrived the following May. We all had a day's holiday. Bonfires blazed throughout the evening on the river bank in the field facing the Royal Oak Hotel where the school was quartered. The local Home Guard, or what was left of them by now, exploded their remaining stocks of thunderflashes. Hymns and patriotic songs were sung with Welsh gusto. I think we all thought the war was over - totally forgetting the Japanese - and we would all soon go home to London once again from where most of the pupils hailed. Back in Coalbrookdale, the long-muffled church bells rang out for hours in triumphant and joyful thanksgiving for Victory.

My great-aunt Sally stood at the foot of the tower, an ear-trumpet inserted in each ear beneath her shiny black straw hat garlanded with artificial cherries. Alas, totally in vain, she was now so profoundly deaf she could no longer hear even the faintest sound although the fabric of the church tower was vibrating with the clangor of the newly released bells. Great-aunt Sally was one of those people whose lasting presence and personality has passed down through the generations, transcending time and space even for those who never knew her except through family tales. My niece Caroline Elkington, considerable artist and poet, is one of those who never having known her is yet still aware of her existence in the collective mind of her wider family. This is what she wrote of both her great great-aunt Sally and of her own mother:

HEARING THINGS
I'm half listening, sort of half here, half somewhere else.
I can hear my mother's voice in the distance, I've heard the same stories for ever.
I must have listened once-upon-a-time, although I can't remember all the details,
The stories seldom change, they cling to each other, affectionate friends,
While Great Aunt Sally weaves in and out like a sparkly magician's assistant;
I never met her but she's been hanging about in the ether all my life.
I heard that she couldn't hear a thing, profoundly deaf since childhood scarlet fever.
I heard that war broke out and she didn't hear it coming,
That she watched all the men leave but didn't hear them go,
That she waited for their return but never heard them come back.
When peace was declared they gave her a black leather ear trumpet;
Filled with optimism Great Aunt Sally picked up her voluminous black skirts

And ran to the church, leaning against the belfry she raised her eyes to the heavens,
Straining every fibre of her being to hear the jubilant pealing of the bells.
But she still couldn't hear a bloody thing. I hate that story.
I can see her crumpling with disappointment like a grief-stricken bin-bag
The useless ear trumpet falling to the ground in slo-mo
And even from this distance it breaks my heart. The stories flood on relentlessly
To Dartford Heath where my mother was stationed at the Woolwich Arsenal
During the war, the din of the guns the only sound she could hear. Towards dawn the guns fell silent and in that moment of pure stillness
She heard a nightingale begin to sing outside the asylum.
She now thinks that it might have been singing all along.
    Only now am I beginning to understand
        that my mother has been singing all along too.

August of the same year, 1945, found Iain Paton and I once more enjoying our summer holidays in Coalbrookdale. The black-out was long gone. Church bells sounded out freely on Sundays and at bell-ringing practice - both banned in the early years of the war when they were to be sounded only in the event of invasion. Iain was the first to hear the news on the wireless. 'Japan has surrendered!' he shouted, 'The war is over! The Americans have dropped a powerful bomb It's no bigger than a golf ball. It's destroyed a whole city! WE'VE WON!! WE'VE WON!!!!!'

The world had changed. It would never be the same again.

3
CHILDHOOD AND WARTIME

The memories of childhood have no order and no end.
Dylan Thomas

It is only right that something should be said about sex in this narrative. We cannot all be like Sir Ivan Lawrence, distinguished QC and Parliamentarian who, being interviewed for a Sunday newspaper, was asked when his first sexual experience took place. He replied, 'Why, I believe it was on the day of my wedding when I kissed my beautiful wife for the very first time.' (He did add that his memory was singularly unreliable.) One must also be diplomatic considering that if these pages are to be read at all, it is quite possible that one's family may be among those who do so and their feelings must be considered. One can confess all to total strangers with impunity, (unless one is famous and confiding to a lady or gentleman of the press). But in general, and in particular with regard to one's nearest and dearest, such total intimacies are perhaps best left to the memory and imagination of the party of the first part - or if one is so fortunate as to have one, to the confidential notebook of one's personal psycho-therapist, perhaps later to be referred to as 'Patient X'. We shall be like the Khazaks of Central Asia amongst whom it is considered unseemly in the highest degree for children to see their parents kissing or embracing in any other manner than that of chaste affection.

Rest assured then, that for the sake of modesty, decency and a quiet home life, we shall approach any bedroom door on tip-toe, closing it gently but firmly behind us as we enter. One must remember that in life, as in the theatre, it is the dress rehearsals which are the most dramatic and revealing times for the actors, rather than the final polished performances to be presented, hopefully, before an admiring audience.

I have very little memory of childhood sexuality. I knew that there was some sort of significance (of which grown-ups seemed to be very aware) attached to the physical differences between little boys and little girls. Children are often curious without being prurient in these matters and I was fortunate I suppose, in that I suffered no doubt as to my own gender. I was a boy, girls were girls and the less the one had to do with the other, the better. It could be said that I and my child peers, friends and school fellows of our strictly single-sex prep. schools modelled ourselves on the attitudes expressed by William Brown of *Just William* fame. We differed with him only in that we thought that Richmal Crompton's hero paid far too much attention to Violet Elisabeth Bott. Without her presence the 'outlaws' had much more fun and could get on with the proper business of being boys together. I still remember at the age of about ten, together with my friend Iain, making stone-deaf old great-aunt Sally understand quite clearly that when we were grown-up, we would have nothing at all to do with girls - they were simply far too soppy and beneath our attention. She smiled and said simply, 'We shall see, we shall see. You just wait!' Dear, dear great-aunt Sally, she was quite right about our rash predictions.

By 1943 and 1944 (when I became twelve) I was becoming more aware that the mysteries of grown-up behaviour in these areas was far more complex and incomprehensible than I had ever realised. When in London from time to time for a week or two during school holidays, I would sometimes stay at the large mansion flat in Fitz-George Avenue where throughout the war the parents of my friend Iain kept open house for so-called (and often self-styled) 'intellectuals', romantic refugees, displaced musicians, writers and artists, servicemen and women of every rank, degree and nationality - the sole criteria being that they must be 'interesting'. Iain's mother was often absent in Coalbrookdale where she played an important role as a pioneer industrial nurse and social worker-cum personnel officer for one of the big wartime factories, evacuated from the environs of Birmingham and now re-established there (Fisher & Ludlow), making wings for Lancaster and Mosquito bombers. She returned to London as often as she could. Iain's father, editor and journalist and occasional war correspondent for the Kemsley Press, lived in London at the flat. It was always full of people. My mother, who was working in Liverpool at that time, sometimes came to stay while I was there during the school holidays and shared a room with Iain and myself. In spite of strict wartime rationing, there always seemed to be plenty of food and drink.

Our mothers often exchanged confidences - as women will - late at night in the room, obviously believing that Iain and I were fast asleep, which sometimes we were not. By that time, although I was not aware of it, my mother and father had already effectively separated, although they were not to divorce until after the war. I knew that we no longer had our own house, having given up the flat in De Vere Gardens after it was badly damaged during the Blitz and by now my mother was living her own life again. Iain's mother was also a lively and attractive woman and living away from home much of the time, busy with war work.

By 1943 the Americans were arriving in Britain in large numbers. Both women were well-connected with a wide circle of friends in London and elsewhere - and to put not too fine a point upon it - with hindsight I think that they were having a ball. From what I heard, they were enjoying it too. I didn't know what to make of it. Neither did I know precisely what it was that they were doing.

In Coalbrookdale I remember a few incidents which must date from then. By that long summer school holiday there were American Army units scattered all over England. It was almost a rare event to see British soldiers anywhere at that time. In Coalbrookdale one only ever saw a few KSLI (King's Shropshire Light Infantry). They were callow youths in ill-fitting battledress, with their forage caps and shapeless berets tucked under the epaulettes of their unbuttoned tunics, fags drooping from their lips. They were probably recruits on leave trying in vain to impress the local talent, who most likely had known them as children together - the progression from spotty youth to roughly uniformed soldier with a bad haircut is no great advance when trying to impress the fair sex. These were the same KSLI who would receive their baptism of fire in June the following year when they landed in Normandy on Sword Beach suffering many casualties in the ensuing weeks in the hard battle for Caen.

All this while the mature and more-seasoned British Army were extended far overseas in North Africa, in the Far East and elsewhere getting on with the war while the Yanks had barely begun to get their act together in preparation for the Second Front. One hardly saw the RAF except on scattered training flights during the day. They were otherwise invisibly engaged in long distance battle in the flak-filled night skies over Germany and Fortress Europe. The Royal Navy were either at sea or their personnel restricted to the coastal ports. However, the soldiers of the US Army and the Air Corps were highly visible. By mid-1943 vast aerial fleets of silver Flying Fortress B17s and B24 Liberators, of Mitchells and Marauders, were cruising high in the summer skies over

Shropshire. Formations of twin-fuselaged P38 Lightnings, of Merlin powered P51 Mustangs and the big single radial-engined P47 Thunderbolt fighters roared over the green fields and woods of middle England (any one of these planes I can still instantly identify half a century later). The Americans stepped in on the ground too - convoys of US Army trucks, tanks and jeeps rolled through the narrow lanes - the occupants handing out chewing gum like confetti as they went. They brought gum for the kids, cigarettes, chocolate and nylon stockings for their elder sisters - and also for the younger, prettier mums and wives whose absent soldier lovers and husbands had already been away for three years and more.

Near Buildwas, on the River Severn, a Company of American Combat Engineers had established themselves in and around a requisitioned country house. Their *entrée* into the local milieu was assured when they sent an amateur concert party of 'talented' (I use this word in its loosest form) performers round the local factories to entertain the workers in their lunch-hour 'workers' playtime' in the works canteens. The workers were now of course mostly women, many of them young and also away from home, sent where directed by the wartime Ministry of Labour. I clearly recall one occasion when Iain and I were taken by his mother - then in charge of medical and welfare facilities at the factory - to one of these performances. To the audience, the performers must have seemed like Hollywood actors. Young, tall, handsome Yanks, wearing smartly tailored uniforms, heavily be-medalled - in spite of their lack of active service. It was sourly rumoured by the British troops of that period that the GIs were awarded the Purple Heart for merely watching the British Ministry of Information's film *Desert Victory*. They played jazz licks on an amateur trumpet and boogie-woogie on an old upright piano. Their every act was greeted with wild cheers and whistles.

I recall one sketch which brought the house down. A gangly southern youth dressed in jeans and plaid shirt plus battered straw hat - chewing a straw and idly rocking on a porch. His 'Maw' enters and says, after a long pause, 'Where's yer Paw?' Similarly long pause before he answers, 'Paw's in the barn.' This is dragged on for several minutes while 'Maw' elicits from her son that 'Paw' has 'hanged hisself'. 'Did you cut him down Son?' '...Nope.' '...Why not Son?' '...He weren't daid yet, Maw.'

The Yanks on the stage in the works canteen taught their willing audience songs like *Don't Fence Me In - Give me Land, Lots of Land* and the

Starry Skies Above, plus songs from the movies like *I'm a Lone Cowhand from the Rio Grande* and *Home on the Range*. Or the one in particular that I remember:

> *The stars at night are big and bright*
> (here a chorus of hands) Clap! Clap! Clap! Clap!
> *Deep in the heart of Texas*
> *They remind me erv the one I lerv*
> (the audience again) Clap! Clap! Clap! Clap!
> *Deep in the heart of Texas*
> (the song then drones on)
> *the sage in bloom, is like perfoom! etc.*

With the chorus of hands continuing 'Clap! Clap! Clap! Clap!' Perhaps mildly prophetic in view of the near plague of venereal infections that were to sweep the ranks of both performers and audience before the Yanks departed for the Normandy beaches the following year. I think that perhaps our own local Americans must have had a lot of Texans or westerners in their ranks - or perhaps they just pretended to be so for purposes of seduction.

Before long the GIs were in clover. No competition from the local men, the only local males left were too old or too young. An adoring and available collection of sex-starved young women were faced with a plenitude of equally willing, wealthy (in British terms), well-dressed and healthy, well-fed foreign soldiery who spoke - or seemed to speak, English. Soon the pubs were full of Americans and their English girl friends drinking warm, weak beer. The cinema queues and the seats were full of embracing couples. Iain and I were amazed. The Yanks were exciting for us too - they were highly visible in 1943 and early 1944. Their airplanes, their tanks that clanked and roared along the narrow country lanes, their artillery parks - all the glamour that had been missing from the war was at last on our doorstep. Neither of us, nor the friends we played with, were very keen on American gum or the sweets they gave us - they tasted 'funny'. By this time, too, my brother Peter was in Canada training as a pilot with the Fleet Air Arm - the 'food' parcels he sent home also contained 'funny' tasting 'candies'.

The American officers at Buildwas had latched on to Iain's mother. The Captain, whose first name only I can remember, Paul, the Company Commander, was tall and fair and his Lieutenant, Alex Gottlieb, dark-haired and wiry. Alex Gottlieb was also a Hollywood film director and producer - after the war I saw his name on the credit titles of several Hollywood movies. I was reminded of this only recently when watching a TV re-run of an early 1948 Doris Day musical - and there was Alex Gottlieb's name as producer - Michael Curtiz directing - so he was no beginner even in 1944. Both of them called frequently at my grandmother's house and charmed both her and great aunt Sally. They sent a jeep around one Sunday to whisk us (my mother and Iain's, plus Iain and I in the role of chaperones) off to lunch in their Mess. I remember careering down the Dale and round Forge Corner at high speed. In the back of the jeep Iain and I excitedly clutched the canvas hood struts as our mothers' hair streamed in the wind. My grandmother was absolutely mortified that her daughter should be seen in such a situation whizzing down the Dale - and on a Sunday!

I still have a clear memory of bucketing in the jeep along a wooded lane near Buildwas, the vehicle hurtling through a flock of chickens from a nearby farm, the jeep screeching to a halt. The driver jumped out and swiftly scooping up two limp corpses and concealing them at his feet, said to my mother as we sped off once more, 'Cap'n 'll be real pleased with these Ma'am!'

I was greatly disappointed at the American Army mess - our lunch was very odd. All our food was served on a single metal tray. There was steak, I don't remember ever having seen such a large piece of meat on my plate in my life. There were mashed potatoes and corn, ice-cream and pie, plus a cup of coffee - all dumped in individual depressions on the tray. Where were the plates? Iain and I were mystified. What was more, our social expectations were outraged. Although the mess hall was in the large drawing room of the house - it was full of common soldiers and NCOs as well as the handful of officers, all sitting and eating the same food together! Even Iain and I knew that this wasn't the manner in which the British Army was accustomed to behave. The Yanks were certainly very strange.

After lunch things looked up a bit. A tall, bespectacled, gangly Master Sergeant took Iain and I under his wing while the officers strolled through the grounds in the August sunshine with our mothers. We were shown trucks and jeeps, we went into the armoury and fiddled with the Tommy guns and then, the Master Sergeant having spoken to the Captain, we went off to a nearby duck pond with a carbine and a Colt automatic pistol and boxes of ammunition. For twenty minutes or so,

Iain and I were allowed to shoot at tin cans and bits of wood thrown in the water for us. After the passage of more than fifty years I am still astounded at this - the free and easy discipline, the disregard of safety - allowing children to blaze away with military firearms, not to mention expending US government property without either excessive care or the filling in of countless forms, at random targets in the middle of the quiet English countryside - on a Sunday afternoon!

Later that afternoon while we were in the Captain's office, the grown-ups talking of this and that, the door opened and in swept a hatless GI, offering an informal salute to the assembly. He said to the Captain, 'Permission to borrow a jeep, Cap'n?' 'Sure, Hank,' replied the Captain, 'Take care now!' The British Army was never like this.

A few weeks after the D-Day invasion of France the following year, I can recall seeing Iain's mother in a flood of tears. It must have been in July at the beginning of the school summer holidays, reading a letter just received from the tall, stooping Master Sergeant. The Captain had been killed in action in the immediate aftermath of the landings in Normandy and his Company had taken heavy casualties on Omaha Beach. By this time my mother had returned to Liverpool, returning home late one afternoon many months later, she found the Lieutenant, Alex Gottlieb, sitting on her doorstep. He was back on a brief leave. 'What else could I do?' I later overheard her say to Iain's mother, 'He had nowhere else to go!'

~ ~ ~ ~ ~ ~ ~ ~ ~ ~

I have no recollection of any sexual matters obtruding into our lives at the prep schools I attended before and during the war. Except perhaps for one day in Wales, when I was haring at high speed down a corridor pursuing one of my fellows, on rounding a corner I collided full tilt at eye-level with the large and shapely bosom of the house mistress in charge of the juniors. We both ricocheted one from the other off the wall, ending up prostrate on the floor, myself lying on top of her outraged form, dizzy with the impact, my head pillowed amid her splendid cleavage. Those few brief moments of bliss as consciousness returned remained as a happy memory for many years. I must have been at least aged twelve at the time for in other respects I was by no means precocious.

If one could, with hindsight, have anticipated any problems it would have been at boarding school in North Wales at Betws-y-Coed where Dulwich College Preparatory School had established itself in the Royal Oak Hotel, otherwise closed for the duration of the War. Our masters and mistresses were the soul of propriety itself with regard to us, their charges. Even the frequent beatings to which we were subjected by the male staff and in extreme cases by the Headmaster Mr. J. H. Leakey (of the famous Leakey family - he later wrote a book about the school's remarkable wartime wanderings called *School Errant*), were I am sure, undertaken with nothing but our own personal welfare in mind and as justifiable and simple punishment for minor infringements of school discipline. In the minds of most pupils such penalties were greatly to be preferred to the dreary and tedious punishments of either writing Latin 'lines' or being forced to learn by heart great chunks of turgid Victorian poetry.

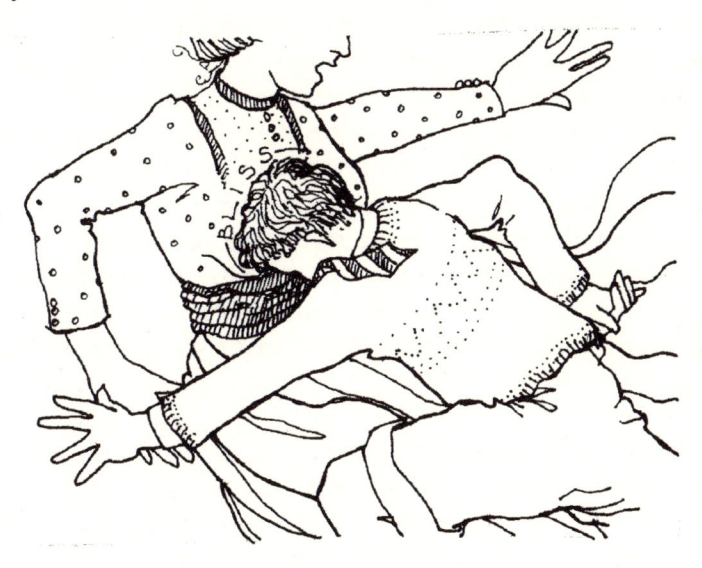

It was a curious period (and I suppose that in a few rare instances it may still continue) when for a century or more British parents of the middle classes should both pay for their male offspring's formal and private education far from home and also for occasional floggings which they themselves would not be prepared to administer to their children. I have two minds about it, although I would certainly not entrust any child of mine to such a system. Unfortunately it induced in me no hankerings for 'discipline and domination' of the kind (if we are to believe the popular press) that numerous MPs, judges and other scions of the public school-educated establishment are reputed to enjoy so freely. It did however induce in those subjected to the system, a certain stoicism in the face of life's vicissitudes.

Transgression of frequently arbitrary and arcane rules, disobeying instructions from one's elders and betters - older was always better in those days - if discovered, led to swift and painful retribution. However, it was not so swift at times when advance warning would be given of a 'headmaster's beating' awarded after accumulating sufficient 'black marks' in the weekly league table, of never less than six strokes of the cane, when the subject was given several hours in which to contemplate the coming ordeal. In retrospect I find it remarkable that mere boys, aged between seven and thirteen, quite cheerfully put up with this regime. Blubbing was a despised mark of dishonour, whereas rushing off to display one's 'stripes' to one's friends smacked of the heroic Agincourt veteran displaying his wounds in the aftermath of St. Crispin's Day!

The recollection of those times helps to re-reinforce my opinion that every child born into this world however deprived or mistreated experiences just as 'normal' a childhood as Little Lord Fauntleroy - if for no other reason that invariably there are no alternatives on offer. Children seldom have choices, they learn from, and God willing, survive the unequal portions they have doled out to them. If they are provided with wealthy, healthy and even-handed parents then they are fortunate indeed. The Spartan conditions in which we lived, the often poorly cooked and inadequate food, lack of heating in winter, icy bedrooms, skimpy and infrequently washed uniform would not be tolerated either by parents or the Social Services in the first decade of the twenty-first century, but fifty years ago it was the norm. Along with many other fellow pupils I endured frequent colds and bouts of bronchial asthma brought about by the chills and the damp. In memory at least our teachers, for the most part, were both competent and dedicated to the welfare of their charges.

Under such a system the cleverer pupil will develop a fairly clear sense of how far one can go without being caught, also of how to avoid being found out. It develops one's ambitions to gain advancement to the point where, if possible, one becomes the person administering the rules rather than abiding by them. Another lesson taught by such methods is the often random manner in which such punishment is doled out, the victim may be genuinely innocent, but simply in the wrong place at the wrong time in the wrong circumstances. The knowledge that both the world and life are frequently unjust - and that there is little one can do about it - is a useful lesson to be learned. To accept one's fate with equanimity, without whinging but without passivity, was always considered a useful quality to be fostered in the administrators, soldiers, sailors and Empire builders for whom this type of education was intended. In these modern times when the average product of the British public school system is most likely to enter the establishment via the City or politics - it is probably outdated and long past its sell-by date.

A family acquaintance once recounted the tale of how as an orphan he was enrolled in the Merchant Navy Training Ship *Conway*. He was, he said, aged eleven or twelve; it was pre-1914. The Captain called him to his cabin, bent the child over the desk and gave him 'six of the best' with a cane. The poor child was then quizzed. 'I expect you are wondering what that is for?' said the Captain. 'Well, yes Sir, I was rather wondering what I have done.' The Captain replied, 'The first three strokes were for your presumption in daring to join this ship in the first place - the second three were simply a practical illustration of the prevailing general injustice which you will soon discover as you progress through life.' Our friend later enjoyed a distinguished career and claimed he had learned a valuable lesson.

Thankfully the flogging of little boys as an aid to education has now virtually disappeared. The only possible excuse for its continuance would be to supplement the excellence and quality of the education which the independent sector still manages to provide. Private schooling can rarely be matched by any system of non-selective State education. Half a century ago those fee-paying pupils who were consistently ill-behaved or disruptive or disinclined to learn (for whatever reason) were expelled by the simple device of asking their parents if their child would not be happier elsewhere - a luxury long denied to the public sector.

Our teachers at Dulwich College Prep School were a mix of capable and dedicated married men plus a variety of bachelors and spinsters either exempted from military service by virtue of age, or in some cases by physical disability, in the case of the men. Teaching for the women was, I think, a reserved occupation. The few younger and fitter masters disappeared from time to time and often returned later on brief visits, to be admired in their (usually) smart RAF uniforms bearing their air crew 'wings' of Bomber Command, which between 1942 and the end of the war, had become the great sink that swallowed up so many lives. (See Note 1, Appendix).

By the time I had taken the Common Entrance exam in the summer of 1945 and was ready to go on to Epsom College (the choice of my parents for no better reason than that my friend Iain was being sent there), the war was already over. That is not strictly true, for it was only the end of the conflict in Europe that we schoolboys celebrated with the good villagers of Betws on the banks of the Llugwy opposite the Royal Oak Hotel on VE Night in May. Bonfires blazed, hymns and patriotic songs were sung while the rump of the local Home Guard exploded their entire remaining stock of thunderflashes. In the Far East and the Pacific the fight against the still largely undefeated Japanese was continuing over vast areas of land and sea - although we had no doubt we would win in the end - as we in Britain had never believed for one moment that we could possibly fail to beat the Hun. For six long years of war in my childhood memory the outcome had always been certain, however dark the news had been. My sister who served in the ATS from 1940 until the end of the war said to me recently that during those years she had never met anyone in the Services, who conceded either publicly or in private, the remotest possibility of final defeat. Such was the never again to be experienced optimism and common purpose of the entire British nation in my early lifetime.

From those times in 1945 the nationality of England really started to fade away and to decline. It was almost as if Britain's history had been concluded, as if a revolution had wiped the slate clean. The character of Britain and particularly that of the English had changed for ever. Within a decade after the war the whole flower and being of England seemed to wither on the stem to be revived only briefly and brilliantly for the Coronation in the spring of 1953 before all the petals finally dropped off one by one. Thereafter the progressive dismantling of British industry, of farming and of fishing, the decline of King Coal, the de-skilling of the once most skilled national work force in the world, proceeded apace. The Merchant Navy and its seamen (all lessons of history ignored) have dwindled to a handful of men and ships. Whether by default or deliberate political intent matters not one jot. The successive governments who allowed this steady demolition of almost the entire framework of everything that had sustained the nation for centuries deserve lasting condemnation. For a few more years the concept of 'Britishness' lingered a little longer in the remaining colonies and outposts of Empire where I saw it fade into forgotten history. It was the British abandonment of Southern Rhodesia that in the end led to the tattered remnants of the Union Jack fading into limbo, like the vanishing grin of the Cheshire Cat. But by then, even many of those who had won the greatest war the world had ever known, seemed to have lost their pride in nationhood and had forgotten their history. Their descendants have never learned it and we have, some sixty years after the end of the war, finally achieved a divided and dysfunctional society.

~ ~ ~ ~ ~ ~ ~ ~ ~ ~

I was of that last generation to be born and mostly educated in an age when scientific and engineering achievements still seemed exciting rather than alarming. The adventure books I read as a child and into my teens were repositories of bigoted racism, of blind patriotism and snobbery. Their defence is that they simply pointed out to the juvenile Briton the comic inferiority of the non-British 'rest of the world'. References to 'niggers, wops, dagoes, gippos and greasers' merely highlighted the popularly held prejudices of the first quarter and beyond of the twentieth century in the twilight of Empire.

The world, as presented to many middle-class children of that era, was for many summed up by the *Boys' Own Paper* (equally looked down on by myself and many of my contemporaries, but nevertheless exerting a powerful and seminal influence). The older copies of the bound annuals that fell into our hands were liberally illustrated with graphic drawings of tweed-suited, knickerbockered English youths in tasselled school caps delivering a straight left to the jaw of some ghastly 'Johnny Foreigner' with bare feet and a sash, whose knife would be sent spinning to the floor - like its owner. George Orwell summed it up perfectly, saying something like this:

'It is forever 1910, the King is on his throne, the pound is worth a pound. The grim grey battleships of the Grand Fleet are surging up the Dover Straits. On the Continent the 'Foreigner' is jabbering and gesticulating. In the East the monocled Englishman with his rifle and bayonet is keeping the Wogs at Bay.'

Magazines like the *Wide World* fictionalised 'true' adventure stories for the stay-at-home blue and white-collar middle classes. Blackwood's *Maga* published the exciting experiences of the Colonial Officers on the frontiers and of the soldiers and far flung colonial administrators who ran the Empire. Fictionalised history was still popular even that from the somewhat turgid but prolific pen of the late G. A. Henty - with such titles as *With Clive in India* or *With Wolfe to Quebec* and some eighty other equally formulaic volumes (we would have much preferred sporting adventures such as the still-yet-to-be-written *With Gun and Bottle to the Dark Continent*). Even by the standards of my contemporaries Henty richly deserved his reputation as a boring, tedious old fart with his pious, po-faced cardboard heroes, his virtuous and heroic young midshipmen and do-gooding ensigns displaying 'grit' and 'pluck' in richly sick-making style throughout the expanding Empire. Percy F. Westerman was another author of innumerable ripping yarns of True British Grit. Over a period of some thirty years he (and his publishers, Blackies of Glasgow) had invented the story of a totally batty shipping line called Whatmough, Duvant & Co., whose tramp steamers were crewed by officers and cadets the author had followed through from the start of their careers in the Sea Scouts. At the age of fifteen I would have loved dearly to follow their footsteps and go to sea - at that time such a career was still possible. I mentioned the idea to my father and he pooh-poohed the notion, wisely perhaps as the rapid decline of the British Merchant Navy in the following years has led to the virtual extinction of the Red Ensign on the high seas. Those halcyon days of the British as a nation of seafarers were soon to vanish. The days of wartime, when every merchant ship in every convoy carried a bowler-hatted Belfast skipper on the bridge, when every engine-room had a chief engineer called Jock or Mac whose assistant was always a Geordie - not forgetting the ever-present Cockney fifteen-year old ship's boy who played the mouth-organ - they were now all fading into legend.

There were others too, Empire Builders all. There was Captain Crouch in Major Charles Gilson's stories - who carried no luggage but 'a pound tin of Bulldog Shag, a big revolver and a box of bullets.' He had a cork foot and did great deeds up the Kasai River in the Congo. The popular advertisements of the time bolstered these images, particularly the pipe-smoking types who read the *Wide World* magazine. Player's 'Digger' tobacco adverts showed nothing more than a smiling gent sporting a full set of Imperial whiskers, a 'wide-awake' felt hat and a scarlet bandanna plus a pipe of the type known in the trade as a 'half-bent Zulu' jutting from his firm and manly jaw - more than sufficient to ensure continual healthy sales of the product. Another favoured brand, perhaps slightly up-market and directed at those who actually bothered to read the advertising copy, was Barney's 'Punchbowl' - sold in vacuum-sealed tins. The hero who smoked this stuff also sported a beard, a frost-rimed parka and a woolly hat with goggles - while ranting on about a 'cache' of supplies lost in an Antarctic blizzard several years before. When re-discovered, his prize unopened reserve tins of 'Punchbowl' were as fresh and as fragrant as the day they left the factory! Until I suppose the advent of the fifties, what was left of the Empire was still seen by many as a vast system of outdoor relief and adventure for the young Briton on the make.

The final loss of the Empire was traumatic. To have been a child educated to believe that half the world belonged to Britain, seemingly for ever, to see the atlases and globes blocked out in solid areas of red, however false the premise on which these allocations of the world were based, to look forward to having these vast lands at one's disposal in the adult world, was a marvellous prospect. The 1926 version of Mercator's Projection used in British schools of that time showed Canada as much larger than the USA, displayed Australia twice and gave the English total ownership of Antarctica. To have them snatched away almost as soon as one achieved adulthood was traumatic. Deep down somewhere in my personal psyche I don't think I have ever truly recovered from the shock. It was like finally discovering at an advanced age that Santa Claus no longer exists.

4
WAR AND POST-WAR SCHOOL DAYS

But, Good Gracious, you've got to educate him first. You can't expect a boy to be vicious until he's been to a good school.
 'Saki', (H. H. Munro)

I had thought of continuing my earlier dissertations on sex by naming this chapter 'Sex and the Single Schoolboy' - to be followed in due course by 'Sex and the Single Airman' and 'Sex and the Single Banker.' But schoolboy sex in these reminiscences must remain disappointingly vague. Either I was too innocent at the time to be aware of any torrid undercurrents in this field, or both my teachers and my contemporaries were equally inactive. I much prefer to believe the latter, particularly at Dulwich College Preparatory School, evacuated as it was to Betws-y-Coed in North Wales for most of the war years.

Our principal preoccupation out of school involved a keen interest in nature. We were also kept busy in organised sports, forestry work when we brashed trees and cleared fire-breaks as our contribution to the War Effort, swimming in the ice-cold river in the summer and, as an older boy, being taken up Welsh mountains by Monsieur Meyrat. Our interest in nature was expressed in splendid wide games in the woods such as 'Cowboys and Indians' as often as not in spite of our awareness of the realities of the continuing war; collecting birds eggs (quite legal in those distant days) and butterflies - and not least, live reptiles. We had slow-worms, grass snakes and (much-prized) adders; the latters' zigzag patterns were the subject of much indrawn breath and admiration as their owners displayed them in their ventilated biscuit tins concealed inside their tuck-boxes beneath their beds. The obsession we had with snakes, in modern psychological practice, would no doubt be interpreted in Freudian terms as denoting our deeply suppressed sexual feelings.

Small boys are surprisingly modest in their persons and even when displaying our behinds to each other to compare the stripes inflicted on us in the course of the fairly frequent beatings we received, it was for reasons of purely clinical comparison in the manner of the veterans of

Agincourt sporting their wounds on St. Crispin's Day. So much for pre-pubertal school sex!

The snake collection and the birds' nesting activities both ended in repercussions and eventual sanctions. Our headmaster, Mr. Leakey was in part responsible for the latter. It was originally his idea that we, the boys, should collect black-headed gulls' eggs from their nesting sites on the small islets of Lyn Elsi, on top of the mountain rising behind Betws. The gulls' eggs, a luxury item in London clubs and restaurants (the eggs being unrationed in wartime) were brought down in their hundreds from the mountain and fed to the school - and greatly enjoyed. I have collected and eaten them again in later years and can vouch for their excellence. I made a first expedition with Mr. Leakey, and again unofficially with two or three close friends to add to our personal collections. It was May and the water in the lake was still icy cold. We stripped to our underpants (as I have explained above, modesty ruled) and we waded, splashed and dog-paddled across to the rocky islands. The transport problem was solved by tying our empty sponge bags around our necks, filling them with the carefully selected freshest eggs - the secret being to take only one egg from each nest containing two, or preferably from a nest containing only one, in the knowledge that the bird would lay more to make up the clutch to two or three. Alas, the local police soon intervened and declared the birds a protected species. In the next county they could be freely taken - but a local bye-law gave the Lyn Elsi birds full protection.

The snakes were yet another matter. We caught them quite easily as they basked in the early summer sunshine in the bracken beds and forest clearings. A forked stick, a cloth bag or a biscuit tin with a pierced lid were the only implements needed - plus a steady hand and the nerve to grasp them firmly behind the head. The few adders we caught were always kept in secrecy as were the larger and more active grass snakes. Alas, secrets by their very nature are prone to leakage as in any closed community.

A master's wife was acting as matron and used to lean her 'sit-up-and-beg' bicycle with its handlebar basket outside the front entrance of the hotel, below the dormitory window which I, as it happened, shared with four or five other boys. We had been handling and admiring a particularly large and very active grass snake (not mine I hasten to add) which then escaped. In our efforts to re-capture the reptile, someone scooped it up and somehow or other dropped it on the window ledge. It then fell out of the open window, straight down and into the basket on the matron's bicycle. We gazed at each other in horror as moments later the bicycle's owner emerged below. Mounting the bike, preparatory to riding home, she gave a piercing shriek and fell off her mount, entangled with the frame and handlebars as if felled by a sudden fit while the large, and now equally alarmed, snake emerged from the basket, made off and vanished across the road into the sanctuary of the riverside garden (much to its owner's chagrin). This incident subsequently led to a search of all the boys' rooms and the discovery of a very fine and venomous adder under one child's bed by a horrified Miss Herbertson. Snakes were then strictly forbidden under pain of at least a headmaster's beating (never less than six of the best) and possible expulsion.

Dulwich College Preparatory School - more usually known as DCPS, was in the forefront of innovative education when as a London Day School on the outbreak of war they evacuated some two hundred pupils first to Cranborn in Kent and not long after moved the entire school as boarders to the Royal Oak Hotel at Betws-y-Coed in North Wales. They were definitely breaking new ground. I joined them in 1941 along with my friend Iain Paton when it became apparent that my grandmother and great-aunt Sally in Coalbrookdale could not really cope with us much longer on a full-time basis. There were also problems with the local schooling. Having come from a London preparatory school, Colet Court, both Iain and I were educationally lost in the local village primary school in the Dale and were two years too young for the High School.

At first I stayed with my other grandmother and Aunt Fairlie at their house some two miles or so outside Betws on the road to Penmachno overlooking the Lledr valley. I cycled to school each day, taking sandwiches for my lunch, while Iain became a boarder. After several months, I too became a boarder - a much better solution for all concerned. At my grandmother's house there was no electricity and doing the plentiful homework I was allocated was a problem in the winter months - candles and dim lamplight and dark mornings and evenings added to my difficulties. In addition cycling to and from the village, a daily total of several miles, with a 'blacked-out' masked bicycle lamp was not easy. Fond as I was of my aunt and grandmother I was pleased to become a boarder - and with permission Iain and I became frequent visitors to their house for Sunday tea.

Our teachers were splendid. Mr. Leakey himself was assisted by his capable and trusted senior teachers from London - Mr. Hatton, Mr. Taylor and Mr. Shepherd, Miss Herbertson plus of course our famous Swiss, Monsieur Paul Meyrat. In addition to teaching us French, M. Meyrat used to take boys up the mountains, scrambling and climbing - even in winter - dressed only in our inadequate school clothes, grey flannel shirts, blue mackintoshes, corduroy shorts and blouses. I never remember anyone coming to any serious harm and the older boys of eleven plus roamed freely and widely in the woods and hills. Discipline was strict, retribution was swift and impersonal, but we were trusted and I like to think that most of us responded in kind.

Our classrooms were basic, some improvised from the hotel's semi-derelict coaching stables, but our teaching and general welfare was probably better than most at that time. The teaching staff (including those in the annexe in the nearby Llugwy Tea Rooms where the five to eight-year olds were cared for) worked long hours, probably for little pay, lodging in local guest houses and rented accommodation. There was always an orderly master or mistress on round-the-clock duty to see that we washed behind our ears at night and awoke at the proper hour in the morning. They used to play scratchy 78 records for us (from their own limited collections, we knew Reginald Gardiner's 'train' noises - 'Diddly-dum, Diddly-Diddly-Diddly-dum' and the *Laughing Policeman* off by heart) in between making announcements over the tannoy system or supervising the plentiful after-hours homework with which we were plagued.

There were other plagues too, of measles or mumps and chicken-pox, but we were hardy and survived. I was stricken with scarlet fever one year, a week before the summer holidays commenced. It was disastrous for I was carted off in an ambulance to the Isolation Fever Hospital at Conway and languished there for six long weeks while my longed for summer holidays in Coalbrookdale dwindled away to nothing before my release - declared infection-free at last. Whatever happened to scarlet fever? In my childhood it was a disease regarded with dread, all sorts of dire consequences were feared. Kept in isolation with another boy from school who had also succumbed, we were forced to lie motionless in bed for the first two weeks, neither permitted to read nor to talk and we were not allowed any food except for liquids. No wonder that by the time we were allowed to sit up, to eat a few invalid slops and eventually to totter a few steps to a chair, we were as weak as kittens. After six long weeks of this bread-and-water regime, our clothes were fumigated one last time, we were scrubbed from head to toe in strong disinfectant and allowed to be collected, weak and pasty-faced, by our grateful relatives. When my own son, aged six or so, some thirty-six years later, developed a rash - to my total amazement the doctor said, 'It looks like scarlet fever. Keep him indoors for a day or two and he can go back to school next week.'

At the end of each term the school hired a special train to take the pupils departing on holiday via Llanwrst to Llandudno Junction where we then dispersed to our various destinations by war-time rail. There were few private cars, with strict petrol rationing for war-important use only. Public trains and buses were the sole means of transport. Some boys, because their homes had been bombed in the cities, or their families scattered because of the war, stayed at the school in Betws, having a high old time being looked after and cared for by the staff who remained. I recall only too well those war-time railway journeys with the Great Western and its chocolate brown-and-cream livery. We always seemed to travel via Chester - trundling along the wastelands of the North Wales coast, those endless miles of seemingly abandoned holiday caravans - no doubt empty because of the difficulties of travel. Rhyl, Prestatyn - rattling past Mostyn and Flint along the muddy shores of the Dee as we shared the cigarette-smoky standing-room-only space in the corridors with kit bag-laden soldiers and shabby civilians. Then Chester, and usually Iain and I together would change for Shrewsbury and then finally take the little, jolting single-line 'stopping' train for Wellington, Dawley, Lightmoor, Horsehay and at last, Green Bank Halt at the foot of Jigger's Bank in Coalbrookdale from where we would drag our suitcases the last few hundred yards to my grandmother's house on Woodside Lane. There we were welcomed and hugged by great-aunt Sally, smelling as always of lavender and moth balls and brandishing her black leather ear-trumpet.

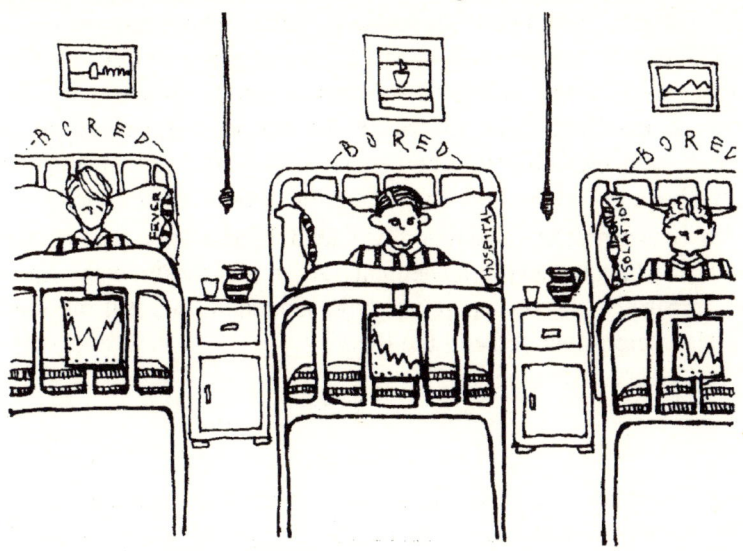

Not all my school holidays were spent in Coalbrookdale as, once the bombing raids on London had quietened down in 1943 and early 1944, Iain and I often stayed in London for weeks at a time, at his parents' large flat in West Kensington. At the age of eleven or twelve, we travelled quite safely alone over long distances by train and bus. We roamed London's museums and parks. We enjoyed the West End cinemas by virtue of Iain's father's free press tickets, particularly the Academy Cinema and the small Studio One cinema at Oxford Circus much used for pre-general release films of the day. Ian and I, school caps removed, mustered as much gravitas as possible in our role as twelve year old film critics for the Kemsley Press. The Academy was small and equipped with luxurious *fauteuils* - or armchairs as we then knew them. Much of the time however we were left to our own devices. Unlike today's children neither ourselves nor as far as I knew, our parents and minders, ever had any qualms about our personal safety on the city's streets. The only danger was from the occasional hit-and-run raid by the Luftwaffe, but

1943 was a quiet period for the Luftwaffe over Britain - one imagines that they were pre-occupied with their Russian Front disasters.

Before D-Day in 1944, our headmaster at DCPS, Mr. Leakey, had contemplated taking the school back to its home in Dulwich, only to be thwarted at the last minute by the random V1 'Doodlebug' Flying-Bombs and the V2 Rockets that rained down on the south of England. A second wave of evacuees abandoned London once more. The last bombs to fall on London were in March 1945. For the last few terms at Betws-y-Coed the school was crowded. In May 1945 the war finally ground to its close. That last summer term saw me reach the age of thirteen, taking the Common Entrance exam before pupils and staff finally wound-up and all decamped back to peacetime London and the anti-climax of Victory.

For no better reason than that my friend Iain, whose parents were ambitious for him to pursue a medical career was destined for Epsom College in Surrey, my own parents, now separated, but still obviously talking, also determined to send me there.

~ ~ ~ ~ ~ ~ ~ ~ ~ ~

Public school sex is a subject of possible interest to the reader, but the doors of memory remain quite firmly closed in this respect. I fear that whatever else might have occurred in the hotbed of homo-eroticism that such institutions are popularly supposed to be, remained largely hidden from me. There were particular and perhaps unusual reasons for this situation which I shall reveal later.

Epsom College was a boys' public school founded in the mid-Victorian era when such establishments became ever more popular. Within easy reach of London on the edge of the Downs, its pupils have always been drawn from middle-class families with a strong medical background - or alternatively where the pupil wished to pursue a career in the various fields of medicine. At least two thirds of the pupils during my time at the school probably met these criteria. Indeed so strong was the medical bias, that upper sixth pupils concentrating on science subjects, could take their first MB exams while still at school.

The boarding house which I joined, known as Forest House, was different from the rest of the school houses in that, at the outbreak of war in 1939, it had closed as the numbers of pupils declined and the school's capacity decreased. At the war's end the decision to re-open Forest House coincided with the return of many teachers who had gone off to fight and with the increased demand for school places - and not least, my own arrival on the scene. This meant that the thirty or so 'new boys' who re-formed Forest House in September 1945 were all of much the same age, thirteen or fourteen at the most. Our only seniors were three or four hand-picked prefects transferred reluctantly from long-established houses who were intended to lead us into the life of the school until such time as we sorted out our own hierarchy. In recent years I have been assured by various friends, whose own careers embraced long association with single-sex public schools, that this strictly limited age-spread was probably the crucial deciding factor that sheltered and protected my continuing ignorance of youthful and boyish same-sex crushes and semi-erotic relationships which were apparently the universal common currency of public school life half a century ago. I am sorry to disappoint my readers in this respect. I sometimes wonder what it was that I may have missed.

It is a very sad reflection on the subsequent life and career of any mature adult who still holds to the maxim that 'school days are the happiest days of one's life.' School days should be formative as well as educative, but for most children and adolescents there is a degree of endurance involved, and for most I would hope, the sense that in the future things can only get better. I do not hark back to my own school days with any great degree of pleasure. I made good friendships at the time, but none that outlasted more than a few years separation. My closest friend from that period, I recently discovered by a chance meeting when his name was mentioned, died some ten years earlier. Lives of such promise as his, brought to a sudden and full-stop before their expected span give an unpleasant jolt to one's own feelings of mortality.

I should have made more of my schooling, but I suffered from the disadvantage of having produced too excellent results in my Common Entrance papers. Last minute cramming for exams I knew would always stuff my head with temporary knowledge. This I found easy to do, being otherwise basically idle in many of my studies. The result of this was that I was placed in the upper fourth form, a year ahead of most of my contemporaries, thus missing out a year of study and basic groundwork, especially in maths and physics which my fellows took for granted. One can make up for these deficiencies in subjects such as English, history, or even languages such as Latin, French and German, all of which I studied. However, if one lacks a numerate affinity with the sciences, then failing to come to terms with the basics and joining the course of study in mid-stream is a recipe for disaster. Therefore instead of being in the top echelons of my own age group, I was discouraged to find myself falling badly behind in the more demanding subjects of maths and physics - chemistry I could just about manage.

In the public school ethos, skill and enthusiasm for team games count for much. Although quite physically able, neither rugger, cricket nor athletics grabbed my attention. Birds' eggs, butterflies and illicit beer-making beneath the floor boards of our house common room were much more interesting. A friend and I once successfully committed ourselves to the sanatorium for a couple of days suffering a severe hangover from our home brew, fortunately misdiagnosed by the matron. As to smoking, I joined the small groups of boys who would slope off outside school bounds to nearby patches of woodland on the Downs. Perching motionless in the upper branches of oak trees above footpaths I first came to realise that the general public at large are oblivious to their surroundings. In wet weather we found a refuge in the parlour of the station master's house (known to its *habitués* as Ma Shag's) at the nearby Epsom Downs station where the pretty daughter would 'stash' our cigarettes and also ply us with tea and cakes. Eventually I came to play in and sometimes captain various 'rag-bag' teams, otherwise known as the Odds and Sods, for rugger and cricket. My team was made up of those boys whose playing skills lacked the finesse necessary to be selected for the Colts or other School First, Second Elevens and Fifteen teams. I enjoyed squash and also rifle shooting on the school's own miniature range. I didn't excel at either but simply competed for my own enjoyment.

Our teachers and house-masters were a mixed bag. Some were definitely quirky and latently (with the benefit of fifty years' hindsight) homosexual. Nearly all were devoted to teaching their subjects well, both driving and encouraging their pupils to succeed. One or two I disliked intensely but I could never deny their ability. Our first house-master was a 're-tread'. He had taught at Epsom pre-war, had retired and subsequently returned to teaching after the destruction by German bombs of his small publishing business. Exceedingly temperamental, erratically short-tempered, and with a young wife and family of his own he was unable, or unwilling, to give his school charges the time and attention that was so necessary.

My main memory of him involves his unwelcome and unexpected late evening inspections of our common room or dormitories. I since discovered that these usually followed on from his visits to the bar of the Drift Bridge Hotel. In a sudden blaze of ill-temper he would find fault and then decide to flog the entire house, excluding the prefects. He always chose to do this in alphabetical order, which meant that I was always the first to be called in - and bending over his desk received the full and undiminished force of his ire with the first six strokes. By the time he had whacked his way through the first half of the house his energy was severely flagging. He would then storm off, announcing over his shoulder that he would punish the remainder the following evening. Of course by that time, he had invariably repented of his own intemperate behaviour and nothing more was heard of the matter - until the next time of course, when once again, and usually blameless, I would find myself at the head of the queue outside his study.

Such incidents induced a certain degree of stoicism in those who underwent that style of education which is perhaps no disadvantage in view of the tribulations of life that we all eventually have to face. But I would not recommend it as a matter of course.

Our assistant housemaster was a young Church of England padre whom we generally admired. He had taken part in the traumatic paratroop landings at Arnhem, eventually spending the last few months of the war as a prisoner. A Scot, in his early thirties, he was a balding bachelor - although his obvious and so far unsuccessful attempts to secure a bride - were the subject of much interest and amusement throughout the school. At field days and other ceremonial occasions when the Cadet Corps mounted march pasts and grand parades, he was a fitting figure, wearing his military kilt and rows of medal ribbons, to take our combined salute.

We may have been at a privileged educational establishment but however excellent the teaching facilities, our living conditions were sparse and lacking any but the most basic comforts. I can still remember sometimes having to break the ice on the surface of the water jugs on our wooden dormitory wash-stands during the winter months. There was virtually no heating in our house common room and we had a weekly, whether wanted or not, roster for hot baths in unlockable and comfortless bathrooms. Our school uniform, a grey suit made from strictly rationed cloth, was worn constantly regardless of summer or winter season. The luckier boys had a lightweight striped blazer for summer wear. Shirts and underwear were changed once a week. Sports kit remained unwashed throughout each term. I remember during much of one winter, probably the severe snowfalls and frosts of 1947, constantly wearing indoors and out, my thick army-issue greatcoat from my cadet uniform to keep out the biting cold.

Our food was subject to the severe rationing and was ill-cooked and basic. In 1947, bread and potatoes were rationed, though they had never been restricted even during the war years, and were supplemented by tins of South African snoek - that bad taste memory that marches along with restaurants serving whale-meat steaks, black, tough and fibrous fishy-tasting lumps. This diet continued for years after the end of the war. All our food was served to us by the college servants, male and female, who were recruited from among the employable but 'differently' abled and handicapped long term residents of the many asylums then scattered around Surrey. They may have inspired second-hand clinical study and observation from those among us intending a later career in medicine - but at the risk of appearing guilty of retrospective political incorrectness, they added little to our redbrick Victorian ambience. Unlike other schools attended and subsequently reported on by my contemporaries, the hand-picked female 'skivvies' (I make no apologies for this term, this is simply the way things used to be) were invariably of such ill-favoured mien, that there was never the slightest suggestion or risk of any sexual liaison taking place.

At other schools such contacts did occur. Many years later, an Anglo-French colleague of mine in West Africa, one Clovis Leplinge, had recounted the tale of his narrowly escaped expulsion from his English public school when he and a friend were discovered *in flagrante* with a comely wench, a school servant they had enticed, not unwillingly according to Clovis, into the cricket pavilion. Clovis' English friend was summarily expelled, while Clovis himself was reprieved only because, as his headmaster had explained, his conduct, although reprehensible, was to be expected because of his 'French' upbringing.

By adolescence, most boys were familiar with the theory and principles at least, of human physiology, at Epsom, possibly more so than usual because of the preponderance of pupils from families with a medical background. Nevertheless I remember one year when our stern and forbidding headmaster, a remote figure to most of the boys - he taught Greek to the classical sixth - introduced a certain Harley Street specialist in these delicate arts to the body of pupils assembled before him in the hall known as Big School. Our headmaster was H. W. F. Franklin, Esquire, MA, Ch. Ch. Oxon, author of *Latin Prose Composition*, Chairman of the Home Office Committee on punishment in prisons and Borstals (fifty years ago this would have dealt with hanging, flogging and bread-and-water regimes - whence perhaps his nickname 'Bloody Henry'). The Harley Street man, said Bloody Henry, would make all matters plain to us. The Headmaster then departed. I can remember little of what followed, most of my companions dozed or surreptitiously read while the Harley Street man droned mysteriously on, illuminating his tedious lecture with medical and scientific slides of anatomical dissections. Occasionally the audience stirred briefly to life as fuzzy projections of naked South Sea islanders, or of remote African tribesmen and women, often scarred or disfigured by parasite or infection, standing rigidly and full-frontally nude at attention before the lens of some long departed medical anthropologist's full-plate camera - were employed to illustrate whatever obscure point our would-be informant was trying to make about sexually transmitted disease or genital abnormalities.

As the lecture drew to its close, Bloody Henry re-appeared, thanked the Harley Street man profusely as we clapped politely. It was a grim outlook for our futures, we decided as we left the hall. If this was an accurate forecast of what life held in store for us. I overheard a fifth former say to a friend as we left, 'Bloody Hell, I had thought of joining the Colonial Service. But that's jolly well put me off. I think I'll put in for the law.'

All was not lost, the general picture lightened - particularly in my last summer term at Epsom. The actor Stewart Granger, an old boy who had left Epsom in 1931, was perhaps in 1948 Britain's most famous film star. He was seen by most boys one sunny afternoon when he visited his Alma Mater. On his arm was the glamourous and ravishingly beautiful young actress Jean Simmons with whom he was then conducting a well publicised love affair. Miss Simmons herself was then no more than eighteen or nineteen - of an age that matched the senior boys. The vision of loveliness she presented (whatever Stewart Granger's motives in displaying her before us might have been) finally expunged from our collective memories the Harley Street man's gloomily depressing interpretation of the 'Meaning of Life.' There was hope, after all!

At Epsom, weekday afternoons were devoted to games and athletics, formal lessons resuming for two hours between 4.30 and 6.30pm (except on Saturdays when the pre-supper hours were free). One afternoon each week was also taken up by the Corps. Joining the Cadet Corps was compulsory, the only alternatives being either the Air Training Corps, or for those of a more pacifist disposition, the Boy Scouts. I quite enjoyed the Corps with its playing at soldiers; drilling, musketry and tactics. The school had its own armoury, piled high with rifles and military kit, employed its own 'professional' Sergeant Major - an ex-Guardsman who ensured that proper standards were maintained.

We held our field days in the spring and summer terms when the entire Corps 'entrained' from Epsom Downs station to some remote Surrey heath with haversack rations, rifles, (bayonets strictly forbidden), blank cartridges and thunderflashes. We stuffed twigs and sticks up our rifle barrels with the blanks and blasted them off at each other, or at any passing wildlife. We skulked through the undergrowth and evaded thunderflashes thrown by the umpires. After a sandwich lunch, those boys who already smoked, as many did, 'skived off' into the bushes with their matches and fags, to re-assemble in the late afternoon in time to entrain once more for our home base. I remember singing the following ditty while we marched to the railway station, emulating our fathers and forebears of the Great War:

> *We are Fred Karno's Army,*
> *What bloody good are we?*
> *We cannot fight, we cannot shoot,*
> *We're the Epsom J.T.C.*
> *And when we get to Berlin,*
> *Der Kaiser he will say.*
> *Hoch! Hoch! Mein Gott!*
> *What a jolly rotten lot*
> *Are the Epsom J.T.C.*

All this was excellent training for the military life that was still to come for most of us.

By 1947 we all knew that, with the re-introduction of conscription by the then Labour Government, we faced at least eighteen months military service after leaving school. Compulsory enlistment in the Army Cadets made sense. The Epsom Corps wore the badges of the East Surrey

Regiment and continued the long established public school traditions of the former Officers' Training Corps which had succeeded the even earlier School Rifle Corps. These cadet forces have a long history. (See Note 2 - Appendix)

I obtained my War Certificate 'A' from the Epsom Corps. I also had a good Schools' Certificate. Had I gone into the Army instead of the RAF for my national service in 1950, I would probably have ended up as a Second Lieutenant in the Pay Corps, enlisting as I did straight from a city bank, but not necessarily so. Several of my contemporaries with similar qualifications who joined the Army became either Signals or Infantry subalterns, at least two of them having a very hard time of it in Korea.

Cert. 'A' one took after three years in the cadets. I never knew anyone to fail. Once one had completed the syllabus, there was a brief and simple written paper followed by a practical of drill and tactics. My entry was examined by a small coterie of young Guards officers and NCOs from nearby Pirbright, wearing impeccably tailored uniforms, dove-grey greatcoats and 'cheese-cutter' caps. The tactical questions we were asked by the subalterns (hardly out of school themselves) were of the following order:

'It is late afternoon. Your section of ten men is pinned down under fire and under heavy enemy mortar and machine-gun fire and sporadic air attack. A large force of enemy tanks is assembling in your rear. A dense cloud of gas is approaching your position from upwind. You have been outflanked by a squadron of horsed cavalry and enemy naval forces including monitors lying offshore are now ranging on your position. What action will you take?'

It was necessary to suppress the urge to reply, as being patently clear to any sensible person, 'I should enquire if any of my section still possessed clean white underpants, and on receiving an affirmative answer I would request them to wave them in such a manner as to be clearly visible to the enemy as indicating our wish to surrender.'

This is not a militarily acceptable solution, the correct answer being, 'Sir! I would wait until dusk, first donning respirators, then swiftly forming my section into tactical blobs, taking advantage of all dead ground and the shadows from the setting sun, I would infiltrate the enemy's lines in the direction of our own friendly forces. At the earliest opportunity I would then make my report to my superior officer.'

In my own case, when asked to drill the squad in my turn, I foolishly let them get too far away for my puny, half-broken voice to order the 'About Turn' within effective earshot, all this taking place out-of-doors on a windy day. My squad was rapidly disappearing in the distance beyond all hope of recall.

'Get a GRIP, laddie!' grated the Guards sergeant - then with a strangulated roar fit to demolish the Walls of Jericho, he bellowed 'AAaaaabbbBBBYTE TURRNN!' Whereupon my squad once more returned to my ineffective charge. It didn't matter one jot - we all passed. In the end the RAF was not in the least interested that I had War Cert. 'A'. What they wanted was previous service in the Air Training Corps. It did however give me a singular advantage over my fellow recruits without cadet experience when the time came.

During the summer half-term holiday in 1948 after I had completed my first year in the sixth form, my father took me out to lunch in a West End restaurant. Having no clearly defined sense of direction as to my future life and career, over a manly half-pint of beer he asked me what I wanted to do. 'I dunno Dad,' is I suppose what I answered. I think he found the school fees made too heavy demands on his purse for such indecision. 'How would you like to be a farmer?' Considering this prospect all too briefly, I conjured up visions of becoming a gentleman farmer, leaning on a five-barred gate overlooking my broad acres. Totally unaware at that time of the implications involved, not least that like Military Intelligence, gentleman and farmer are callings almost diametrically opposed, contradictions in terms. I agreed.

The die was cast, my school days were definitely over.

5
A Farmer's Boy

I'll plough and sow
And reap and mow
And be a farmer's boy-oy-oy-oh!
I'll be a farmer's boy.
From a traditional country air

I was not totally unsuited to the agricultural life. I made a passable farmer's lad for the best part of a year, working on two mixed farms in Cumberland's Eden Valley. My father had arranged for me to go on to agricultural college following a year's practical experience. The rub was, that no-one ever bothered to explain to me what future career openings might lie ahead. If someone had said to me that after a while I might have concentrated on forestry, or land agency - or perhaps have entered the Colonial Service as an agricultural officer, then I would probably have stuck at it. As it turned out, working through a full farming year - weeding, hoeing and pulling turnips, milking smelly, wet cows, haymaking, harvesting, hedging, mucking-out byres, scything weeds and thistles, herding stupid, woolly sheep - all in the unforgiving wet and muddy climate of northern England finally convinced me that at the age of seventeen, my future - whatever it might be - did not lie in that direction.

The reason of course that I had fallen in so swiftly with my father's suggestion was that having always enjoyed country life and pursuits - spending part of my idyllic summer holidays with a school friend on a Lake District farm, fishing and shooting - I mistakenly thought that actually 'working' on a farm would allow me to carry on a sort of rural Utopian existence. How wrong I was.

I was employed on the now long-outdated principle of farm pupillage in that my father paid a premium to my employer on the basis that while working I would actually be taught something worthwhile about the theory and practice of farming.

Reality was very different. Farmers like all craftsmen are reluctant to disclose the secrets of their trade. Farmers' children soak up this information with their mothers' milk. The outsider is left to glean whatever nuggets might be left lying around. Asking questions does not necessarily lead to answers because the knowledge sought has never consciously been formulated before. 'Why lad? That's just the way it's allus bin done.' I was not paid a wage. My father sent me a weekly allowance as pocket money and I was simply used as unpaid extra labour.

The first farm only lasted a few months. I was sharing the farm house, the cooking and all the chores with the young and recently qualified farm manager. I remember that we lived on scrambled eggs from the hens, home-cured bacon, porridge made of milled oats from the cattle feed (replete with rat droppings) and butter that we churned ourselves - after skimming off the cream from the milk that was sold to the Marketing Board. There were only the two of us who lived in the ancient and uncomfortable farmhouse plus the cowman who lived in his tied cottage and looked after the stock. It did not work out. I simply did not know enough to take on the responsibility that was needed. I had to learn to milk. I couldn't drive the tractor to begin with - and when I did (almost entirely self-taught) I left a trail of destruction in my wake. I could not harness the Clydesdale mare single-handed, then back her into the shafts of the cart. I could not control the pair of sheepdogs (Fly and Spot) working two fields away, Indeed I did not know what it was I was supposed to be telling them to do. I could not dose a flock of sheep or drench a cow without all the expensive pills or the medicine landing on the floor. When I milled the corn for the cattle feed I let the sacks overflow and the chute and the mill run dry from the loft above so that the hammer-mill's 'hammers' flew off in all directions, whanging and ricocheting off the walls like bullets. I was not popular at times. All these simple tasks could have been done by a fourteen year old farm lad brought up to it, standing on his head.

The first job I was given was to lift a field of several acres of mangolds - swedes or turnips to the uninitiated - to be stored for winter fodder. It was October - cold, muddy and at times frosty. Having pulled your individual turnip free of the ground with the left hand it is then topped and tailed with the turnip knife, a short sickle with a spur at the end of the blade. Then the whole process, known as 'snagging,' is repeated several thousand times for two to three weeks, morning and afternoon until the field is littered with the bulbous roots. It is hard on the back from the half-bent posture the harvester needs to adopt. As a tedious agricultural chore it is only equalled by the springtime task of hoeing and 'singling' turnips. As well as being as boring as watching paint dry it is hard physical labour.

Having lifted the turnips, my next task was to lead them back to the farmyard for storage. After several weeks I was now dreaming turnips. I took Jess the Clydesdale mare - having learned at last that to stuff a draught horse's head through its collar and hames, it is necessary to turn the collar upside-down, swivelling it around once past the ears. I finally mastered the art of sorting out the harness, the halter and bit (without getting bitten or stamped on by Jess's huge, feathery feet), backing her between the up-lifted shafts of the two-wheeled farm cart and hitching up all the various hooks and chains. I would ride on the cart-shaft to my turnip field and lead Jess back by the halter, once the cart was laden.

I became over-weeningly confident in my own abilities, a serious fault in the young. Heaving the roots up into the cart was a monotonous task and after a while I tried to load more and more turnips, piling them high in the interests of efficiency. Part of my route back to the farmyard lay across a recently ploughed field, at right angles to the furrows. As I led Jess by the halter the heavily laden cart lurched across the ridges. At first a single turnip bounced over the front of the cart, striking Jess on the rump and making her go faster. The faster she went, the more turnips fell on her - shaken out of the carefully constructed pyramid of mangolds that I had loaded. At the third or fourth blow she received, she bolted, rearing her head and shaking me aside like a rag doll. From my hands and knees I watched in disbelief as Jess galloped like a racehorse in a steeplechase, turnips flying in all directions, as the cart behind her leapt and corkscrewed from furrow to furrow. At last, reaching the dyke, topped with its dense thorn hedge, Jess, still in the shafts, flew over the hedge-top like a Grand National champion. By the time I caught up with her, to my horror, I found Jess on the far side of the hedge, suspended over a ditch by the shafts, while the cart and its few remaining turnips was jammed firmly behind her on the other side of the dyke. In the end we had to cut Jess (unharmed at least) out of her harness. The cart was badly damaged.

Equally my efforts with the Fergusson tractor were not appreciated. Armed with this post-war piece of cutting-edge technology and a half-hour or so of basic instruction I demolished gates (that had mysteriously closed themselves since I last careered that way). I modified the hydraulic drawbar almost beyond economic repair when trying to attach a trailer whose towing-hitch failed to match up to that of the tractor.

I believe the final straw was after some three or four months when the cowman - having been kicked by a cow - was off sick for several days. The farm manager had gone away for a couple of days and I was left in sole charge of milking the dairy herd of some thirty cows over what turned into a very long weekend. I will not go into detail but suffice it to say that the milk yield immediately fell by a third and a week or so later the fractious and nervous cows were still yielding well below their expected capacity. I had ceased to be of any economic advantage and, because of my lack of experience, I was something of a liability. Inevitably we parted.

I stayed at my next farm for another eight months or so. It was a much larger four hundred acre mixed farm which, as was the case in those far off days of cheap labour and little mechanisation, could call some eight men into action (including the family) at times when they were hard pressed. The cowman was a German ex-POW as was another of the farm's workers. Both had fought on the Russian front. There was the horseman, Wattie, who lived in the loft over the kitchen. He was an elderly man, over fond of his beer, who started each morning coughing and spluttering over his first cigarette of the day, which he fashioned from newspaper and his hand-rubbed Black Twist pipe tobacco. I learned a lot, and more than enough to absorb the lesson that my future did not lie in the muddy fields and cow-byres of a post-war north country world of farming.

I was just seventeen when I returned to London with a certain sense of relief. Within a few months I had, by devious means and various introductions, obtained a position with a city bank, the then Chartered Bank of India, Australia and China, in Bishopsgate. I had become a Foreign Staff Probationer with the view that, at the age of twenty-one, I would be posted to the Far East where lay the bulk of their business. When I was first interviewed by the secretary of the bank, to whom I had an introduction, I said to him with all the candour of youth, 'Of course I'm no good at maths at all. I'm very bad at adding up and that sort of thing. I only got a poor pass in School Cert. - and that was after sitting the exam twice.'

Airily he replied, 'Doesn't matter one jot, my boy. When you get out East there'll be plenty of native clerks to take care of all that. Don't worry about it!'

Shortly before this incident I had been taken out to lunch at the Normandie restaurant in Knightsbridge with my mother and an old family friend, a retired Colonel and bachelor, who we all knew as 'Boysie'. He had finished his career as Comptroller of the Governor General's Household in Australia. Before joining the Army in 1914 he had started off his working life in a city bank. My mother had engineered this particular meeting as she - like all worried mothers - had decided that I was unsettled and uncertain as well as anxious about my future.

Over coffee Boysie didn't mince his words. 'Your mother tells me she's very worried about you. Doesn't know what will become of you, all that sort of thing, what?'

'I suppose so...' I tailed off, not really knowing what to reply, as my mother hadn't broached the subject before lunch, keeping her concern under wraps.

Boysie continued, tucking into the 'mouse-trap' cheese and biscuits, dabbing at his grey toothbrush moustache with his napkin. By 1949 I think the government restriction that in a restaurant one could only have either cheese or pudding, but not both, had finally been lifted. His balding pate glistened with brilliantine. 'Well now, you're a well set-up sort of lad aren't you? Fond of cricket and all that sort of thing?' I felt obliged to answer, 'Well, yes, of course!' Trying to sound enthusiastic about the subject, which was very far from the truth.

'There now!' said Boysie triumphantly, turning to my mother, 'I told you there was nothing to worry about. The boy likes cricket - obviously nothing wrong at all. Right as rain!'

6
NATIONAL SERVICE - RAF, 1950-52,
CALLED UP AND BROKEN DOWN

*Every man thinks meanly of himself for not
having been a soldier, or not having been at sea.*
        Samuel Johnson

One night not long ago I dreamed that I had my call-up papers again. The classic anxiety dream. I had a train to catch in twenty minutes, my uniform was creased and faded and no longer fitted properly. My wife had gone to work. I had no breakfast. A troopship was waiting on the tide to sail off to some nameless war. The webbing straps on my kit were hopelessly tangled, 'idle' brass and blotched with verdigris and mould. Where was my passport? Why did I need a passport? Foolish question! So that I could desert if I didn't like it, of course. I needed some comforting book to take with me to read through the endless days ahead - but nothing more would fit in my already overstuffed kit bag. Dear God! Just look at my rifle, the web sling slack and greasy, unblancoed, dirty, its barrel choked with a mass of rust and dirt, the battle peepsight still missing from the slide, kicked off in that panic on the train in Malaya. There was going to be trouble with the Armoury Sergeant, my pay docked when that was found out. Perhaps I would be put on a fizzer - Oh God!

Then I awoke, deeply uneasy and disturbed. My wife was sleeping quietly beside me. A bar of bright light shone from beneath the bedroom door. Was there some shadowy presence outside on the landing? Who or what would I see beyond the door? The ghost perhaps of an eighteen year old boy, hardly a man? Would I recognise him? Treading softly I opened the door into the pool of moonlight streaming through from the bathroom window, its cold brilliance sharply outlining the Lake District fells fading into the distance of a crisp October night, nothing else. I had a pee, gazing out on the moon and went back to bed.

As I write these lines it is half a century since October 1950 when I received my final call-up papers for my national service at the age of

A.M. Pamphlet 250

MY HUSBAND OR SON (OR OTHER RELATIVE) IS SERVING IN THE ROYAL AIR FORCE

WHAT DO I DO?

1. **Question:** If I want to write to or about him?

    Answer: You always quote his number, rank, name, and initials, in that order. If you do not do this, unnecessary delay may occur; and you know how much the receipt of regular mail means to men serving away from their homes.

2. **Question:** If he is overseas and I want to send him an urgent message of a private nature?

    Answer: You write to the Officer Commanding Records, Record Office (C.1), Royal Air Force, Gloucester, for a C.S.N. Cable Form. You give his full number, rank, name, unit and relationship. The scheme is operative to and from :—

    (i) All countries in which R.A.F. personnel are serving, except Canada, South Africa, Newfoundland, U.S.A., and West Indies.

    (ii) R.A.F. personnel serving in H.M. Ships (including Troop Transports).

3. **Question:** If I want to find out the facilities there are for communicating with him by Air Mail when he is overseas?

    Answer: You enquire at the nearest Post Office.

4. **Question:** If I lose his address?

    Answer: You write to the Officer Commanding Records, Record Office (C.1), Royal Air Force, Gloucester, requesting to be put in touch with him.

5. **Question:** If I have his address but am worried because I have not heard from him for some weeks?

    Answer: (i) You write a letter to the Commanding Officer of his Unit.

    (ii) If he is overseas and you have not heard from him for over two months, communicate with the Officer Commanding Records as shown at Answer No. 4, when a wireless message will be despatched to his Overseas Unit requesting details of his general welfare and for him to be interviewed and urged to write home.

eighteen in 1950. Never in my previous recollection have I dreamed of my time in the RAF in such a way. If I were in tune with the present times, with which I have long since fallen out, (for all the similarity I find between now and the days of my youth - I might just as well have been born in Albania), perhaps I should sue, claiming damages for Post-Traumatic Stress Disorder, or volunteer myself for some (publicly funded of course) in-depth personal counselling? I still sometimes think of those days; the farce, the boredom, the many compensations of comradeship in far-off barrack rooms in distant lands. I sometimes talk of those times in the Services with my contemporaries who served. All have tales to tell, some to make you cry with remembered laughter, some to reduce you to tears with the loss and futility.

~ ~ ~ ~ ~ ~ ~ ~ ~ ~

If one includes World War Two, (although some would have it that there was only the one war, the Great War - part one being merely temporarily suspended to allow the Germans a breathing space and time to re-arm), national service conscripted all fit young men for a period which lasted more than twenty years until it finally fizzled out, along with the British Empire, in 1962. This excludes Northern Ireland - of whose wartime population some 38,000 nevertheless flocked to volunteer, both Catholic and Protestant - perhaps even more surprising were the 43,000 men and women from the Republic of Eire who also volunteered to join the British Forces. Between 1945 and 1962 alone 1.8 million men were conscripted. The length of service varied from the duration of World War II hostilities to as little as eighteen months between 1947 and 1950 when it was extended to two years - some poor bastards captured by the Chinese in Korea actually served for more than four! With the conscripts of 1915-1918 that meant that almost without exception every British generation of the first half of the twentieth century had either personal experience of the Armed Forces or had family or friends who had served. It is a period unique in this country's history, unlikely ever to be repeated, during which Britain truly had a Citizens' Army, a mass of non-professional civilian soldiers, sailors and airmen, many of them reluctant heroes. Indeed why the need to volunteer when you were almost certain to be conscripted willy-nilly?

If one knew one was bound to serve, then one accepted it without exception. The only exemptions were by virtue of age, physical disability (eg bed-wetting or flat feet - if properly certified - were both sufficient reason, but unlike the American services, shaven armpits and perfume were not considered a disqualification). Further exemptions were for reserved occupations such as farming, mining, or the Merchant Navy, in wartime a much more dangerous calling than most. Between 1939 and 1945 there was a one-in-four chance of a merchant seaman being killed - higher than in any of the other three services - and their pay ceased the moment their ship sank. The young Ulsterman or Jerseyman, one envied perhaps - and then wondered why so many of the former volunteered for three years regular service. Was it a badge of manhood perhaps? Of my generation most had older relatives who had served, many of them during the Great War, both men and women. It was a rite of passage accepted almost without question.

There were no teenagers in my youth - they remained an American invention. Holden Caulfield and *The Catcher in the Rye* were still light-years away in the future. One moment one was at school, a child of thirteen or fourteen in some cases, the next moment one had a job and was working for a living. Such role models as we had were our elders, who had all been through the mill in one way or another, at war either as Home Front civilians or in the Forces. My father had been a soldier in the 1914-18 war, my sister had served throughout the London Blitz as an ATS driver with an AA battery, my brother had been a Fleet Air Arm pilot, my brother-in-law was a Hurricane pilot in the Battle of Britain and still serving in the RAF, a rare survivor of 'The Few.' My godfather died with *HMS Hood*. Even my great-aunt Sally had worked in an aircraft factory in 1917 stitching up Sopwith Camels. Any number of other relatives, few of them professional soldiers or sailors or airmen had served, some had been killed or wounded. My family background and experience was common at that time. Being called-up was simply a part of growing-up for whole generations of young men. With hindsight I eventually came to understand the reason why, that like so many of my generation I was blessed with a superfluity of maiden aunts, who without children of their own channelled their affections and modest fortunes towards their nieces and nephews. A large proportion of the generation of young men (as always the strongest and the fittest) who fifteen or twenty years earlier would have married them and fathered their children had marched off to the Great War and had died in their hundreds of thousands in the slaughterhouses of Flanders and the Somme.

Most adolescents of the immediate post-war period were conformists. Any opportunity to be different, or to form a sub-group of one's peers was almost non-existent. 'Yoof Culture' had it even been suggested would have been bizarre. Clothes, food and fuel were rationed. Cars and motor bikes were few and far between and definitely not for the young. On the wireless those who were 'with it' listened to the American Forces Network with its traditional jazz and Big Band recordings - but the 'with it' then included people in their thirties. Foreign travel, even if one had money, was severely restricted by the £25 annual limit that one could take out of the country. Adolescents of eighteen (the legal age for drinking) rarely frequented pubs, apart from the fact they mostly couldn't afford it, they were not made welcome. The actuality faced by most young people meant either that they lived at home on low wages, or that they were still at school.

Family ties and discipline were stronger than today and such vestigial social services as there were did not take kindly to anyone who dropped out of the system. A job of some sort was always available even for those with minimal skills or abilities. The minority who planned to take a degree or to complete an apprenticeship had the Hobson's choice of deferring their national service until qualified - or of joining up at eighteen and deferring their further education. No wonder there were few rebels in the grey, pinched years of post-war Britain. Non-conformity was a luxury that few could afford or imagine. By the standards of the 1990s both rich and poor led lives of material deprivation. Average expectations were limited to simple achievable goals. Horizons were still clouded by the war years and by the thirties' Depression.

In most closed tribal societies, the adolescent young of both sexes become a special group. The difficulties of transition from child to adult are dealt with by treating the teenager as a raw recruit to the mysteries and duties of the fully-fledged member of the tribe, both male and female. Looked at cynically, one could say that they recognise the bolshie aggressiveness of the pimpled youth and the moody pubescent maiden and by locking them away in bush-camps they can then be painfully and ceremonially circumcised, cicatrised, frightened half to death, taught tribal lays and lore by their elders and betters, instructed in their duties as warriors and wives until allowed final entry into 'proper' society. By ritualising puberty they thus obviate the worst effects of Shakespeare's

cheerless complaint:
> *I would there were no age between sixteen and three and twenty, for there is nothing in the in-between but getting wenches with child,*
> *wronging the ancientry, stealing, fighting.* A Winter's Tale.

It is a fortunate society that has no teenagers. Allowing for early physical maturity with modern improvements in nutrition and healthcare, Shakespeare's wilderness years could almost be re-set between thirteen and twenty-five. These are the very age limits which today encompass the majority of petty, or not so petty, criminals. The average young male of the forties and the fifties was most likely to find his anxieties, his antisocial urges and aggressions comprehensively channelled in other directions by drill-sergeants, petty officers, foremen and chief clerks - even perhaps being clipped around the ears by the local 'bobby' on the beat. The system did not tolerate the wilfully disobedient, the unruly or the simple, idle layabout lifestyle that most of us would have preferred to adopt given half a chance. The ways and means of enforcing a disciplined conformity were quite ruthless and usually, although not entirely, effective. To break the system required the qualities of a masochist, an unrelenting, determined masochism, which few possessed - and in any case were few in number. The Army for example swiftly recognised the infamous Kray Twins for the incorrigible eighteen-year old villains they were, locked them up for several months, first and briefly in the Tower of London as deserters and then in a detention barracks before dishonourably discharging them back into Civvy Street. The genuinely incompetent had a hard time of it until they were recognised as such and shunted off into some quiet backwater where they could do no harm while some sort of role was found for them.

I had already had my medical in late July 1950, in some dismal civic hall in Shepherds Bush, just after my eighteenth birthday. At that age today one would be allowed to vote, whereas in 1950 that anniversary was still three years off, and my employers, the Chartered Bank in Bishopsgate, did not allow me a cheque book until I became twenty-one. A motley gang of youths had been assembled for the medical. A crew of attendants and doctors marshalled, sampled and examined us - teeth, ears, throat, eyes, feet, chests. Fixed and moving parts were prodded perfunctorily, 'Say Aaaah. Say ninety-nine. Cough. Fill this bottle. Read this chart. Fill in this form. Do HURRY UP THERE!'

There was an air of general unease among the group of milling youths - understandably. There were nasty little wars going on all over the world, some not so little, some promising to get bigger. On the 25 June 1950 North Korean tanks and infantry had crossed the 38th Parallel. The British had already promised troops to reinforce the Americans. By July of 1950 the war was going badly - the Americans were then leading their 'Great Bug-Out' fleeing south to the small enclave at Pusan that would still provide a toe-hold for the United Nations to recover the peninsular. British 'Z' Reservists were being sent to Hong Kong to replace units already on standby for Korea. In Indo-China the French were having an increasingly tough time with the Viet-Minh led Communist rebellion, who also posed the same threat to the British in Malaya where the terrorist campaign was now giving us a bloody nose, (although the Malayan communists saw themselves both as liberators and also as part of the mainland Chinese Eighth Route Army). There was a healthy reluctance abroad to go into the Army. As far as I could make out we all indicated our choice as the Navy or the RAF. 'Fat chance,' we were cheerfully told. 'Ten-to-one you'll all be wearin' black boots and battledress with a rifle and pack and on your way to Korea before you know where you are.'

At the Chartered Bank in the city a few days later the accountant called in all the junior clerks and foreign staff probationers of the same age group awaiting our call-up. There were several of us and I was sent for first, being then, as now it would be correct to say 'alphabetically' challenged. I had no idea what to expect. The head office accountant, a powerful figure in a city bank of those days, was a small and dour Scot approaching retirement. Without preamble he said, 'You'll be leaving soon for your military service. When you've served your eighteen months, will you be coming back to the bank?' Being young, naive and taught to tell the truth, I said, 'I'm not really sure Sir. I don't know. I haven't yet thought about it.'

'What a pity,' said the grey, forbidding Scot. 'Had you said yes, the bank has just decided to pay those who agree to return their full salary while in the Forces, plus a bonus of £100 when they come back.'

That was a savage blow, a thoughtless slip of the tongue had cost me dear. A year-and-a-half's full pay, plus a substantial bonus - nearly £500 in all - a small fortune. I tried hastily to back track, but he would have none of it. I went from his office severely chastened.

I suppose I learned a lesson. It was an unfair approach. Of course I told the others, all of whom solemnly promised to return, which they did, it would have been foolish not to. They all collected two years salary plus bonus (national service was extended by six months by the Atlee government within a few months of the Korean War starting). Several only stayed on for a month or two and then left. I went back when demobbed in 1952 re-claiming my job as was my right, stayed on for nearly two years and got nothing for my honesty.

At the beginning of October I received my marching orders: 'Report to RAF Padgate on 17 October 1950.' A travel warrant was enclosed together with a postal order for four shillings - my first day's pay - and looking back on it, I suppose it was the equivalent of the old Recruiting Sergeant's King's shilling. If I failed to turn up as ordered, I would be a deserter. Looking back again, I don't know what my mother felt at the time. The Navy, the Army and now the Air Force had in turn taken her brood. My brother and sister had served for most of the war, my brother trained overseas as a pilot, returning to Britain in time to see out the last year of the European conflict still training as a carrier fighter pilot. Had the Japanese not folded in August 1945 he would almost certainly have gone to the Far East. My sister in the ATS having been a driver with a London AA battery throughout the Blitz, finished in 1945 as a War Office driver ferrying Generals and VIPs. Now, I, the youngest child was going off, perhaps to war again. I think that people today have long forgotten the demands, and the duties, that King, Country and the Empire imposed on its citizens, and with how little complaint those demands were met.

RAF Padgate, near Warrington, came as an unpleasant shock to many recruits. Bleak, uncomfortable huts, cold and damp October mists added nothing to the depressing atmosphere. A cheerful, elderly - or so he seemed to us - medal be-ribboned Irish Leading Aircraftman (LAC - then a rank of consequence in the RAF) took charge of us. Doubling us around, trying to instill some sense of order into the ill-assorted rabble that we were. We were issued with ill-fitting uniforms from stores, bearing out the old service joke about the two standard sizes, 'either too large or too small' and a small mountain of kit. Then it was off to the camp barber for a regulation haircut with the added indignity of having to pay a shilling for the crude cropping. No matter that one had a 'civvy' haircut the day before, the treatment was the same. Then for more medicals and a brief swearing-in ceremony. This was followed by a lecture or two, an eye-opening session on fatigues in the grease-soaked 'Tin Room' of the smelly cook house. All our civilian belongings were parceled-up under supervision. We were allowed a paperback or two to read, while everything else bar pyjamas and a toothbrush was sent home.

We were not to receive our eight weeks basic training at Padgate. Our draft of one hundred recruits was destined for RAF Hereford (today the Regimental Depot of the SAS). We spent a week at Padgate in what by today's standards would be called squalor. In an adjoining hut a recruit committed suicide, hanging himself in the 'ablutions' causing a brief flurry of concern. Another fresh-faced young lad down from the Orkneys had to be cut out from his long flannel combinations - complete with strategic flaps - into which he had been sewn for the winter. Our Irish LAC, inevitably named Paddy, showed us how to wear our ill-cut uniforms, how to assemble the crazy tangle of webbing straps and haversacks and how to pack our kit bags. Now we knew why we had not been permitted to keep any personal belongings. It was not simply so that we couldn't desert as we had thought, but that there was not an inch of excess space. Brasso, blanco and boot polish all had to be bought from the NAAFI canteen at our own expense. In between shuffling us to and from the cook house for unappetising meals Paddy gave us a few cheerful elementary lessons in 'bull', warned us not to lose any kit nor to steal it from our mates. The Airman's Credo was quoted: 'Thou shalt not take unto thyself nor covet thine oppo's kit, neither shalt thou borrow thereof in his absence lest thy sins thrust upon thee the fist that by its quickness doth blacken the eye of the offender.' He taught us how to stand in a semblance of a straight line and to watch out for the drill corporals and sergeants into whose tender care we would be passing and who 'would have us by the short and curlies' if we transgressed.

We must have been dispatched by truck or coach to Hereford. My memory has failed me, but there was no way our shambolic draft could have been allowed to travel by train. The few friendships struck up at Padgate were just as quickly broken down again as on arrival our Flight was re-formed into three sections each with their own hut and Corporal Drill Instructor. The quarters were similar to but better than Padgate. They were also much cleaner (owing to the superhuman efforts of our predecessors as we were soon to discover). We had sheets and mattresses on our beds rather than the rough blankets and straw 'biscuits' we had endured for the previous week. This raised our expectations.

These improvements in our meagre lot were soon superseded by the all-pervading presence of the Corporal Drill Instructors (DIs) whose job it was to systematically break us down over the next few weeks - to strip us of our 'civvy' mentality, to shout, to rage, to scream, to insult, to instill in us the automatic, disciplined response of Pavlovian dogs. They taught us not to question orders, to spend all one's waking hours not involved with drill or instruction, in 'bulling' boots, brasses, webbing, rifles, floors, buckets and the 'ablutions.' Our skills included ironing and pressing coarse serge trousers to knife edged creases, polishing boot studs and eyelets to a glittering sheen for kit inspections, buffing-up mess tins to a brilliance with which Perseus could have bedazzled Medusa to death. Not a speck of detectable dust was allowed to soil the floor. The window panes were polished diamond bright. One shuffled across the gleaming linoleum with strips of blanket beneath one's feet.

Perfection was the order of the day, every day. A hint of dried Brasso behind a cap badge signified idleness. A brush shank not scraped sufficiently white or a bed frame out of a strictly measured alignment, would bring about a tirade of recrimination, of colourful threats, of suggestions of varying and lucidly expressed opinions as to the recipient's ancestry, his limited past, present and future prospects. All this was usually achieved with a minimum of four-letter abuse. It has always been a source of wonder to me how such histrionic verbosity was achieved by certain NCOs. An 'act' it certainly was. Did they have handbooks of military insults? Did they practice in front of mirrors? The authentic outraged flush, the bullfrog swelling of the throat - was it all accomplished by some arcane system of mental and physical exercises? However it was done, and probably still is for all I know, the individual on the receiving end must not by any twitch, wink, facial expression or manner give the slightest suspicion that he thinks it is all an act. To do so risked charges of insubordination, or of the old catch-all accusation of 'dumb insolence' and serious consequences to follow.

I have seen callow recruits reduced to tears, standing stiffly to attention in front of some NCO screaming face to face a torrent of abusive recriminations for some minor error in military dress or deportment. For the victim to move or to respond in any way other than rigid subservience is simply to provoke the aggressor to further excesses. There are no defences. All thresholds are breached at this early stage of the recruit's indoctrination. Any degree of personal esteem and mutual respect between ranks which is part of the ultimate aim of basic military training is still far off. An overly-coarse or genuinely foul-mouthed NCO in my brief service experience was a rarity and neither liked nor respected. This was all the more curious considering the rapid deterioration in the average recruit's own vocabulary in the company of his fellows, where however gentle his upbringing might have been, the F word in all its limited variety rapidly became the common currency of our daily discourse.

The conversion of a civilian, willing or unwilling, to a serviceman is not an edifying spectacle for those of a faint-hearted disposition. The first few weeks of our basic training were actively devoted to stripping the last vestiges of 'Civvy Street' from our existences. The constant carrot dangled before us was that at the end of our first four weeks' incarceration our Training Flight might, only 'might', be permitted a forty-eight hour pass. That was provided that we had progressed and improved to the state where we were fit to be seen in public, off the base, as representatives of the RAF. A thin glimmer of hope had appeared on the horizon of our seemingly timeless existence in this limbo of screaming NCOs, of 'bull' and drill, of boring lectures in military law, on rank and precedence, of repetitive drills and exercises and of already spotless equipment being made ever more perfect and presentable.

I was very lucky in comparison to most of my comrades in this temporary misfortune. I had been a boarder at an English prep. school, followed by public school. To quote the Duke of Wellington, 'After Eton, a barrack room seemed like a perfumed boudoir.' Indeed the living conditions of an RAF recruit in 1950 were somewhat better than they had been at school. The water was hotter, the food was probably better, the barrack room with its coke-fuelled 'Arctic' stove was warmer. I had been in the Cadet Corps for three years. I knew all my basic drill movements and commands. I had been screamed at by Guards NCOs while taking my War Certificate 'A'. To strip and clean a Lee-Enfield rifle held no mysteries. I could already name the parts from muzzle to butt-trap in my sleep. By avoiding drawing attention to myself (the NCOs had plenty of softer targets), by doing everything competently, I got by much better than many of my fellow recruits to whom everything in our strange new life was unexplored territory strewn with mine fields for the unwise and unwary.

Communal living without any comforts of home and family, strict discipline, the stress of being shouted at without warning, detachment from the so-called 'real life' left behind in Civvy Street was of no great moment or consequence to the few of us who had already endured the same sort of upbringing. For those of us weaned on boarding school regimes, familiar with drill and military trivia through our Cadet training, it was perhaps too easy. For the majority, who had never left home or ever slept away from the bosom of their family in all their brief lives, it was a rude awakening. Our ages ranged from eighteen to as much as twenty-two or three (in the case of those who had deferred their call-up for one reason or another). Our occupations ran the whole gamut - apprentices, clerks, civil servants, students, trainee-this and trainee-that, greengrocers, librarians, labourers, a handful of graduates. Young men from every class and region of Britain.

The difference between ourselves and the youth of today was that if we had left school before call-up we had, almost without exception, been in some sort of paid employment and being recruited for the RAF it was a pre-requisite that we could read and write. Literacy was more universal at that time, although I subsequently heard from friends in the Army that not a few of their comrades were functionally illiterate. Letters had to be both written and read for them and written instructions carefully explained. But then the Army would have taken over and all but the most recalcitrant dyslexics would have been taught (probably by numbers, for that is the Army way of doing things) a basic literacy by the time their service was completed.

I don't remember any particular friends from that time, although towards the end of our training the three of us who were already destined for the Far East, Alan Stephenson (Steve) with whom I shared all of my service, and Dave Teague who was posted to Kai-Tak in Hong Kong, were sticking together. As for the rest, we were all in the same boat, good mates for the present, comrades in temporary misfortune, ships that would soon pass in the night.

We were ceaselessly drilled - foot drill, arms drill. If it rained we drilled under cover in vast echoing hangars. I suspect that those same hangars today still echo to the shouts and screams of NCO instructors of the SAS. We were endlessly lectured on basic foot and infantry drills, on musketry, on military law, on RAF ranks and procedures, on service administration, on King's Regulations, crimes and penalties and on our rights. By this stage it came as no surprise to learn that we had none except the 'right to some pay, and to some leave' both unspecified - everything else being a 'privilege'.

We were shown lurid and frightening films on venereal diseases - no doubt intended to put us off sex for the entire period of our service - or even longer. We were told that the male projectionist had fainted and had to be carried out from the camp cinema during the showing of one such film for WRAF recruits. We were tested as to our 'aptitudes and abilities'. We answered those early multiple choice papers and fitted strange shapes into matching apertures, to determine the slot we should subsequently occupy in the great RAF Scheme for the Universe. This was comforting for we felt that those of us who wished to be mustered as despatch riders, drivers, trainee air crew, air-sea rescue crewmen, firemen, air traffic controllers, aircraft riggers and fitters, gunners, armourers and mechanics - would all achieve our goals. We little realised that this was all a cover-up for when our names would all be mixed up in some giant hat and drawn at random. Cooks, clerks, storemen, medical orderlies, general dogs' bodies in the main, requiring little or no formal training, were our destinies.

The only one of our whole Training Flight who was allocated what we considered a desirable 'trade' was a big, soft, ungainly Jewish lad, a founder member of the Flight's 'Awkward Squad' for remedial drill, who found the greatest difficulty in simply standing up straight in the vertical position. He was popular because of his cheerful disposition in the face of multiple adversities. His buttons popped and his beret would fall off his frizzy red hair in the first breath of wind. When commanded to 'fix bayonets' both rifle and bayonet would somehow detach themselves from his grasp and end up on the ground. He turned left when he was ordered to turn right. When marching he was always out of step - frantically trying to match the swing of his arms (but not his feet) to those of his adjoining files. In short, he was a disorganised disaster both on and off the parade ground. He reduced our Sergeant and Corporal Drill Instructors to spluttering incoherence, once drawing the comment from our Cockney Corporal DI, 'PULL YOUSELF TOGETHER AIRMAN!! You're like a fart in a colander. You can't make up your mind which way to go! WOT ARE YOU, YOU 'ORRIBLE LITTLE MAN??' Eliciting the time-honoured reply, 'I'm a fart in a colander Corporal.'

To what trade was this paragon of unco-ordination allocated? To our uproarious disbelief and amazement - at the end of our training he was sent off to become a despatch rider! I often wonder what befell him. That same Corporal DI on one occasion while berating us for our ragged performance, shouted, 'Right! You 'orrible lot. Get it all together now like this!' Whereupon he quoted (or more likely shouted):

'It was on the China Station
The Navy gave a demonstration.
They sunk a junk with jets of spunk
From united masturbation!'
'NOW YOU 'ORRIBLE LOT - GET IT ALL TOGETHER LIKE THEM SEX-STARVED MATELOTS! ...ON THE COMMAND - SQUAAADDD!!'

Not a single soul dared the faintest titter, until falling out for a smoke some ten minutes later when tears of mirth ran down our cheeks.

~~~~~~~~~~

As Aircraftmen Second Class, we were the lowest of the low. By the end of the first four weeks of training we were deemed smart enough, and presumably 'conditioned' enough to be let loose on a 'forty-eight', a weekend pass from the camp. We had learned to wear our uniforms with an acceptable degree of smartness, our foot drill was becoming sharp and precise. The snap, crackle and pop of a well executed movement en masse was a cause of pride. Our instructors also must have felt some sense of achievement in bringing about this transformation upon such a shambling, disparate and ill-assorted group of civilian recruits who had been turned over to them only a brief month earlier. This was also reflected in our NCOs' manner. They were definitely becoming more reasonable towards us, although equally still not to be trifled with. Their quirks and foibles, their sense of humour were subjects of discussion among the recruits. They were now only part-time terrifying objects of fear. They had achieved their primary objectives. They were gradually moulding us into the conformities that the Service demanded.

7
PICKING UP THE PIECES

*Don't tell my mother I've joined the Air Force,
she still thinks I play the piano in a brothel.*
Old RAF joke.

Our basic training had now run half its course. Five gruelling weeks after passing through the gloomy portals of Padgate we were now thought fit to be exposed in public. We had learned how to wear our uniforms correctly, a difficult art considering how poorly cut and ill-fitting they were. We knew how and whom to salute if we passed a uniformed officer in the street which was unlikely to happen except on railway stations as the British officer class in peacetime of whatever rank has always inclined to wearing mufti outside the barrack gates, unlike our more militaristic European cousins who were prepared to cut a dashing figure in public.

From our pay of twenty-eight shillings a week (£1.40 pence) we managed to buy our cigarettes, our half-pints of thin NAAFI beer, sweet tea and cakes, sometimes egg and chips in the brief hours free from the demands of bull and square-bashing, not to mention ever more supplies of boot polish, blanco and Brasso. Those married recruits, of whom there must have been at least a dozen in our Flight of a hundred men had allotted a large slice of their weekly pay to their wives. Some of us had even managed to save a few shillings. We had travel warrants to exchange for bus and train tickets. We were ready to hit the high spots, whatever they might have been in 1950 post-war Britain - with winter setting in.

On that long-awaited Friday afternoon we were given the order to dismiss earlier than usual. Coaches for London, Manchester, Birmingham and even Glasgow were drawn up near the Guard room at the main gate. Vigilant NCOs looked us over seeking real or imagined faults. RAF Police with their razor sharp creases, white webbing belts, pistol holsters and red armbands looked down their noses at us from beneath the 'cheesecutter' peaks of their white-topped caps. From time to time they would stamp their gleaming boots to settle the lengths of chain that kept their trousers neatly folded over the tops of their white gaiters. All the while they were eyeing us up and down for the undone button, the greatcoat collar turned up 'improperly' or for the slightest hint of 'idleness' in the bearing of the recruits who jostled for the buses. It took a year or two, well back into Civvy Street before I could walk past Military Policemen patrolling in pairs at main line railway stations, a common enough sight until the early sixties, without experiencing a frisson of unease, half expecting to be asked for my pass or checked for some real or imagined shortfall in demeanour or dress. It was one of the Pavlovian reactions of our generation.

With our impeccably blancoed small packs, blocked into the proper shape with strips of cardboard, containing washing gear and a change of socks, slung across our shoulders we boarded the coach. We were FREE! Two whole days of liberty lay ahead. How simple joy became unconfined once the coach was clear of the camp! Fags were lit, tunic buttons loosened on our 'best blues.' Songs were sung: 'I've got sixpence, a jolly, jolly sixpence - to last me all my life,' sadly relevant for many of us in our parlous state, hoping to borrow ready cash from indulgent mums or wives and girl friends at home. We sang Guy Mitchell songs - *O My Truly Fair* or, 'She had a dark and roving eye and her hair hung down in ring-er-lets etc.' We whistled choruses of *Pedro the Fisherman*.

We read copies of *Reveille*, well-thumbed *Tit-Bits*, *Lilliput* (in those days a pocket-sized publication with short stories and jokes - as was *Men Only* - not the hard-porn imitators of Playboy that these became in the seventies). *Men Only* then might have had a few art-study pin-ups one could have shown to an elderly maiden aunt with impunity. In 1950 the youthful prurient voyeur had to make do with the strategically airbrushed photos or cunningly held beach balls in the pages of *Health and Efficiency*, itself posing as a handbook for naturists, where the girls were always playing volley ball. H & E finally ceased publication in 1996 - its long dwindling sales and later hushed and unspoken allegations of paedophilia being replaced by top-shelf porn. (See Note 3 - Appendix).

For the more literate, tattered paperback Westerns were brought out from small-pack or pocket and if one was really lucky, the latest Hank Jansen novel. Whatever became of Hank Jansen? Who still remembers him today? He's not totally forgotten. I asked a contemporary of mine, now an ageing barrister. The inner wheels of his legally-trained memory whirred soundlessly for a few seconds. 'Hank Jansen?' he mused,

'Quite horny for his time. Near pornographic trash. Titles? I remember Trooper Higginbotham, en route for our tank training course at Catterick in 1950. He was reading *Women Hate Till Death* in the train.' Hank Jansen was the all-time master of pulp fiction, read universally in barrack rooms, on remote airstrips, in jungles, in deserts and on board destroyers ploughing lonely oceans. He was the author of a hundred titles with lurid covers - usually involving a pneumatic, busty girl - lightly clad in torn wisps of fabric, bound and straining against some mustachio'd villain, who was sinister and obviously foreign. I cannot remember one title, not one plot, but read every one that came my way, as we all did. They were the common currency of the lonely conscript and the barrack room, more valuable than cigarettes, almost as precious perhaps as a letter from home. Conjecture was endless about the author. 'Cor - he must be a millionaire at least!' 'No, no! Not so. He was a small, but rich and bespectacled ex-railway clerk living in Croydon.' Whatever the truth, the nation owes Hank Jansen a great debt for relieving the tedious boredom of so many servicemen for so long. I have since heard (can it be true?) that 'Hank' was any one of half a dozen authors of pulp fiction who were supplied with pre-titled lurid covers and told to produce 30,000 words that more or less matched up with the book wrapper. This was a situation brought about by post-war paper rationing whereby limited supplies precluded quality products but 'mushroom' publishers who appeared overnight could claim the same allocation of paper for their trashy publications. The market was such that almost anything sold. Forty years later, on behalf of your many readers, a belated, 'Thanks Hank!' Whoever you were or wherever you may be.

The weekend 'forty-eight' passed in a flash. I probably ate and slept in a state of mindless relief not to be confined in a barrack room with thirty or so other farting, swearing, snoring, and belching unfortunates at the beck and call of the sadistic (as we then considered them to be) Drill Instructors who dragooned our daily lives.

I remember visiting a pub near my mother's West Kensington flat, with a prosperous uncle who was staying that weekend. The pub was a Victorian relic of cut glass mirrors and dark, oak panelling - propped up outside by huge buttressed beams to stop its imminent collapse into one of the derelict bomb sites that bordered the North End Road. I was wearing uniform. It was hardly worth changing into civvies for such a brief respite. My uncle offered drinks.

'I'll have a gin and tonic,' I said. My uncle was outraged, 'What's wrong with a pint of beer?' I have never had the stomach or capacity for the British obsession with beer - although I tried desperately at times to like the copious draughts that are considered part of a Briton's manly heritage. But the unpleasant sloshings of one's overloaded gut, the frequent urination and the vomiting that accompanies or more often precedes intoxication are too much of a price to pay for conformity. I digress, the weekend was swiftly over. Late Sunday afternoon in the foggy winter's day of a post-war November saw me in the Waterloo Road amid a throng of uniforms outside the old Union Jack Club, scrambling aboard our coach back to face once again the harsh realities of our recruit training. One of our fellows failed to return to Hereford, a young married lad. We never saw him again but we were told that when he was eventually arrested he would be forced to undergo a full period of basic training again after six weeks 'inside.' 'Eeeow! Poor bugger,' we said to one another.

The remainder of our basic training was endured stoically. The final weeks dragged inexorably on towards Christmas. We marched to and from the cook house in the rain. We attended weekly pay parades, learning the drill procedures necessary to receive the single £1 note and little pile of silver and copper coin that we were due. The weather grew colder and we needed the coke-fired Arctic stove which heated our hut, filling it with fumes which dulled our brass and shed a thin layer of dust over all. The sergeants and drill corporals still shouted insanely at our real and imagined faults. We were still being threatened with a transfer to the Army and hence to Korea (where the war now went badly with increasing losses as the Allies fought to retain their toehold position on the Pusan Peninsular).

Ninety nine per cent of us smoked. Anyone who didn't was thought either odd or perhaps a potential athlete - which was the only understandable excuse - but even athletes normally smoked in those days. Every hour in the training schedule there was a ten minute break to fall out and have a fag. 'Ten minutes to wait, so mine's a Minor!' was De Reske's advertisement for their mini-cigarette. Their larger cork-tipped and filtered fags were regarded as pansified, more suitable for tarts and nancy-boys. Given a choice we would all have smoked Player's or Will's Capstan or Senior Service. They were all full strength, un-tipped 'real man's' smokes. But as we were near beggars we couldn't be choosers, for as well as the cost, the more popular brands were in short supply and unofficially rationed. We had to smoke poor substitutes like Bar-One or Turf made from Empire tobacco from Rhodesia, or perfumed oval Egyptian and Turkish brands. Even these were too expensive and we fell back on thin and weedy Minors or Woodbines which were sold in packets of five and were more paper than tobacco. Parcels from home were cakes and cigarettes or chocolate and sweets that were still rationed. I suppose on reflection that smoking dulled our appetites for food which was certainly no disadvantage as the cook house provided little more than a basic diet.

If we were still hungry by the evening, as many of us were, and if we could afford it, soya-link sausages, or egg and chips in the NAAFI made up the deficiencies. With hindsight, the married recruits must have had a hard time of it living on what was left of their pay, although I think that a small official allowance was also paid direct to their families.

As part of our training we were gassed. We were first dabbed with a droplet of mustard gas which we had to neutralise, then forced to march round inside a gas hut wearing our masks while a tear-gas canister was released. To prove the respirators we wore were effective we were ordered to remove them while doubling around before being released choking and gasping, eyes running, to collapse on the ground outside. Foolishly a few recruits gulped at a flask of gin which they had been told would relieve the acute distress. It didn't. It seemed to induce instant projectile vomiting, which made the rest of us without the benefit of the gin feel better. That of course was the last exercise of the afternoon. Recovery followed in our own spare time with the usual 'bulling' and cleaning to occupy the remains of the day.

We fired our musketry course. Some most unlikely lads proved first-class shots or marksmen, though they had never fired a rifle in all their previous lives. I was never more than an inconsistent first-class shot with a rifle except at 'snap' targets where I excelled. Our shooting was done with weapons supplied by the armoury. Our own 'drill' rifles were unsuitable being deliberately loosened up at various points - the bands and swivels to such a degree that the barrels were loose in the stock. Small coins or loose screws were sometimes hidden under the magazine spring so that they rattled and banged and jingled as they were struck with the flat of the hand during arms drill. 'One, Two, Three! Crash! Bang! Wallop!' This kept the NCOs happy - but woe betide any poor sod whose rifle was so loose that it shed parts or visibly wobbled on parade.

I have forgotten the names of our NCOs. My copy of the official photograph of our training Flight has long since disappeared. I can still conjure up their faces without effort. The sergeant and three corporals were a microcosm of the nation. The sergeant was a small stocky Scot who could equally have worn a kilt. He had a tight little face with black button eyes and a snub nose and a long upper lip. He could have been a dead ringer for Andy Stewart fronting the White Heather band on New Year's Eve twenty years on. He was, as befitted his rank, slightly remote. However, as well as being witty, he was also a man we thought we could trust to be fair.

One of the corporals was a tall, dark Welshman. Sardonic and unpopular, he was all that the sergeant was not - vindictive, abusive without being funny, loud and unreasonable. Fortunately he was not in charge of the hut I was in although we all felt the rough edge of his tongue on the drill square. He mocked the men he was directly in charge of. He formed a 'zoo' of several of his meeker recruits. When the mood took him in the evening before lights out was sounded, he would order his 'zoo' to perform according to the animal alter-ego he had given them.

The cock would crow, the pig would grunt, the rabbit would hop and the monkey would be forced to caper and gibber in front of their embarrassed fellows who were grateful that they had avoided their tormentor's personal attention. The fact that we put up with this treatment was a measure of the new identities we had thrust upon us, as well as a measure of the control and discipline we were subjected to. I know that matters came to a head one wet, windy night. The corporal - maybe in his cups - returned to his bunk room at the end of the hut, switched on the light, screamed the sleeping occupants awake and ordered them to jump out of the windows and double around to the door in their pyjamas or underwear before allowing them inside again. I think someone must have either complained, or the sergeant heard of it, for following that particular incident the 'zoo' was disbanded.

My own section corporal was a tall and fair-haired Home Counties Englishman. Rumour had it that in Civvy Street he had been a golf professional. He might have been for all I know. He was unforthcoming but strict and as our mentor we had little to complain about. The third section corporal was a cockney, short in stature, long on wit and a holy terror to us all. Wickedly humourous, wildly funny on occasion, he was a dangerous man to laugh at on parade. He taught us coarse and hilarious rhymes to match the sequences of various manoeuvres. All four NCOs were impeccably smart, confident, paragons of the drill square and each in their own way taught us much about coming to terms with RAF life.

Three of our Flight applied for a commission. Why I put myself forward I do not know. With hindsight I suppose I felt that I owed it to my education (such as it was - today it would barely qualify me for a place on a job seeker's course), or to my upbringing, or even perhaps to myself. It was a foolish and time wasting move. My Army Cadet training was hardly considered - only the Air Training Corps seemed to have any validity in the RAF. I was called before the Flight Commander for a preliminary interview. I cannot recall what was said but my application was approved and passed forward. I went before a Board of three more officers. I must have been most unconvincing fluffing my way through unreal answers to such questions as, 'Why do you want to become an officer?' I probably replied with some such approved nonsense as, 'I want to serve my country,' or 'I think I can be of more use as an officer.' Rather than, 'Well, the food's probably much better in the Officers' Mess and I'll get more pay, get to wear better-fitting clothes and tell other people what to do!' In reality it was a very foolish move with under two years' service in prospect of which two months had already passed. Officer training would have been a further six months. The options would have been limited. Air crew opportunities at that time were as scarce as hens' teeth for national servicemen unless they were prepared to sign on as a regular. More likely - either as happened to a friend - a commission in the RAF Regiment, square-bashing for much of the time or even more likely in view of my limited civilian career - a posting to the pay branch on some dismal base in the UK or Germany.

Relief was at hand. Some two weeks or so before the end of our training the Flight's postings came through for our future destiny. None of them seemed to bear any relationship to our earlier aptitude tests or preferences. Storemen, cooks, orderlies, clerks, medical attendants were what we were to be. Where were the air sea rescue postings? The despatch riders, the mechanics, drivers, signallers and fitters? Not amongst our lot! 'Not too late to change,' we were cheerfully told. 'If you want a trade of your choice - sign on as a regular!' 'Not bloody likely!' we chorused in reply.

All was not lost. Of the hundred or so men of the Flight, five of us had immediate overseas postings, of whom I was one. I was to go to the Far East as something called a 'Clk/Org u/t.' This meant that I was to be a clerk, presumably in some 'organising' capacity and I was to be trained 'on the job.' Considering that some seventy-five per cent of the Flight had volunteered for overseas service, the fact that only three of us (one of them myself) out of the five chosen, had actually volunteered was a good indication that the random 'square-peg-in-round-hole' policy was in full swing.

The idea of going to the Far East was suddenly much more exciting than any off-chance of a commission. I withdrew my application without any great opposition. I said that as I was already planning a future civilian career with the Chartered Bank in the Far East, I would take the opportunity now offered. I was accused of wasting everyone's time and sent off with a flea in my ear. I felt much better immediately.

Of the five of us with overseas posting, Dave Teague, Alan Stephenson (Steve) and myself immediately got together and became a group apart, the other two of the five were lesser beings posted to Germany. It even affected our final period in the Training Flight as our passing-out parade loomed. I still regret having missed taking part. After eight weeks intensive square bashing the Flight (even the members of the 'awkward squad' now hidden in the depths of the centre ranks) now moved and drilled as one man. The

NCO's formerly incomprehensible screams and strangled commands were now responded to as if by a corps-de-ballet. Our steel-shod boots crashed on the ground in unison. We no longer had to shout, 'One, Two - Three, One!' as we wheeled and turned on the parade ground. Rifle parts jingled in time with the slap of palms on butts. Arms were presented in a manner fit to stand guard at Buckingham Palace. There is a simple delight in being part of a well-drilled squad. The Snap! Crackle and Pop! of a perfectly executed parade ground manoeuvre offers a certain 'buzz.' The concentration demanded in the timing and teamwork becomes a matter of pride. The NCOs must have felt it too. The culmination of their work in creating a disciplined, willing squad out of a group of ill-assorted, shambling youths who had fallen into their clutches a few brief weeks before must have held satisfaction for them. The final passing-out parade was the NCOs' moment of pride as well as ours - only we didn't have to start it all over again in two week's time as did the drill instructors.

The day before the final parade, Steve, Dave and I had been ordered to report to sick quarters for our overseas jabs. By the following morning we were sick and feverish, our headaches and stiff arms were accepted as more than sufficient excuse not to take part. Nevertheless the final parade was a spectacle I enjoyed watching and I was sorry not be taking my part. Because of the cold December weather, greatcoats were worn, and because of the rain and the spoiling effect it would have had on blanco and brass the Flight was bussed rather than marched down to the drill hangar where the parade was to be held. We went too as onlookers, determined not to miss it. The Station Commander, with various other officers stood on a dais as our Flight was put through its drill, as sections and as a Flight, marching and counter marching, every possible combination of parade ground drill was demonstrated at the peak of perfection.

Except for the grand finale. 'Flight will advance in review order!' This is a command that sets off a sequence of movements carried out on its one final word, you have to count the number of steps forward and come to a crashing halt as one man. Now the Flight was drawn up at attention in review order in front of the saluting base, (having already overcome the difficult obstacle of fixing bayonets as one man, generally no better than a fifty-fifty chance). The order was given, 'SAALLLOPE - HIPE!' in preparation for the next order to follow, 'GENERAL SALUTE! - PREEEee - SEENNNT - HIPE!!!' (This final word 'Hipe!' will be recognised by any ex-serviceman - it was, and probably still is, a common euphemism for the word 'Arms.' However hard you try you cannot bellow 'ARRRMS!' as effectively or decisively as 'Hipe!').

From our position at the back of the hangar we clearly saw one of the 'awkward squad' hidden in the rear rank. To 'slope arms' from 'attention' calls for the performer to hoist his rifle briskly in a vertical direction, hurling it upwards with his right hand while simultaneously catching it across his chest with his left hand moving horizontally before transferring the rifle with the right hand, once more to the left shoulder. This is all very well and it is a movement normally executed without mishap by a well-drilled squad. In this instance however, not just one, but three random 'wild cards' entered the equation. The first was the useless eight-inch 'pig-sticker' spike bayonet attached to the rifle, with anyone of average height the point is well below the shoulder. Second, add to this an ill-fitting bulky greatcoat, tightly belted at the waist and thirdly our man who we were watching closely. On the command 'HIPE!!' he drew his rifle smartly upwards and catching the bayonet point neatly in a fold of his greatcoat, impaled himself in the armpit. As the rest of the Flight continued with their 'present arms' movement, our lad, whose beret had now fallen off in his efforts to unspike himself, was rescued by two watching corporals who marched smartly from the sidelines to the rear of the ranks. Grabbing him by the elbows, they retreated as swiftly as possible dragging him along still clasping his rifle firmly to his right bosom with his highly polished heels scraping the ground. No-one else seemed to take any notice of what had happened.

We were all 'passed-out.' No-one was sent to Korea. Our final party in the NAAFI canteen on the night before we left was a stunning success. At least half the Flight became drunk on the weak canteen beer. Our Flight Lieutenant congratulated us before hastily departing. Our sergeant and corporals, who had bedevilled our lives for the eternity of the past two months, chatted and showed signs of humanity. Even the sergeant made a speech, sang a rude song and told us how well we had done before departing for the Sergeants' Mess. The three corporals in their turn gave dramatic monologues or sang a song - then discreetly left. We in our turn sang, smoked, drank recklessly and told jokes. Choruses of *The Foggy Dew* rang out. Geordies sang endless verses of *The Blaydon Races*, and *The Lambton Worm*. A 'flat earther' from Norfolk gave us a memorable rendition of *The Pheasant Plucker*.* The Scouses nasally

---

* The chorus of which goes something like this:- 'I'm not a pheasant plucker, I'm a pheasant plucker's son. And I'm only plucking pheasants 'til the pheasant pluckers come.'

intoned *Dirty Maggie May* until told to shut up. We all sang *The Harlot of Jerusalem, The Good Ship Venus, The One-Eyed Reilly* and *Barnacle Bill, the Sailor* and scatological versions of hymns such as *Life Presents a Dismal Picture*. I suspect that most of these songs have long been forgotten. Modern youngsters, deprived of a period in the Services, are probably condemned to sing nothing wittier than football supporters' chants.

At last by 22.30 hours the orderly sergeant on his rounds came in to hear the final renderings of that dreary but popular 1950s' ballad *Goodnight Irene* while several pints of beer wobbled and slopped about on top of the upright NAAFI piano:

Last Saturday night I got married.
Me and my wife settled down -
But now that we are parted,
I'll take a little walk down town.

The chorus was endlessly repeated in a maudlin dirge, 'Goodnight Irene, Irene Goodnight.'

The memory of it doesn't improve with the passing years but it's a damned sight better than choruses of the *Earwig Song* which is the best that modern youth seem to manage these days - ''Ere we go, 'ere we go,' as they stumble down the street. (Do French soccer fans sing, 'On-y-va, on-y-va, on-y-va'?) I feel a measure of regret for those who never had the opportunities their fathers and grandfathers had forced on them all those years ago. I suppose some of these songs are still sung in such male-bonding groups as rugby football clubs where vast quantities of post-match beer may still be swilled from chipped enamel jugs, but they are no longer widely known. Singing these ribald choruses was a universal rite of passage for the young serviceman.

At about 1am (01.00 hours we would have said by then) we were awoken from our drunken and cheerful slumbers on this our last night at Hereford. Fire alarms sounded and lights flashed as fire tenders raced past down the lines of huts. Someone went to the door and said, 'Bugger me! The NAAFI's on fire!' So it was, but we turned over and went back to sleep. In the morning we found out that the fire had started at the back of a settee where someone had left a smouldering cigarette end. We looked at the smoking ruins and shrugged our collective shoulders. It was someone else's problem. We had finished our square bashing. We were off on leave for Christmas!

8
ESCAPE THROUGH THE HOLE IN THE WIRE

...the snare is broken and we are delivered.
Prayer Book

I allow myself a wry smile when I hear people call for the re-introduction of national service as a cure for the supposedly disordered youth of our present times. Those who can make such a suggestion after more than four decades since conscription ended show how little they understand the changes that have taken place both in society and in the broader world outside Britain's shores. Until the late 1950s Britain's armed forces still straddled Western Europe and the Mediterranean, plus there was a major presence in the Far East (apart from the sub-continent) and in the remainder of the largely intact colonial Empire. There were some 30,000 servicemen alone in the Canal Zone in Egypt. There were bases in Libya, Iraq and in the Gulf, plus little wars to be fought in East Africa and Malaya. The Navy's fleets still sailed the oceans. The RAF's planes flew the long supply routes from Britain as far as Japan and Korea. Atom bomb tests in Australia and the Indian Ocean soaked up ships, men and materials. Yesterday's frontiers have shrunk to contain a Little Britain with a small, selective, highly trained nucleus of techno-oriented military forces.

Any possible advantage to the professional Armed Forces (and these would be few) in absorbing and attempting to train large numbers of basically unskilled and often functionally illiterate young men would be outweighed by enormous disadvantages. The cost would be horrendous. The facilities to house and clothe and equip such numbers no longer exist. The Swiss are one of the only European nations for whom military conscription seems to work efficiently. Their national character is such that they can accept the fact that every adult male can be a trained part-time soldier who keeps his uniform in the wardrobe and his rifle in the broom-cupboard under the stairs, ready, in theory at least, to turn the entire countryside into a killing ground for any foreign army daring to invade. The Swiss can do it. We can't. It's too late to turn back the clock. Our society in those post-war years was homogeneous and close-knit in comparison with the Britain of half a century later. Our differences then were easily bridged in comparison with the gulfs that divide our population today.

There is no civilian alternative version of national service that would work or would change the individual character in the way its protagonists visualise. Without removing civil rights, you cannot impose a strict, rigid discipline on large numbers of unwilling people. My generation and those preceding had no choices in the face of the different set of realities that faced the nation. As the educationalist Kurt Hahn said, 'For more than forty years the schooling of Europe's youth in the first half of the twentieth century was incomplete without learning the art of cleaning a rifle.' We should all thank whatever God we follow that it is no longer so.

~ ~ ~ ~ ~ ~ ~ ~ ~ ~

After Hereford, and with our basic training safely completed, the three of us who were 'on draft' to the Far East met up in London over our Christmas leave. We half-anticipated more of the same treatment we had already experienced when the time came to sit it out in our transit camp awaiting embarkation, however we would now be better adjusted to the culture shock, with the full submersion of self into the lower levels of the RAF. The constant round of drill, PT, fatigues, kit inspections, parades, basic weapons training and lessons in Service structures and procedures was now over we hoped. In our imaginations the drill instructors still bellowed at us eyeball to eyeball, 'When I say MOVE! You MOVE!! and don't stop moving 'til I tell you. On the double - MOVE!' We expected further doses of the NCO's classic observation on inspecting the work of a fatigue party, 'These ablutions look like a SHITHOUSE!' This was what we were prepared for as we reported to our new RAF station somewhere in Staffordshire in the depths of winter. It was the beginning of January, 1951.

In temperament as well as in fact, I had now become 2492975 Aircraftman 2nd Class Adamson, P. M. I was one of the latest arrivals in that humble but honourable rank that stretched all the way back to, and beyond, the somewhat better-known 338171 ('May I call you 338?' wrote Noel Coward) Aircraftman 2nd Class Shaw, T. E. when he re-enlisted in 1925 at the age of thirty-seven. Unlike 'Shaw' of Arabia I do not recall myself or my comrades being excited about our coming service. Apprehension perhaps better described our feelings being as yet neither 'sprocket nor cog' in the machinery of the RAF. It was as exceedingly ill-fledged 'sprogs' that we checked in at the main gate of RAF Hednesford.

The transit camp at Hednesford still remains something of a mystery in my memory. It was perpetually shrouded in grey winter drizzle and fog so that one never perceived the limits of the camp. There were endless lines of wooden, tin-roofed huts, shabby stores and offices. It was silent in contrast to the constant noise and bustle of Hereford. Here the parade ground was empty and deserted. Small knots of 'erks' shambled around aimlessly in the rain, huddled under their waterproof ground sheet capes, from one part of the camp to another. In all the intervening years I have never re-visited the limbo where Hednesford once existed. As a military base it must have long vanished. I doubt if it ever closed - it could have simply dissipated into nothingness. We heard that it had once been an Army camp and was condemned as 'unfit' during the Crimean War. This I could believe, although realistically it probably dated back only to the Boer War or perhaps to 1914-1918. Whatever the truth, in January 1951 it was little more than a dump in the throes of military decomposition.

Our draft had now swollen to some fifteen airmen. We were housed in a damp and dirty Nissen hut already populated by a handful of RAF cooks. After the brisk and purposeful atmosphere of training we were now left to our own devices for much of the time. The cook house staff who shared our billet set the tone.

A short (and I have to admit, unfairly prejudiced) dissertation on Service cooks will not go amiss. Cooks in the Services before the present days of catering college standards and *cordon bleu* messing always occupied a peculiar niche of their own. Outwardly ill-smelling, ill-favoured and bad-tempered in equal measure - their trade seemed a repository of indifference and indiscipline. They acknowledged and answered to no-one except their own immediate hierarchy. Orderly Officers and NCOs rarely dared to criticise them. Airmen were expected to complain about the food indirectly through the usual channels (whereby one expected little and got even less). 'Other ranks' trod carefully in their presence in case, as always happened in the end, one fell into their clutches on cook house fatigues. Their temperament always veered close to the edge of insanity, pulsing with stress and irrational rages that could explode at any minute. Under the post-war regimes of rationing and shortages they specialised in 'cordon noir' cookery - primordial soups of the 'brown Windsor' variety; blackened and luke-warm cold boiled spuds, glue-like porridge with dry and fibrous lumps, gristly and gobbety rissoles. There was greasy, watery, boiled mince, smelly cabbage, and the occasional delight of a perfectly steamed suet pudding with jam and runny custard. Except perhaps for the more able cooks who aspired to the sergeants' and officers' messes, they were a hump-backed and villainous crew who never ate or tasted the food they served us. Instead they lived on bacon butties, fried eggs and chipped china mugs of strong, sweet tea, thick with condensed milk which they brewed up over the coke-fired Arctic stove in the billet we shared.

Having said that, the three or four cooks with whom we shared our hut sometimes relented and gave us bacon butties in exchange for cigarettes. They always provided a bonanza of tea, tinned milk and sugar for brewing up in the hut. From somewhere they had looted a stack of five-pound tins of wax floor polish which they used as fire-lighting fuel for the coke stove. Coal and coke they also had in plenty. Thanks to them we were at least warm in the vicinity of the stove, but we left the cooks much to their own devices. They played their own games of cards sitting around on their unmade bunks with greasy gumboots on their feet, or dirty white submarine stockings with their smelly toes exposed. Unravelled sweaters clothed their upper limbs and torsos.

Perhaps because of the cooks we suffered no inspections. The only NCO we saw with any regularity, nominally in charge of us, was an elderly sergeant also awaiting passage to the Far East. During the first week we were issued with tropical kit from the camp stores. We examined this with interest, marvelling. There were jackets - bush, khaki - other ranks for the use of, three; shorts, KD, three pairs; trousers, KD, two pairs; underwear - because the stores had run out of tropical cotton underpants we were issued extra knee-length woollen winter issue to bring us up to tropical scale! Then there were blue 'Airtex' short sleeved pyjamas, knee-length khaki hose, issue sunglasses and extra towels. 'My God!' we said, 'No expense has been spared, we really must be going after all!'

We paraded in the rain every morning at eight. We were sent off for more medicals and more jabs. We were detailed for daily fatigue parties by NCOs who had no more interest in us or the pointless tasks they allocated than we in them. We 'skived' off to the warmth of the NAAFI at the first opportunity every morning. We eked out our meagre pay on 'char and wads' to supplement the awful food the cook house slopped out which was far worse than anything during our recruit training when we had been 'fine set' and always hungry. We read and swapped books and magazines, 'charped it off' on our straw paliasse beds - no bed sheets here, just grey issue blankets. We smoked, played cards and swept up some of the dirt and dust when we could stand it no longer. We practised packing and unpacking our kit ready for the 'off' which never came. The mass of kit never quite fitted in packs and kit bag. There was never enough space for our 'issue' gear, let alone any personal items.

There was never news of our draft on 'orders' or from the orderly room. Our own sergeant, also in transit, was powerless to give us any useful information. Like RAF Hednesford itself, we languished in limbo, not yet knowing whether we were to go by sea or on a trooping flight to the Far East. We were allowed no weekend passes but one 'forty eight' per month. The weekends were dismal. The cooks, who seemed to have every weekend off, and who were often absent during the week

- two had a job moonlighting in a transport 'caff' several miles away - volunteered the information that there was a hidden gap in the perimeter fence not fifty yards from our hut, giving on to a minor road not far from a main cross-roads. We rapidly re-assessed our situation. There were no roll calls between Friday mornings and the following Monday. There was little risk of our draft being shipped out at short notice although we had already had two weeks embarkation leave before reporting to the transit camp. The sergeant, who guessed what was afoot, warned us to leave a telephone contact with our 'oppos' who would remain in camp on rotation, for if our draft was called while we were absent, it would not be a simple matter of AWOL (absent without leave) - but desertion.

From then on it was simple. For the next two months, every Friday after parade and roll call, half of our draft - seven or eight men slipped away back to the billet. The only glitch was if the fortnightly pay parade was called for a late Friday afternoon. Collecting greatcoat and small pack they crept away silently through the mist and drizzle at ten minute intervals, so as not to attract attention, through the cooks' private hole in the wire fence. This was followed by a brisk walk, marching smartly down to the cross-roads full of confidence, as if in legitimate possession of a genuine weekend pass. A lifted thumb on either the north or southbound lane of the road and within a matter of minutes one was in the passenger seat of a car if very lucky, or in the cab of a lorry, or if not so fortunate, sitting uncomfortably on a pile of potato sacks in the back of a truck. In uniform, hitching a lift was always 'a piece of cake' in those far off days. One's benefactors had almost always been in the Forces themselves at some time and knew the form.

Until nearly the end of March 1951 we endured being 'on draft.' Our week days were suffered in monotonously increasing cold and squalor as the winter dragged on. The fog and drizzle became sleet and then freezing fog and snow. Being away two and sometimes three weekends out of four lightened our dreary boredom. I went home to my mother's flat in West London. I went to the cinema on borrowed money, saw a few former friends, carried on a hopeless and desultory affair - entirely chaste - with a student nurse with whom I had fallen passionately in love. Songs and melodies of the period still recall for me a time of empty longing and sweet despair - *Bewitched, Bothered and Bewildered Am I*, *Far Away Places with Strange Sounding Names*, *Moon over Malaya* the last crooned by Jimmy Young, no less! Then there were any one of half a dozen movie melodies by Doris Day - *Give Me Something to Remember You By* or perhaps Guy Mitchell and the gang belting out *She Had a Dark and Roving Eye*. As Noel Coward once remarked, '...extraordinary how potent cheap music is.' But in those days one could at least hear the words the vocalists sang, however banal the sentiments might have been.

Except for our monthly official 'forty-eights' we avoided the main line railway stations. The risk of being picked up by the Military Police wasn't worth taking. Without a rail warrant too the cost was more than we could afford, so it was mainly by dint of hitching that I travelled to and from London without any difficulty. Travelling by train was equally uncomfortable and cold, delays were frequent. If one left the camp (legally that is) after standing down on a Friday afternoon, it was quite likely that by 11pm that night one would have got no further than Crewe. I have memories of spending half the night on a platform bench at Crewe, huddled up in my uniform greatcoat against the fog and cold of the Midlands (it was always foggy) waiting for some long delayed train from nowhere to arrive. Crewe is one of those strange insubstantial towns that one only encounters when passing through by rail, or by changing trains. I have never been there by any other means and sometimes I think that Crewe's existence, rather like the mythical village of Brigadoon, is only triggered by a supernatural event - but rather more frequently perhaps, by the magical arrival of a railway train on which I still sometimes unaccountably find myself.

At last the date of our deliverance was announced. Our now shambolic and disintegrating draft fell into shape again. The absent members were telephoned and hurried back, scrambling through the wire fence into the camp for the last time. It was early April 1951. Almost six months of our expected two years service had already slipped by. With hindsight it is no wonder that so few national servicemen in the RAF were given any skilled training, so essential for a highly technical arm of the Forces - there simply wasn't the time. It took a three year engagement as a regular to make it worthwhile to teach a man a skilled trade from scratch and two years to train air crew. Things did change, but many months later when, because of the demands made on the overstretched Forces, efforts were made to train more men in skilled trades. But by then our intake's roles were already pre-destined.

In full 'Christmas Tree' marching order, criss-crossed with webbing straps, girt about with mess-tins and waterbottles, our kit crammed into every nook and cranny of our packs and kit bags we went by train to RAF Lyneham in Wiltshire, then as now, a centre for the RAF Transport Command's world-wide flights. We were back in an organised purposeful environment. The RAF seemed to be in working order once more contrary to the impression we had received since our basic training. We passed the night in comfortable, clean barrack rooms. The food was superb after the inedible slop of Hednesford.

By the next afternoon we had re-packed our kit, taking only our small packs on our persons. Everything else was loaded as cargo. Out on the apron was a real aeroplane! A four-engined prop-driven Handley Page Hastings was already warming up. It was tiny by today's standards. I saw one again recently in the Imperial War Museum's collection at Duxford perched on its twin undercarriage, dwarfed into insignificance by the modern jet transports nearby. Our flight was a trooping/ambulance run to Korea. Half the seating space was taken up by triple-banked layers of canvas stretchers for the return trip with casualties from the battle front. It carried no more than forty passengers - several less with the stretchers - and the bucket seats (rear facing of course for safety) were allocated to officers and NCOs - why not? What else is rank or privilege for? I was given a stretcher near the door on the lower level. We were off on what was supposed to be a three day flight to Singapore via North Africa, Iraq, Pakistan, Ceylon and then across the Bay of Bengal to Malaya.

We were airborne by dusk, flying south across France and over the Mediterranean to Libya. I had only ever flown once before, at the age of fifteen, in an open-cockpit Miles Magister piloted by my brother from Croydon to the Isle of Wight. So, as with most of us on the draft, it was an exciting experience. It was an advantage to have a stretcher as while flying overnight, one could sleep fitfully. The NCO quartermaster supplied us at intervals with foul-tasting tea or coffee from huge flasks, with wedge-shaped sandwiches of cheese and corned beef. Smoking was forbidden - only the crew could smoke on the flight deck and tantalising wisps of cigarette smoke drifted back to us through the night. The cabin lights were extinguished and outside the four great piston engines drummed and roared, exhaust stubs glowing red. The Hastings transport was unpressurised and with little insulation from cold and noise I remember that sleep came slowly.

By dawn we were over the Mediterranean. With sunshine and bright blue sky and foam-streaked sea below we roared on to North Africa. We were all wide awake, peering eagerly out of the windows like models for a recruiting poster. Flying at no more than five or six thousand feet and often less, one can watch the world below. The drawback is that one is more subject to the atmospheric vagaries of the weather with all its concomitant clumping and bumping.

Soon a sandy coast and scrubby brown desert was rushing beneath us. We were strapped in our stretchers and seats by the time a cluster of white buildings and a tarmac runway appeared below. As we bumped and lurched through the morning sunshine, flaps down and engines throttled back - we made what was my first foreign landfall. There was a great 'CRASSH! BANGG!' followed immediately by screeching noises and a strong smell of burning rubber as the aircraft slewed and yawed, gradually juddering to a halt facing sideways across the runway. I still have a very clear recollection of the moment of touch-down seen from my bottom stretcher right next to the cabin door. The door, springing from its frame by the forces that strained and vibrated the airframe to its limits, momentarily revealed a gap of several inches through which I could clearly see sand and scrub and tarmac whizzing by at high speed.

With my fellow novice airmen I was impressed. I thought that this was perhaps the RAF's normal manner of landing. We were not at all alarmed by the seemingly near-terminal violence and unexpected gyrations of our otherwise smooth flight from England to North Africa. The more experienced service passengers sitting in the front of the cabin displayed white faces and perspiring brows as they staggered from their seats in a display of haste to get out into the open air, lighting cigarettes with shaking hands. The Hastings sat on the edge of the runway with a definitely lopsided, bucolic attitude as we ourselves lurched off in a rattling crew bus for the white cluster of buildings set amid palm trees and flowering shrubs. This was Castel Benito, lying south of Tripoli in Libya, a British staging post on the RAF routes to the Middle East and beyond.

The bursting of the tyre on the main landing gear, for such it was, delayed our further departure for several hours while the RAF ground crews replaced the wheel, re-fuelled and I hoped checked out the safety of the Hastings for undue strains before our onward flight.

In 1951 the former Italian colony of Libya was still virtually run by the British in the aftermath of war. Ghaddafi was still a toddler, clutching at

Castel Benito, Libya, April 1951. The flower 'pots' are bomb casings.

his bedouin mother's skirts. King Idriss had yet to come to the throne of an independent nation the following December. In the comfortable transit mess that early morning at Castel Benito we were fed fresh coffee and rolls, orange juice and fruit such as most of us had never seen. We were served deferentially by efficient Italian waiters in crisp white uniforms. Outside the sun shone brilliantly. The sky was bright blue with puffs of white cloud. The air was soft, warm and scented. It was a revelation of sheer delight to most of us. It should be remembered that in post-war Britain, foreign travel was almost totally unknown. Package tours were still light-years away in concept and in imagination. The only prospect of overseas travel for the great majority came with enlistment. We new recruits had been raised in wartime austerity. Our recent experience and expectations had certainly never led us to believe that in the space of a short overnight flight from dreary old England we could be enjoying such delights, like Hollywood film stars, from whose screen antics our visions of the high life were derived.

We bought cheap cigarettes from the kiosk, luxury brands like Senior Service - full-size, untipped, packed in sealed tins of fifty - all for the price of a scarce packet of puny ill-flavoured Woodbines back home. We sauntered outside in the warm sunshine. Life was beginning to look good.

After several hours idling in the sun, lunching on 'cold collation' we took off again on what we hoped was to be the uneventful next leg to RAF Habbaniyah in Iraq, to the west of Baghdad, with a short re-fuelling stop at the old wartime desert airfield at El Adem near Tobruk. Flying due east in the afternoon sun, the blue sea of the Gulf of Sirta unrolled beneath followed by flat brown sandy scrub, low rolling hills and wadis, with the occasional road and settlement along the shoreline of the Libyan desert. We dropped down at El Adem, as smoothly and efficiently as our previous landing had been bumbling and violent. At El Adem our stay was brief, barely time for a smoke, to watch and note the Libyan Levies in slouch hats and khaki serge who manned the airstrip defences for the RAF. Airborne once again, we continued east towards Egypt, out over the sea again as the sun descended behind us to the west.

In the early dusk we started the last few hundred miles run-in across Jordan to Iraq. By this time Steve and I had swapped our stretchers for seats with two sergeants who wanted a couple of hours kip. Looking out over the wing root to port, Steve pointed at a slim trickle of black oil running out from the inboard engine nacelle, quivering and glistening in the slipstream, trembling into nothingness on the trailing edge of the wing. We decided it was nothing unusual.

Several minutes later I prodded Steve awake, dozing over a paperback thriller. I pointed out of the window again at the inboard engine. The trickle of oil was now a thickening ribbon. From the trailing edge the slick was now wobbling off like black treacle into space. Was this normal, we wondered. After a while the quartermaster came round with more luke-warm Thermos-flavoured tea and squash. We drew his attention to the apparent oil leak. He said nothing but swiftly vanished forward again into the flight deck closing the cabin door behind him. After a few moments one of the flight crew came through, peered for a minute or two out of the window and disappeared again. Over the next ten minutes, one by one all the crew repeated this performance in turn. By now it was getting well into dusk. We listened anxiously to the beat of the engines. As it grew darker, with the cabin lights still unlit, we could see the exhaust stubs glowing more and more alarmingly red. From the wide open cooling gills occasional fiery bursts of sparks erupted - to vanish instantly into the night. A crew member came back and peered with a torchlight out along the wing. There were a series of abrupt, clattering bangs, more showers of sparks as the propeller ceased to rotate, by now clearly feathered. We flew on eastwards across the desert on three engines.

I have distinct memories of this stage of the journey. Firstly we were given no direct information by the crew. One or two of the officer passengers went through to the flight deck from time to time where the door was now kept firmly closed. Secondly, over a period of fifteen minutes or so, various members of the crew ambled the length of the cabin aft to the toilet compartment at the rear, returning with what were quite clearly their parachute packs from one of the lockers. I have been assured over the years that I must have imagined this and that I am a victim of 'received' memory. But I don't think so. Others have said it was probably a joke.

Landing safely and smoothly at Habbaniyah in the star lit desert night was an anti-climax. The air was warm and soft, a dry breeze gently wafted strange but pleasant smells around us. Our draft was led off to an airmen's mess hall where we were fed and then bedded down in a comfortable hut where we found all our kit already off-loaded and dumped.

The third day of our journey dawned with the news that we were there for at least twenty-four hours while our Hastings underwent an engine change. Habbaniyah as I recall was a vast, flat, sandy dust bowl interspersed with low buildings including aircraft hangars, wire fences and gun pits. The only vegetation to be seen were a few shrubs planted in oil drums and the occasional feathery casuarina tree. Low ramparts of sand rimmed the distant boundaries of the base. The few British RAF personnel we saw seemed outnumbered by the armed RAF Levies wearing khaki serge and strapped-up bush hats. (See Note 4 - Appendix).

At Habbaniyah I had my first encounter during my service with a senior ranking air officer which placed me in a position for which my training to date had left me unprepared. After breakfast a few of us had gone to the stores to draw more bedding for our extended stay. On the verandah outside, laden with blankets under each arm, I noticed to my great alarm a tall KD clad officer approaching. The quantity of 'scrambled egg' on his cap plus the thickness and profusion of the blue-black rings on his epaulettes indicated at the very least an Air Marshal. He displayed every sign of wishing to address me. I was familiar enough with the esoteric arts of 'sitting to attention,' even with the expected and unnaturally strained posture of 'riding a bicycle at attention' when one was unable to otherwise salute. At that time the bed-ridden in military hospitals otherwise unable to move were expected to 'lie at attention.' Nobody had ever suggested what to do when one's saluting limb was otherwise occupied with a bulky and unwieldy burden. Fainting on the spot I ruled out as being overly dramatic. Being without benefit of bicycle, bed or chair I drew myself up as smartly as possible at a semblance of attention, laden arms akimbo like a paralysed washer woman.

'Everything all right, airman?' he said. 'Sir!' I replied, stamping my feet in approved fashion. Apparently satisfied, he moved on to chat to our elderly (thirty-five-ish?) sergeant, who to my great surprise did not seem to treat him with any exaggerated respect, chatting easily about our mishaps and delays en route.

The rest of our stay was uneventful. We changed from our blue serge into KD for the first time, our khaki bush jackets with their bright red shoulder flashes synonymous with far-flung service in the outposts of Empire. (Alas, I believe long since replaced with SCP - definitely unromantic Stone Coloured Polyester in the 1960s.) We were now off to the tropics. We took off the following day to fly down to Karachi where another RAF staging post manned by a small detachment still serviced the transports flying through. By the 1960s all these trooping flights were re-routed through Gan Island which was itself finally closed down in 1976 when Far East trooping became no more than a trickle. We flew across the Tigris and Euphrates, the twin rivers of ancient Mesopotamia, following their course down to Basra, then out over the shallow waters of the Persian Gulf. From six thousand feet the clear greens and blues of the sparkling sea were a revelation. Coral reefs, rocks, shallows and depths were clearly delineated as if on a coloured contour map. Toy ships trailed herringbone wakes as they lay seemingly motionless on the painted ocean below. We sped on high above, cruising between and around the towering monsoon thunderheads at an effortless 180 knots.

I remember that it was on this leg of the journey that I discovered a major drawback to lengthy unpressurised flight - or at least as far as I was concerned. The cool, unnaturally bone-dry air jetting out through the nozzles of the ventilating system at altitude made my nose and eyes stream uncontrollably. Then and on later long distance flights with the RAF, I realised that I would never have made a flier. I have never in my life been either sea or air-sick, but I imagine that if the discomfort matches the other symptoms I used to experience, then I would much rather stay on the ground given the choice.

Our Hastings transport flew into Karachi as it grew dark. It had been raining heavily and the heat was damp and oppressive. We stretched our legs and smoked our fags and drank tea with sandwiches from trestle tables in a hangar. We were guarded by rifle-carrying bandoliered soldiers in grey, baggy, shirt-waisted robes and turbans. They smoked our proffered cigarettes through their clenched fists. Were they there for our protection, or to stop us breaking out or perhaps to establish a bridgehead and re-claim the Raj?

Of the long overnight haul down the west coast of India to Ceylon I remember nothing at all. Just after sunrise we landed at RAF Negombo, a few miles to the north of Colombo. The real tropics now surrounded us. Serried ranks of coconut palms, steaming heat, lush flowering shrubs. Black kites and huge piebald crows lurched and hopped about in the sunshine. Ceylon had been independent since 1947 but there were still British bases on the island, including the great naval base at Trincomalee on the north-east coast. We were led into a reception hall where smiling, shiny dark-skinned Sinhalese in spotless white cottons elegantly gave us tea - with the compliments of the Ceylon Tea Growers' Association (or some such organisation). I think Negombo must also have been the civil airport for Colombo as the combined purchasing power of a group of near penniless RAF transients would hardly have been enough otherwise to warrant the expense of such an exercise in public relations.

The final leg of our trip lay across the Bay of Bengal and down the Straits of Sumatra to Singapore at the southern tip of the Malayan Peninsular. There were other intervening RAF staging posts en route as I was later to discover when I flew the following year from Singapore back to Ceylon in a shorter-range aircraft, but our Hastings could do the long hop in one. By now we were *blasé* about flying. We were into the fifth consecutive day of our journey. I think we had probably had enough of travelling into the unknown. Flying was boring. We needed a positive destination, showers, food and drink that was fresh, not luke-warm from metallic tasting vacuum flasks and curling sandwiches.

A run-in over low lying islands, the shallow mud-coloured sea dotted with huge fishing platforms on stilts with their cantilevered dip-nets passed below in the late afternoon. With a now familiar bump and a screech of tyres we were down at Changi. The huge monolithic bulk of the infamous prison was clearly visible not far off. The airstrip itself, finished after the end of the war by the British, had already been largely constructed by the slave labour of the Allied prisoners-of-war from Changi Gaol and its surrounding camp where the Japanese had kept them in atrocious conditions for the long war years.

Steve and I, whose destination this was, said goodbye to Dave Teague with whom we had shared all the iniquities and vagaries of service life for the past six months. Dave was bound for Hong Kong and RAF Kai-Tak. We shook hands, wishing each other good luck and promising to keep in touch. Dave was a good chap all round, a 'mucker,' a 'mate.' We never saw or heard from each other again.

The Hastings and its crew continued on its slow world-wide wanderings, like an albatross, to pick up the war-wounded and weary from Korea and return with them once more to far-off England on the other side of the world.

9
SINGAPORE

Please God - make my knees brown
Airman's prayer on first wearing KD shorts

RAF Changi was my first experience of living in the tropics. Steve and I with the others still remaining from our UK draft were quartered on the upper floor of a white, two-storey barrack block with a red-tiled roof, set about with tall shade trees. Our quarters were uncrowded and spacious, being mainly for transit personnel and where we now awaited our unknown final postings. It was an eye-opener to the young lads that most of us were. The damp heat of Singapore caused us to sweat buckets at the least effort. We marvelled at the sunshine, at the sudden downpours of torrential rain, at the exotic scents and at the lush vegetation that surrounded us. Looking out from the wide, shaded verandahs onto the glossy, rattling palm fronds and leafy branches that sheltered us from the sun we watched the brightly coloured birds that flew and chattered and squawked amongst the luxuriant foliage. Those of us new to the tropics gazed in astonishment at the *chik-chaks* - the tiny transparent lizards that scuttled upside-down across our barrack-room walls and lofty ceilings.

Our barrack block was a few hundred yards from the Changi airstrip, its single runway surfaced with linked, perforated-steel planking laid over coconut matting. The few RAF Dakotas and Hastings transports that flew in and out barely disturbed the tropical torpor that all too soon overwhelmed us. The Changi RAF squadrons and the headquarters of the Far East Air Force shared the scattered airport buildings with the fledgling local airlines established since the end of the war.

In the near distance, looming up over the coconut palms that fringed the airfield was the great square bulk of Changi Gaol - the focal point of the crowded camp that had so recently been the noisome and notorious home of so many Allied wartime prisoners.

We found ourselves living almost in the open air, the big double-louvered verandah doors on which we hung our now unwanted thick woollen serge RAF 'blues,' were permanently hooked open to allow the breezes through and ceiling fans slowly stirred the somnolent atmosphere. We lay on our *charpoys*, 'charping it off' (already learning the lingo) in the heat of the day. Reading, writing letters home, smoking fat, cheap, luxury cigarettes - Players, Wills' Gold Flake or Capstan, unfiltered full-strength Virginia 'men's' cigarettes - bought from the Changi NAAFI with the proceeds of our first pay parade. Our wallets were now modestly stocked with Straits dollars and our pockets jingling with square copper one cent coins.

Miraculously our four shillings (20 pence) a day pay had almost doubled overnight with an extra three shillings and eight pence overseas allowance (a total of £2.68p per week). In 1951 national servicemen were only paid two-thirds of a regular's pay - except for the last six months service when we would receive the full rate for whatever rank we had achieved. Here we were, luxuriating (for the moment anyway) in tropical idleness, while the poor national service squaddies serving at the front in Korea were putting their lives at risk for their basic four shillings a day - their cost of living and other circumstances not thought to warrant any additional allowances.

The 'old sweats' on our floor initiated us into the mysteries of dealing with the Chinese 'Sew-Sew' women, who wore wide, black pyjama trousers with their white high-buttoned cotton jackets, their glossy black

June 1951, 0715hrs. Barrack room verandah - crisp, clean KD ready for the office.

hair scraped back into a tightly fashioned bun. The 'Sew-Sews' sat cross-legged on the verandah floors deftly snipping and stitching while they altered our KD shorts to considerably less than the regulation length of 'two inches above the knee' (it was vital to keep at least one pair at the proper length for formal parades). These women darned our socks, sewed on buttons and cloth badges - all for a few cents - jabbering, shrieking with laughter and shouting raucous and incomprehensible jokes the while to their friends on the landing below. The *dhobi-wallahs* (also Chinese) came and collected our *dhobi* (more lingo), bringing it back within a few hours crisply pressed and crackling with starch, all for a few cents more.

Chinese 'sew-sew' darning our socks.

There was a Tamil bearer outside on the verandah who for similarly puny sums blacked our shoes, washed out all the blue 'blanco' caking our webbing straps and packs, bringing it back clean and dry, the brasses glinting in the sunlight looking shinier and brighter than they had ever seemed in our square-bashing days. The bearers made up our beds (white sheets and green cotton bedspreads), each evening, letting down the neatly rolled, musty smelling green mosquito nets that hung on the wall behind each bed.

The grim and dreary England of 1950 was fast vanishing from our collective consciousness. The England of pre-fabs, of derelict city bomb sites, of rationing and cold foggy winters, of dour post-war gloom was slowly sliding away behind us. This was the life for us!

For a few days we lived in this pleasant state, uncertain of our immediate futures, not even knowing whether or not we would stay with our 'mates' with whom we had suffered the long months of winter misery at Hednesford. Who cared? We were young, resilient and for the moment well fed and comfortable which was always a bonus for the lower ranks, the groundlings of the Air Force. We knew full well that our immediate future was not and could not be our concern or responsibility. Whatever might happen to us was out of our hands. We lived solely for the moment. It was a useful lesson to learn and one that I have always tried to hold on to. We came to realise that there is nothing else in life but the present, neither past nor future exist. One has to take note of the past and learn its lessons, equally one should have regard for the future - but that apart, it is only the present that is life, each moment unique and complete - and final.

After Hubris, comes Nemesis. Within a few days our postings were through. We re-packed our kit for the umpteenth time, paid off the few dollars we owed the bearers (*dhobi-wallahs*, knowing we were in transit had wisely insisted 'No tickee - no washee!') We strapped on our clean-scrubbed webbing and departed, some up-country to Kuala Lumpur or Butterworth, near Penang, others to the airfields on Singapore island, the bomber station at Tengah, to Changi itself or to the old RAF airfield at Seletar in the north of the island, some five miles east of the causeway that crossed the Johore Straits to mainland Malaya. Seletar was where Steve and I and one or two others were now posted.

An hour's journey in the back of a three-tonner, wire netting protecting the open sides beneath the canvas hood - we were still too green to realise why - gave us our first sight of the teeming streets of downtown Singapore.

Before the arrival of prosperity and of the now ubiquitous air-conditioning which drove the indigenous Singaporeans behind closed doors and soundproofed glass, all human life was conducted in the narrow alleys and crowded streets. Along the old shaded 'five-foot' ways backing onto the open-fronted shop-houses, or leaning out of the shuttered windows with their fluttering poles of washing, people screamed at one another. Deep storm drains lined roads that were crowded with pedal rickshaws, hawker stalls, taxis and trucks. Red-scarved Hakka women (gangs of celibate labourers who by dint of sheer numbers moved the red earth of Singapore from point A to point B before the advent of the bulldozer) shouted at each other from beneath their wide-brimmed coolie hats and stray chickens added their cackle to the din.

The tropical Chinese could rightly lay claim to being the noisiest race on earth - in the noisiest city in the world (perhaps barring Hong Kong). On the crowded pavements were people mending shoes, repairing bicycles and bashing pots and pans. Carpenters made furniture on improvised benches amid a riot of blaring radios, conversations were yelled across the street, challenging the motor horns, bicycle bells, Malay music, Chinese music, Indian music all mingling in one giant cacophony of atonal dissonance punctuated with rasping 'Hoicks!' as Chinese throats were cleared in preparation for juicy expectorations.

'Bleedin' f......g 'ell!' shouted our sweating driver, jamming on the brakes and throwing his passengers into an untidy heap of bodies and kit bags on the floor of the truck as we came to a busy crossroad. 'Effing bloody Chinese funerals. Can't effing bloody wait to bugger off out of this bleedin' world into the next f.....r!' He continued ranting in this vein, not in any spirit of racial rancour or sense of white superiority, but simply the age-old frustrated despair of the British serviceman bemoaning the seeming inability of the native peoples of the Empire to behave in a rational manner. It was all a jumbled nonsense to us seeing it for the first time. But interesting.

A high speed convoy of open builders' lorries and taxicabs careered across our front in the manner of the Keystone Cops, packed with wailing professional mourners (apparently the louder they shrieked, the greater their remuneration). One truck bore the coffin (if my memory still serves me right - perched precariously on a heap of building sand), shrouded in fluttering red banners. A second carried a brass band at full discordant blast, scattering firecrackers as they zoomed off into the distance. Chinese funerals I later learned always chose circuitous routes to their hillside-situated cemeteries. High speed also thwarted 'devils' and evil spirits (by repute unable to negotiate corners or strategically positioned mirrors). Girt with flags and banners, ladling out showers of paper money and firecrackers, jumping traffic lights - 'red' is a lucky colour to the Chinese - for with sufficient velocity and disregard the chances of ill-luck following the deceased into the after-life can thus be reduced to an acceptable minimum. Ordinary pedestrians also dart across the road against the lights, risking life and limb in hair's breadth escapes, but thus evading any evil spirit that might too be following them. They smiled their thanks at the sweating driver who has hooted and honked his way past, his alertness and skill with chancy brakes alone saving them from death or injury.

Such smells there were too - of rancid drains (unable as we were then to isolate the putrid effluvium of the durian fruit), of joss sticks, flowers and strange cooking odours. It was all a delight and source of amazement. Once through the city the flat landscape opened up into village after village, past jungle thickets and the low hills of Bukit Timah - the highest spot on the island. We drove past the orderly ranks of trees in the rubber plantations. Then at last our truck reached the civilian shops and bars of Seletar Village lining the road that led down to the impressive white stucco gates and guardrooms of Seletar itself, with its familiar RAF Police strutting and preening. This was to be my home for much of the next eighteen months.

~ ~ ~ ~ ~ ~ ~ ~ ~ ~

At the age of eighteen (and three-quarters) I had now become a very small cog in a very large military machine. Like my fellow national servicemen I knew little of the background to what was going on around us in South East Asia. We were simply glad to have avoided Korea. But even had we known more I doubt if our attitudes would have altered one jot. In any case we had no choice to be anywhere else. The possible consequences of exercising too much free will could have ended badly - probably in the 'glasshouse.' In early 1951 much of the British Empire was still in place. We were British too and if we thought about it at all, we felt we had a right to be where we were. We were people of our time. Britain still remained a homogeneous monocultural society in spite of being riven by deeply rooted class divisions. We were all brought up with the mores and education of the thirties and forties. Our elders who had won the greatest war in history may have converted to socialism - but that hardly extended as far as the great areas of the atlas still coloured red! With God's great gift of hindsight a little background history will fill in the gaps of my own knowledge at that time of what was going on around us.

~ ~ ~ ~ ~ ~ ~ ~ ~ ~

In 1951 the Malayan Peninsula, from the far northern border with Thailand down to the great trading island of Singapore at its southern tip, was in turmoil. Following the end of the Second World War in August 1945 the peoples of the old colonial territories of South East Asia were unwilling to lapse again into their subordinate roles as vassal states of their former masters, France, the Netherlands and the British Empire. The United States' colonisation of the Philippines in 1899 after the Spanish American War - for whom Kipling penned the sage advice, 'Take up the White Man's burden...' - was yet another matter.

The swift and overwhelming victories of the Japanese in 1942 had pricked the fictional bubble of white colonial supremacy once and for all. The native peoples now claimed both the economic and political freedom that they felt had been withheld and was at last within their grasp. In Indo-China the Viet-Minh rose against the French the moment the Japanese conceded defeat in 1945. The French were so weak and disorganised that for a while the British occupation forces in Indo-China were forced to enlist the aid of the still present (and armed) Japanese army in fighting off the Communists who sought to seize power before the French re-assumed control. There were to be thirty years of tedious and costly warfare before the Viet-Minh finally achieved their goal.

In Indonesia in 1945, encouraged by the Japanese who had already

The Singapore waterfront, 1951.

installed him as head of a puppet government, the firebrand Dr. Soekarno had assumed the reins of a nationalist government before the Dutch forces could return in sufficient numbers to recover their vast, rich, sprawling Empire of the East. As in French Indo-China, again the British occupying forces attempted to 'keep the seat warm' - this time for the Dutch. Vicious fighting ensued between the British Army (mostly Indian troops - for by now many British soldiers had been demobilised) and the Indonesian rebels. Once again, the Japanese awaiting repatriation were not disarmed 'for their own protection against reprisals.' The Dutch finally withdrew in late 1946 after much bitter fighting and heavy casualties (particularly on the rebel side) leaving the Indonesian people, or so they thought, in command of their own destiny under Soekarno after one hundred and fifty years of Dutch rule.

In 1947 India, Ceylon and Burma had achieved independence, not without much internecine bloodshed in India as the British withdrew. In Malaya there were also nationalist stirrings. The single decisive factor that precluded a post-war rush to independence there was the ethnic and religious make-up of the population. Chinese immigrants (since the nineteenth century) and native Malays were the main constituents, almost equal in number, and were themselves in conflict. The Chinese were the energetic, go-getting businessmen. They were the contract labourers, mechanics, traders, builders and in general, except for those engaged as rubber tappers or tin miners, townspeople. The indigenous Malays were Muslim peasants, self-sufficient agriculturists and fishermen with little interest in changing the status quo - particularly if it meant the Chinese gaining power and influence at their expense.

Significantly, the rulers of the Federated Malay States and Straits Settlements were themselves all Malay. The interests of the Chinese and Malay populations were thus directly opposed. The minority populations of Indians, mostly of Tamil origin, were mainly employed as labourers on the rubber plantations and the Sakai (today known as Orang Asli), simple aboriginal hunters living in small settlements in deep jungle, were of small account. The Sakai people had little contact with the outside world and were suborned and used by both sides during the long years of the Emergency. The British were the planters and businessmen for the big trading companies, the colonial policemen, administrators, teachers and advisers.

Historically, the Malayan Communist party had always been mainly Chinese and following a series of illegal strikes in the late thirties they went underground (to avoid likely repatriation to China). The Japanese occupation had made the British and the Communists into uncomfortable bedfellows on the same side and the latter provided the main resistance to their mutual enemy. There were very few British or Allied personnel around in Malaya until 1944/45. Of these perhaps the most notable was Colonel Freddie Spencer-Chapman (author of *The Jungle is Neutral*) and later the members of Force 136. But the British had exercised very little influence, apart from supplying arms, and the Communists who now called themselves the Malayan Peoples' Anti-Japanese Army were following their own agenda with the aim of seizing power in post-war Malaya.

Into the vacuum left by the collapse of the Japanese in late 1945 and before the arrival of British forces in any numbers, the Communists, now renamed the Malayan Races Liberation Army, started to gain more and more influence in the south and in western Malaya among the Chinese squatter settlements in the bigger towns and on the jungle fringes. Chin Peng, the Communist leader, given a post-war OBE by a grateful British Government had actually marched in the great Victory Parade held in London in June 1946 with a small contingent of his wartime guerrillas (I must have seen him when I watched that last nostalgic flowering of the Empire from the Mall). An uneasy truce existed until 1948 while the MRLA gained strength and influence - still principally among the Chinese, although they did include some Malays. At the end of 1948 the MRLA came out into the open and actually assumed power in some areas.

They had planned to overpower the small police forces and in one fell swoop, to murder and assassinate British planters and officials. Lacking essential support from the Malay population and being poorly co-ordinated the operation went off at half-cock. The British Government swiftly declared a State of Emergency and adopted a strongly defensive posture - and the Communists went back into the jungle once more.

By April 1951 when I arrived, things were not going well. The 8,000 or so active Bandits or CT's (Communist Terrorists) as the MPLA were now known, were on the offensive from Johore State in the south to Perak in the north. The previous year some two hundred and twenty-nine members of the Security Forces, soldiers and police, the latter mostly Malays, had been killed. Three hundred and forty-four civilians had also lost their lives. British troops - having forgotten or lost their jungle fighting expertise so hard-won in Burma - were also suffering casualties. British rubber planters were in the forefront of the civilian losses up country. Many of them were veterans of the Japanese prison camps or ex-servicemen and, hardened as they were, their losses were mounting. Morale was low - at best the British were only holding their own. Had I known a little more of this at the time, I might have felt a little less cheerful. From the northern shores of the Crown Colony of Singapore the rattle of gunfire could sometimes be heard at night, echoing across the narrow Johore Strait from the mainland. Between 1948 and 1960 some five hundred and twenty British servicemen were killed as were 1,297 Malayan Police of all races and some 2,473 civilians, mostly rural Chinese, but also including many British planters who lost their lives during what is now largely a 'forgotten' war.

In Singapore itself, the illegal Communist Party were organising strikes and committing sabotage. Inter-racial tension between Malays and Chinese intermittently burst into riots and violence. In December of 1950 serious rioting had occurred involving the cause of a young Dutch girl, Maria Hertogh. Separated from her parents during the war she had been brought up by Muslim foster parents. When her Dutch family at last traced her to Singapore and tried to seize her back, she was forcibly married at the age of thirteen to a young Malay school teacher from Kelantan. The Singapore Courts upheld the rights of her natural parents - and in the ensuing riots the Malays went 'amok.' Nineteen innocent Europeans (including an airman, Corporal Peter Bell, from Seletar, who was down in the city to buy a car prior to the arrival of his wife and infant son - still two days off Singapore in a troopship) were killed. Some were dragged out of cars and buses and beaten to death by the mob. Two hundred more were injured as cars, buses and houses were burned. At the time the weather was widely held to blame. Unusually no rain had fallen during the days of rioting. Had it done so, many believed the Malay rioters would simply have gone home to avoid getting soaked. But equally to blame had been the authorities. The mainly Malay police at that time were unwilling to antagonise their fellow Malays and passively barricaded themselves in their police stations. The Gurkha police and the British military police were withdrawn and the Singapore government dillied and dallied about curfews or calling for military aid. Finally the troops went in, making a brief show of force which had scattered the mobs. No wonder our RAF Bedford three-tonner was shrouded in wire netting as protection against stoning. Until a few weeks before the drivers had all been armed and escorted.

I suppose we vaguely knew what was going on. We listened to the wireless from time to time (the BBC Overseas News on the Tannoy system) and read the local *Singapore Free Press* and the influential *Straits Times*, plus the few UK newspapers that fell into our hands, mostly the weekly overseas omnibus editions of *The Daily Mirror* (with its thick yellow covers - and what a marvellous newspaper that once was). We also read the bundles of strictly local newspapers that fond mums at home dispatched by Forces' mail to their offspring serving in the far-flung outposts - wherein hard news from the Empire rarely made the front pages. Basically I suppose, we didn't really care. We were there, we were a generation of young men to whom military service and a life of little comfort was the norm. Our motivation was the social climate from which we came. We were both protected and armoured by our youth. That was enough for us to be getting on with for now.

10
SELETAR - BROWNING THE KNEES

Get some in!!
Customary exhortation to sprog airmen exuding naive innocence.

The arrival of our small draft at RAF Seletar had no more noticeable effect than that of a tiny pebble dropped into some huge pond. Within the space of a few days we were given clean bills of health by the Station MO (yet another embarrassing FFI - a 'Quick Flash' as elsewhere described). We 'moon men' - so called by our elders and self-proclaimed betters because of our fish-belly white bodies - were given billets on the top floor of a two-storeyed barrack block in the east camp overlooking the parade ground. We collected rifles from the station armoury. They were then kept chained in the wooden racks at each end of our barrack room, the rifles' bolts removed and labelled in a separate locked box in one of the sergeants' bunks. Unlike most RAF stations, at Seletar corporals shared the same open-plan barrack floor with the rest of the airmen.

We learned about the *dhobi* arrangements. We shared and paid for the services of one of the Tamil bearers who cleaned our brasses, blacked our shoes, made up our beds and swept our floors. This was a hitherto unknown and unexpected luxury - even in Civvy Street few of us had mothers half as accommodating as this. We found our way around the airfield, to the east and west 'camps' separated by the long runway extending to the shore of the Johore Straits, to those hubs of social life - the NAAFI, the Malcolm Club, the mess hall and the Astra Cinema - and were allocated duties in whatever trade we were supposed to be already qualified for or to undergo further training.

Steve and I found ourselves reporting to the headquarters of 390 Maintenance Unit, Far East Air Force - about a hundred yards away around the parade ground from our barrack room. The 'square' was the personal territory of Station Warrant Officer 'Joe' Bollard - to be crossed at one's peril. One of his unwritten rules was 'Keep Off My SQUARE!!' We joined the three or four other clerks who manned the HQ Registry under the eyes of Sergeant 'Smudger' Smith and Pat, the WRAF corporal, who between them ran the office for the adjutant, a much harassed Flight Lieutenant, and for the CO (a lordly and much less harassed Group Captain).

I fail to recall in any detail what our clerical duties, real or imagined, involved. I am sure we were not over-burdened in this direction - unlike the 'hard-skilled' technical and engineering tradesmen and fitters of the Aircraft, Engine and Radio Repair Squadrons. They composed the core of our unit and kept the Far East Air Force serviced and flying. They worked in the hangars on the far edge of the airfield and supplied spares and servicing parties throughout the Far East, wherever the RAF might fly, as far as Kai-Tak at Hong Kong and Iwakuni in Japan (from where the Sunderland flying boats patrolled Korean waters for the United Nations).

To begin with almost all the airmen who shared our barrack room in the east camp were young national servicemen, most of us newly arrived and undergoing some sort of trade training, before being allocated to a more permanent job within the unit.

~ ~ ~ ~ ~ ~ ~ ~ ~ ~

By the early 1950s the RAF was in difficulties with its personnel. As always during times of so-called peace the forces of the Crown were paying the price for the incurable habit of every British government, for reasons of economy, of allowing the armed services to fall far below the lowest level necessary for safety and need. (See Note 5. - Appendix)

All that is now history. My problems in 1951 were more immediate. History, statistics and the underlying problems of the Malayan conflict hardly concerned me. I still had eighteen months in the RAF to look forward to before I could resume a civilian career. For the meantime where better than an interesting time in the relative comfort of the Far East to sit it out? The military historian John Keegan has rightly classified the Malayan Emergency as a 'small war' that provided young British national servicemen with 'a highly enjoyable experience of tropical soldiering.' In my case that was certainly true, but I would argue that few of the young soldiers who found themselves floundering through the jungle swamps in momentary expectation of a murderous ambush would have agreed with him at the time.

Short Sunderland Flying Boat - keynote post-war aircraft at Seletar.

As I have said before, I retain only hazy memories of my everyday duties. We must have filed things. We certainly learned to type - after a fashion. We dealt with signals traffic, shuffled papers and other 'bumf' (service abbreviation for bum fodder) and undoubtedly we made and checked lists - the latter so essential to any bureaucracy. In retrospect I am amazed by the sheer sweep and all-encompassing scope of the organisers and administrators who ran the British Empire, the armed forces and civilian services, the Colonies and Protectorates and the dependent territories. This was done mostly without prejudice and with a degree of impartial and unselfish efficiency that has long since vanished - together with the legacy of a working infrastructure - in many of the places that were once ruled by Britain. I remember a sense of 'service' as still in existence. The costs must have been enormous. The numbers of people involved beyond counting. It is no wonder that within fifteen or twenty years of the end of the war, UK Inc. was just beginning to crawl out of bankruptcy as it shed the diminishing relics, if reluctantly, of Empire. The final bottom line of the Imperial balance sheet had been an expensive luxury!

We national servicemen, newly arrived at Seletar in April 1951, modelled our behaviour on that of our older comrades who exhibited the regulars' attitudes and experience of a more relaxed service life in the tropics. Their knees were browner for a start. The old sweats' KDs were faded and had achieved that cardboard-stiff texture that can only be built up by being saturated in the *dhobi-wallah's* starch for months on end. Their speech was larded with words and phrases whose meanings had to be learned. *Tiffin* was now the mid-day meal, *gharry* was any form of road vehicle, *lekas-la* was 'hurry up!' Charping it off was how we spent the hot afternoons dozing on our beds. Many of the words were not peculiar to the Far East but common service slang from India and the Middle East. To 'take a *dekko*' meant the same as to 'have a *shufti.*' *Bint, bibi, chico* and *cushy* all became everyday words and phrases. Scraps of kitchen Malay were thrown in - *banya bagus* (very good); *terimah kaseh* (thank you); *berinti-berinti*! (stop! Useful in buses); *nanti-la* (wait!); *makan* (food); *satu, dua, tiga* (one, two, three). *Besar, kechil-kechil* meant big or small - the latter pronounced, 'kitchy-kitchy.'

We 'moon-men' with our milk-white knees listened and practised, sending our KD shirts and shorts to the *dhobi* every other day to get rid of their obvious newness. 'Please God - make my knees brown,' was the substance of our evening prayers. The 'old sweats' told us scornfully to,

'Get some in!' (meaning service - or experience) if we ventured an opinion in their hearing. Unlike the aircraft fitters and the army, we humble clerks were unable to shed our shirts in working hours. Newly arrived soldiers were often ordered to do so in the tropics, to acclimatise them to the effects of the sun. We sweated damply in our airless offices.

Having arrived with nothing but our issue kit we needed to find some civvies for our off duty hours. It is an extraordinary quirk of the British serviceman that, given any choice in the matter, they will rarely socialise in or out of barracks wearing uniform. Without civvies one could hardly go down town into the Singapore flesh pots some fifteen miles away. If in uniform off the camp, one was immediately subject to scrutiny by the ubiquitous military police whose attentions were always best avoided. Outside the main gates of Seletar was the camp's own village with the shop-houses of the Chinese and Indian businesses lining the five-foot ways and the road that led into Singapore. Tailors, curio shops, camera stores, chemists, bars, eating houses and hawker stalls - nearly all were there because of the trade from the airfield. Unlike Changi which handled civil air traffic at that time, Seletar was a closed military base for service personnel and government-employed civilians only. The base was strictly guarded inside the long perimeter fences.

The local shops were a revelation to us after the post-war austerity we had left behind in Britain. We bought casual shirts and slacks, shoes and ties. The range was eclectic and to our delight included American 'Arrow' and 'Greyhound' soft-collared shirts until then only seen in flash US magazines, plus a whole choice of ready-made trousers. One could have clothes made-to-measure for little more than the price of the off-the-peg items. Shoemakers would cobble you a leather pair of loafers for a few Straits dollars. To fully appreciate what this meant to us, I think it was necessary to have been brought up in Britain during the war and then to have experienced the increasing deprivations of the immediate post-war period. The Seletar shops remained open until late at night, another entirely new concept.

We also found ourselves for once with money in our pockets, a hitherto uncommon experience for most of us. As AC2s we were receiving our basic twenty-eight shillings (£1.40 pence) plus a further twenty-six shillings per week overseas allowance. Our accommodation and food were all found. We didn't even have to buy cigarettes. We now received a 'free issue' ration of at least two hundred fags each month, frequently more. These were round, vacuum packed tins of fifty, of full-size unfiltered cigarettes. The best of all were the tins of full-size 'Pusser's' Woodbines, usually only issued to the Navy. I can still remember with pleasure (although I have long since given up smoking) the faint 'hiss' of air as one pierced the vacuum seal followed by the rich aroma of export quality tobacco as the cigarettes were revealed.

It is difficult to put our pay into proper perspective. In simple inflationary terms comparing 1951 with 1996, a conscript AC2's £1-8s. per week, plus the overseas allowance that we received, was together worth about £37 in 1996 terms. It was 'starvation wages', peanuts in fact, about the equivalent of a single man's dole and less than one sixth of the basic pay of a modern British army private. Our needs and average expectations were so much less, that what are now everyday necessities to all classes of western society were then luxuries possessed and aspired to only by the fortunate few. We certainly didn't feel ourselves to be deprived in any way. There were a minority who probably did feel the pinch. Some conscripts made a weekly allocation of seven shillings (35 pence) from their pay to their families - in some cases wives! Not a few national servicemen allocated this to their mothers who they hoped would save it for their return if it was not needed for helping out with the family coffers. There was also another unspoken motive for making such an allocation home. Unless this was done and a serviceman then subsequently died or was killed, then the family - sometimes a mother whose sole support might be her son - would receive no compensatory pension.

The Straits dollar current in both Malaya and Singapore was worth then about 2s-4d. - or twelve pence in our modern decimated currency. In 1951 former British POWs of the Japanese were given a final 'pay off' of £72-10s., equivalent to about £1,000 in 1996. Workers who survived the Burma Railway were given an extra £3 each (£42.00) in recognition of their sufferings. This is an exemplary illustration of how our average expectations have altered in the last fifty years.

I think that only regular airmen received a marriage allowance in 1950 which was paid direct to the wife at home. There was very limited married housing available overseas which effectively meant that generally only senior NCOs qualified to have their wives with them. Married officers often lived off-base if no other suitable quarters were available for them. In the various squadrons in which I served, there were always a proportion of young married airmen living a bachelor life in a crowded barrack-room, separated from their wives for up to three years and more, if overseas. How these marriages survived such lengthy separations I do not know, nor care to imagine.

The money that we did receive was in effect, pocket money. All our other needs were met, including food and quarters, our kit only had to be paid for as it needed to be replaced. Many of us in Civvy Street had spent our time being 'skint' - we now had cash burning holes in our pockets. Compared with back home the choice and range of goods in the local shops was much wider and cheaper (much of it exported from Britain). We could afford to eat and drink in local eating houses - most of us didn't save a penny from our pay - if we did, we simply accumulated a pile of cash kept in our bedside lockers for leave or for some special purchase. Few of us had a bank account though perhaps a money order could be sent home by the Pay Branch, but otherwise it was safe. Theft of personal property among the occupants of a barrack room was almost unheard of.

We were of course paid in cash. Pay Parades were a fortnightly occurrence on Fridays. The men of a Flight were drawn up in their ranks, usually in a hangar facing a blanketed trestle table behind which sat the Flight Commander, the pay clerk and a paying officer. Hats were worn and in a working unit some attempt at formal dress was made - no bare chests. The drill was formal, a man's name was called, to which he responded, 'SAH!' came smartly to attention and announced in a loud voice his 'last three.' (The last three digits of his service number). As to the 'last three' some wags were in the habit of shouting out gibberish such as 'Knife, Fork and SPOON, SAH!' in the full knowledge that it would be misheard and no notice taken of what was merely a formality anyway. Marching smartly forward he would halt before the table and salute, remaining at attention. The pay clerk would give the correct cash to the officer who would then count it and announce the total, handing it over to the airman who received it in his left hand, moved two steps to the rear, saluted again, and marching off, fell out, leaving the parade. This was where I found it of advantage to have my name beginning with 'A.' I usually didn't have to hang around but unfortunately the occasional paying officer would vary this routine by paying out in reverse alphabetical order. (See Note 6 - Appendix).

Our barrack rooms were comfortable in a Spartan fashion with high ceilings and slowly moving fans stirring a faint breeze. They were airy rooms with tall double-louvered doors giving onto long shaded verandahs. On the ground floors the verandahs were fringed with two feet deep storm drains which both led away the torrential rain which fell almost daily the year around and also kept out snakes which were common enough. Our beds were metal framed, but at Seletar we were back once more to the old-fashioned 'donkey's breakfast' - the three straw-filled 'biscuits' that were used instead of a mattress. In the mornings our communal bearer piled up the 'biscuits' at the head of each bed, folding the sheets and green cotton bedspread and a single grey blanket on top together with the pillow. The bearers also swept out and cleaned during the morning. Later in the course of the day the bearers would make the beds down again for when their owners came off duty for a late afternoon or post-*tiffin* snooze.

On the wall behind each bed was a taped-up roll of green mosquito netting which was rarely used as Seletar was kept relatively free of mosquitoes and other irritating insect life. The nets were used sometimes if it became too cool after constant rain or if the occupant was desirous of a modicum of privacy in what was otherwise an unremitting round of public living. As I have noted before - having lived through dormitory life at school for many years - barrack-room life was a considerable improvement on the former being both more comfortable and more civilised.

The key to one's survival, remembering that many of the airmen were regulars serving a three-year overseas tour with no home leave compared with the maximum year-and-a-half of the conscripts, was the 'bed-space.' Each man's bed was contained within an area of about eight-by-four feet. Each man had two lockers, one upright and one low enough to write on, lined one side and on the other, across a narrow space, another man's bed with lockers on the opposite side. Thus a whole barrack floor containing maybe as many as a hundred airmen was broken into two-bed sections with a wide central space between each pair. There were simple wooden chairs, the bed also served as a seat. Within those constraints our quarters were clean and a man's bed-space was personal and sacrosanct. The barracks had all been built during the late 1920s and '30s - and had undoubtedly been occupied by the Japanese conquerors a few short years earlier though there were now few traces of their stay.

During my year and a half in the Far East, I moved quarters two or three times around the East Camp at Seletar in the first months while I was still in Headquarters (I later moved to the West Camp and the Radio Repair Squadron). The 390 MU Headquarters building (See Note 8 - Appendix) that I first worked in bore (and still has) the date 1931 over the entrance.

The pathway to the main entrance was flanked by a pair of magnificent fan-shaped Traveller's Palms. (When last seen by me in November 1995 these trees had long since vanished, replaced by a pair of seedlings in pots). The HQ building was not far from the extensive flying boat sheds and slipways on the edge of the Johore Straits. Nowhere had air-conditioning. Apart from the cold stores for food I doubt if there was an air-conditioned room on the base. Down town in Singapore the only building I recall that had this facility was the old Cathay Cinema which we frequented from time to time as much for its breath of cool air as for the popular films we watched (mostly American musicals with Chinese sub-titles!). What remains of the Cathay is dwarfed today by the towering skyscrapers that now dominate the city. The HQ Registry office where I sat out the long hot mornings and even hotter afternoons was immediately over the Headquarters' entrance. The wide shuttered windows and ceiling fans providing the only cooling system.

The Cathay Cinema, Singapore, 1951

11
NORTH TO PENANG

If you can't take a joke - perhaps you shouldn't have joined.
RAF saying.

Life as a low-ranking AC2 'Plonk' in the RAF soon settled into a routine. Unlike some of the conscripts the regular serviceman finding himself on a tour of duty in an overseas posting didn't often look for excitement - he keeps his head down, gets stuck into the job if he is a tradesman, writes letters home or to his wife if he is married - and saves his pay until it's time to go back to Blighty. The 'old sweats' sometimes regarded us as a swarm of mildly irritating insects, as they grumbled and complained at our ineptitude.

The 'military life' only really lends itself to low comedy during times of mass conscription. Service life isn't at all funny when all are there by choice rather than compulsion, whatever current vicissitudes there might be. Rudyard Kipling's army stories such as *Soldiers Three* and his classic poems about their lives in *Barrack Room Ballads* are all basically tragic. Even when trying to be funny his characters are soldiers by choice, even if by default of any other trade being available to them. They are never mere civilians in uniform carrying out an unfamiliar role. The Army (or the Navy or the Air Force) is both their family and their calling. They are where they are because that is the life they have chosen.

I like to think that a leavening of national servicemen was perhaps good for RAF morale in a country such as Malaya in the 1950s where a shooting conflict (never formally declared as a war but simply 'The Emergency') was in progress. In the army most of the close-quarter jungle fighting was undertaken by conscripts, who were in reasonably good heart even if at times they were somewhat 'reluctant heroes.' The RAF in the Far East was a different matter altogether, where probably no more than ten or fifteen percent were national servicemen compared with the thirty-three percent in the home-based RAF in 1952.

The conscript airmen tended to stick together. We were younger than the run-of-the-mill regulars and we probably had more wild oats to sow but then we had less money with which to do it. Few of us were family men and, with the prospect of at the most an eighteen-month overseas stay in the Far East, we could almost pin up our demob calendars on the back of our bedside locker doors on arrival, ticking off each numbered day on the chart, ending with a crude drawing of a ship or a plane. '540 days - and an early breakfast to go! Roll on demob!!'

To begin with I think that many of the national service airmen could not believe their luck. Seletar's barrack rooms were spartan enough and discipline was reasonably strict, but it wasn't irksome, and one soon learned the parameters and conventions beyond which it was inadvisable to stray. On the base there were NAAFI canteens; the Malcolm Club; the local WVS provided a library; the Astra Cinema showed up-to-date films - and also had a stage for theatricals; there was a luxurious swimming pool built in the late 1930s complete with a bar that served food (sausage, egg and chips), beer and ice-cream (during the war the pool had been badly neglected by the Japanese until towards the end it became a cobra-infested, semi-submerged paint store). The Seletar Yacht Club was for all ranks and opened in 1934 on the initiative of a Wing Commander Burling and the late Air Marshal Sir Arthur McDonald, (then a junior officer and incidentally an Old Epsomian - although a pupil at Epsom more than twenty years before myself). There were a few basic civilian shops such as cobblers and barbers inside the camp - and immediately outside the main gate was Seletar Village with its shops, bars and restaurants, that catered almost exclusively for the airmen of the base. The object I suppose, of all the sports facilities that were provided and the RAF's emphasis on physical fitness was to provide as many amenities as possible for what was mainly a young bachelor society, ie. to make them too tired in the evenings to pursue 'other' activities. In particular the activities took their minds off the women and drink that were widely available in down town Singapore city at the weekends.

After some months had passed I made myself known at the small branch of the Chartered Bank that opened two or three mornings a week with a sub-branch office across the road from the Base H.Q. building. I introduced myself as a member of the London staff to the manager, whose name as far as I remember was Cresswell. He was a former wartime RAF officer and arranged for me to go down town one Saturday morning and meet up with some of the junior expat staff I had known in

London. This was to be a revelation and if it was a reflection of the civilian career I had already chosen for myself then I had chosen wisely.

As arranged, I called in at the palatial head office of the Chartered Bank on the Singapore water front, dressed in my newly acquired and somewhat cheap civvies and tie from the Chinese and Indian tailors in Seletar Village. A strikingly smart Sikh messenger ushered me deferentially to the chief accountant who called over Robin Fox* whom I already knew from London. Robin, a fair-haired and genial young man (with a shiny black Ford car!), later showed me around town. I think we had a beery lunch at the cricket club on the *padang*, probably watched the cricket for the rest of the afternoon and then went back for dinner at the Chartered Bank bachelors' mess. In Robin's quarters we drank several *stengahs* in the verandahed and pillared old colonial house which were well furnished and comfortable with chintz and rattan. Ceiling fans gently stirred the warm air.

Being a Saturday night they all dressed for dinner - spotless, crisp white linen and shark skin jackets, starched shirts - I felt a little out of place in my shirt and slacks, but no matter. The bank's own crested silver and glass gleamed on a mahogany table. The food was served by an army (or so it seemed to me) of silent and efficient Malay servants. These privileged young men were the paladins and future moguls and taipans of Far Eastern commerce. If I could join their august company in a year or two, then so much the better. Robin drove me back to Seletar later that evening, leaving me with much to think about in my narrow iron bed in the barrack room. The future rarely turns out as one expects.

Since 1949 there had been a few WRAF at Seletar inhabiting a strictly 'off-limits' barrack block in the East Camp. In such a social climate one needed to be persistent to the point of obsession to engage their off-duty attention - they were quite out of reach for the relatively poorly paid conscripts. It will probably bring down richly-deserved contumely on my head for me even to suggest that most of the WRAF probably enjoyed an active social life in the company of the much better paid Australians from the RAAF bomber squadrons at Tengah. Anyway by 1952, from a wartime peak of 181,000 in 1943, the WRAF were now fewer than 10,000 in total of whom barely 1,000 were in overseas postings. Apart from the delightful WRAF corporal, Pat, in 390 MU HQ, I

---

* Within the year I believe Robin Fox had contracted tuberculosis, was sent home and sadly that was the end of another promising career in the Far East.

only knew one or two of the others by their first names. Singapore must have been a 'plum' posting for these girls.

It was quite possible for an airman to spend his entire tour without leaving the confines of the base unless officially required to do so when on duty. Singapore's oppressive climate did not encourage strenuous physical activity and after a while most airmen simply adapted to a fairly lethargic routine which involved occasional NAAFI drinking sessions, getting 'tanked-up' (but rarely drunk) on the excellent Tiger draught beer, infrequent trips into down town Singapore at the weekends, the camp cinema, a meal perhaps in Seletar Village - invariably egg, chips and sausage - the local cuisine except for run-of-the-mill curries was generally ignored. Not a lot of activity in other words, but an awful lot of charping it off - which is a very similar activity to 'Egyptian PT,' ie. 'deep breathing in the horizontal position with the eyes closed.' For those so inclined there was the sailing club and various other special interest activities for off-duty and leisure pursuits. However my lasting impression remains that the majority of us took little advantage of these apart from the luxurious swimming pool, the Astra Cinema, the NAAFI and the Malcolm Club.

Working hours I think were from 07.30 until mid-day and then 14.00 until 16.30. Wednesday afternoons in the RAF were supposed to be set aside for sport on which the authorities were very keen. Not a lot went on - it must have been very discouraging for the station sports officer! Because of this mid-week half day off, on Saturday mornings we worked until midday.

The messing was good, far better than back in still half-starving Britain. At *tiffin*, the mid-day meal, there was always a wide choice of dishes including curry and rice and fruit salads. Cooked breakfasts were always available for those who wanted bacon, sausage or eggs with which to bump-start their day's activities. If one gave the mess hall an occasional miss in the evenings or at weekends there was always the NAAFI for egg and chips or Seletar Village for a mixed grill.

Our *dhobi* was collected and returned the following day by the Chinese washermen. Our KD uniforms, shirts, slacks and shorts soon became so saturated with starch that they were as stiff as boards when first put on in the morning - one had to 'punch' one's limbs through sleeves and legs, almost ripping the cloth apart by force. It may sound uncomfortable, but it wasn't - the stiffness permitted cooler air to ventilate the body, and anyway before long the day-time sweat and movement both softened and creased shirt and shorts. Virtually all our 'bull' was attended to by our Tamil bearers. As well as all our service kit they pressed our walking-out 'civvies', they cleaned and swept the barrack-room, made our beds and generally kept us tidy with little effort on our part. The Chinese 'Sew-Sew' women did all our running repairs. If one had to be in the Services - this was the way to do it.

The flip side of the coin was boredom. After a while most of us I suppose became too idle in the oppressive and usually unchanging damp heat of Malaya to take much advantage of the facilities that existed for physical exercise. At the beginning too, when I was mainly living and working in the East Camp, the *dhobying* was almost certainly responsible for most of the minor afflictions which plagued us. Many newcomers suffered from the electrifying irritation of prickly heat until one learned to drink enough and one's sweat glands responded by perspiring freely. As the *dhobi* was simply done in cold water, cross-infection was the principal cause of Chinese rot, crutch-rot, foot-rot, tinea and ringworm, impetigo and other fungal or bacterial skin afflictions which few of us managed to avoid. It was pointless to report sick - the MO and his minions simply painted the affected parts an indelible bright purple with Gentian Violet - generally without effect. After a while we all discovered that the Chinese pharmacy in the village sold an ointment - a highly painful mixture of carbolic, benzine and sulphur - which was particularly agonising when applied to the crutch but which resulted in clean, new skin within a few days.

There were few formal parades apart from 'colour-hoisting' mounted by a small detail morning and evening. Each unit in its turn mounted the weekly CO's parade with the station band in attendance or even our small group of pipes and drums, (it is a pleasure to march to the skirl of the pipes). Guard duties came round quite frequently, perhaps two or three nights a month either in the bomb dump set amid the extensive rubber plantations on the base, or at times of Muslim festivals, when the beginning and end of the month of Ramadan for example rendered the RAF Regiment Malay auxiliaries hors-de-combat, the task of guarding the wire perimeter from the rickety searchlight towers fell to the airmen. I was normally excused guard duties as two or three times each month I was on the roster as duty clerk from 18.00 hours to 06.00 the following morning in the empty and deserted HQ building. Here one had a bed frame, a mattress and mosquito net in a small ground floor room - if the telephone rang, any messages required logging. Every two hours or so during the night one had to visit the Signals Centre a short distance away - a solid, fortified concrete cube (still there in 1995) with a spider's web of aerials suspended above it - to collect the latest batch of signals that might have arrived from anywhere in the world. It was mostly prosaic material concerning aircraft spares but still requiring to be logged. At the best, it provided a night's privacy and solitude away from the barrack-room, but otherwise it was a hot and mosquito-ridden way of passing the time. As with guard duties one was left 'free' until 10.00 hours the next morning.

I almost preferred being on guard duty as long as it didn't rain, or a fierce 'Sumatra' sweep through in the early hours before dawn - a sudden squall from the west with tearing wind, torrential rain and thunder, lit by blinding flashes of lightning. If one was in bed in the barrack-room, the verandah doors banged until someone got up and closed them tight, the temperature could swiftly drop by as much as twenty degrees. One searched for a blanket and waited for the storm to pass, knowing that all too soon it would be dawn. Sumatras rarely lasted more than half-an-hour. Reveille at 06.30 would sound on the tannoy system (not always - for we also had one or two proper buglers) and one would rise to a grey, sodden, sunless day, waking to the loud 'click-clack' of Rolls patent razors being stropped. If returning from guard duty after such a storm you would be cold and wet through, with rain-drenched soggy KDs to be discarded and your rifle needing to be oiled and dried before it rusted in front of your eyes. It was on mornings such as this that one regretted that the 'ablutions' and the showers provided only cold water, usually a matter of indifference in the steamy heat that normally prevailed.

A moonlit and solitary two-hour stint (two of two-hours on, four hours off during the night) amid the rubber trees of the bomb dump listening to the whine of the mosquitoes and the creaking stridencies of the crickets or the eery silence before dawn when even the crickets were quietened, I found stimulating - perhaps because I didn't have to do it too often. We kept a weather eye open for the approach of the guard sergeant or perhaps the orderly officer on his rounds, which was not difficult because they had sense enough not to creep up or try to catch unawares a jumpy sentry with 'one up the spout.' The guard-room provided *charpoys*, bully beef sandwiches and that oddly metallic-tasting luke-warm sweet tea from an urn, replenished during the night with fresh supplies from the cook house. I also occasionally did a spell on the wire perimeter fence, perched high up in an *attap* roofed watchtower with another airman for company for the night. We would man a dim searchlight which we soon learned to use sparingly - its beam, barely penetrating the layers of mist rising from the nearby creeks, clearly acted as a flare path for swarms of night-time insects which homed in on us. In any case the light still left huge pools of darkness between ourselves and the next watch tower some hundred yards distant. Break-ins were frequent through the fence, but more for purposes of simple theft rather than CTs (Communist Terrorists) intent on creating mayhem. We would be visited during the night by a fifteen hundredweight truck bringing us more of the villainous-tasting tea and curling sandwiches.

There was also a picket boat guard which patrolled the Johore Straits off Seletar where the flying boats lay at anchor. A national service airman was detailed for this one night to make up the numbers of the usual Malay auxiliaries. Issued with a Sten gun, which he inadvertently dropped when attempting to board the small RAF Marine Section pinnace in the dark, the notoriously erratic and unreliable sub-machine gun spontaneously discharged its entire magazine of thirty-two 9mm rounds indiscriminately into the well of the boat, inflicting (fortunately non-fatal) wounds on most of its luckless crew, excluding the guilty party. He was subsequently court-martialled but acquitted, quite rightly, on pointing out that his training had omitted to provide any experience whatsoever of the Sten.

I passed several months in the 390 MU Headquarters Registry before being posted to the West Camp as orderly room clerk with the Radio Repair Squadron. It had become tedious in the extreme and before I moved I got into the habit of keeping myself closely informed as to what 'courses' or other details were looking for volunteers (or pressed men if no volunteers were forthcoming) - Part 1 and Part 2 Station Orders were closely scrutinised for such opportunities. As well, there were frequent calls for escort details for up-country ammunition shipments. Willing volunteers were always in short supply.

When I tot up the time I managed to engineer away from Seletar it adds up to nearly three months in total. In retrospect it is no wonder that Warrant Officer Pugh, with whom I worked in the Squadron Office, sometimes became irritated - although otherwise invariably good

The Union Jack Club, Singapore, 1951.

humoured - at my frequent absences.

I took two periods of fourteen days leave in Penang, staying at the small RAF leave centre at Tanjong Bungah* on the north-east coast of the island, not far from Batu Ferringhi, which is now the site of serried ranks of major resort hotels. In 1951 and 1952 the palm-fringed beaches were deserted except for a few Malay fishermen and their huts. Very few servicemen seemed to take advantage of these exotic amenities and most airmen, if they bothered to take leave, either slopped about on the base or booked themselves in for a few days at the Union Jack Club in Singapore.

Tanjong Bungah (Flower Cape) was a large, formerly private, cliff-top house with its own small beach. It was run by the WVS for no more than about thirty, or perhaps forty personnel at a time. If there were any WRAF, they stayed in the house while the airmen bunked in a pair of single-storey wooden bungalows in the extensive gardens. The house had teak floors, open jalousies, gentle breezes, capacious mosquito nets

---

* I recently unearthed an old NAAFI receipt for my 14 day stay at Tanjong Bungah, Penang, in July 1952. Full board for the period totalled just over 55 Straits Dollars - equivalent of about £3 - and less than a week's pay and it included free travel. As a humble national serviceman, I reckon this was good value.

hanging over cane-latticed *charpoys*. In the garden bloomed the scarlet flowers of hibiscus, bougainvillaea, alamander, scented frangipani flowers and the rustling fronds of the coconut palms - it was an idyllic setting. On both leaves I went with Steve - who was now in a powerful position in the HQ Movements Section (eventually being promoted to corporal), whereby he had direct access to 'indulgence' flights to RAF Butterworth, although by choice on the second occasion we travelled by the mail train overnight to KL and then the following day on to Penang. This was shortly after a Valetta transport aircraft had crashed at Butterworth, with no fatalities it has to be said, but during the emergency landing it had demolished several Hornet fighter-bombers* parked on the airstrip - reducing the severely frightened passengers to near hysteria.

I enjoyed travelling by comfortable passenger train - as opposed to Third Class (Military) on escort duty in a freight wagon. As always when up-country one had to take one's rifle and a cotton bandolier of fifty rounds and in spite of the slowness of the journey there was always cold Anchor or Tiger beer and a decent curry to be had from the buffet car. I was particularly fond of the fish curry they served, but one day seeing an Indian gentleman tucking into what appeared to be rice and curried tomatoes, I indicated to the Chinese steward that for a change I would have the same. 'You no likee! That not ploper for Blitish soldier - only Indian can eat!' he warned. Ignoring his protests I insisted that he serve me the same dish. The steward went off clucking like a hen. Steve observed that the Indian diner appeared to be sweating buckets and was frequently mopping his brow as he shovelled in the fragrant tomatoes. Steve wisely stuck to the reliable curried fish. What I got was a dose of the red-hot runs, a burned-out and semi-paralysed gullet, plus an insatiable thirst - all as a result of trying to eat what turned out to be a dish of curried 'banana' chillies.

Arriving by train in the late afternoon of the second day's travel at Prai on the mainland, one then took the ferry across to Georgetown, (today there is a long road bridge), sailing through the harbour with its ocean-going ships and swarms of sailing junks and *sampans*. On landing we hailed a pedal-driven trishaw to check in and leave our rifles and bandoliers at the military police armoury, then caught a bus out north along the coast to Tanjong Bungah.

The WVS ladies ran the place superbly. There was a bar, a gramophone and scratchy old 78 rpm recordings of Deanna Durbin singing

---

* A single seater variant of the wartime 'Wooden Wonder' the De Havilland Mosquito.

Beneath the Harbour Lights of Home, of Howard Keel and the *House of Singing Bamboo* from the film *Pagan Love Song* also starring the perpetually water-logged, swim-suited Esther Williams, who sang where 'You don't have to count sheep - that's for Little Bo Peep. You can sleep 'til the sun peeps through.' Another record was the first ever double-track recording of Les Paul and Mary Ford's *Somewhere There's Music - How High the Moon*. There was a small library of mainly Hank Jansen-type novels, a pleasant dining room, gardens with rattan steamer chairs, a quiet beach down under the cliff where the water was murky but still unpolluted - unlike today one could swim freely or fish off the rocks. The food at the centre was superb and so was it in the bars and restaurants of Georgetown.

There were bicycles for us to explore further afield and there were frequent trips in a three-ton *gharry* laid on for us to swimming 'holes' up in the hills behind the town and to what are now the tourist haunts of the Kek-Lok-Si Pagoda and Penang's famous Snake Temple where the WRAF girls shrieked satisfactorily as the comatose Russell's vipers were draped over their unwilling shoulders. An RAF launch took us on day-long trips

The harbour at Georgetown, Penang.

to the island of Pulau Rimau off Penang's south coast where giant manta rays rose horizontally out of the water splashing back like huge table-tops in showers of spray. Compared to contemporary life back in the UK this was paradise!

There were weekend dances (also organised by the WVS) at the Army leave centre not far away, but these were fairly grim affairs as I recall, one visit was enough. The squaddies tended to rowdiness and to drink too much. The girls who attended were not the cheerful, raucous, Chinese taxi-dancers from the downtown dance halls, but specially invited (and closely chaperoned) mostly Anglo-Indian and mixed-race girls. They were pretty, dark, sparrow-legged, in purple taffeta dresses with glistening permed hair and their mothers watched them like hawks whenever a young soldier with slicked-down hair and Hawaiian shirt offered to partner them in a fox-trot or a waltz to the laboured strains of an off-key band. Any lovelorn soldier who fancied his chances with any of this lot - short of marriage - was on to a dead-cert loser. The atmosphere lacked spontaneity and we swiftly made off elsewhere.

We rarely, in any case, socialised off-duty or on leave with the common

The shoreline at Tanjong Bungah, Penang.

soldiery. They were unpredictable and in any case we had our own oppos and mates. downtown in Singapore there was occasional late night trouble leading to scuffles between the various services. If it was a proper inter-service brawl, traditionally the RAF and the Navy usually sided with each other against the Army, presumably because they were otherwise outnumbered. This was the case except on one notorious occasion when ships of the US Pacific Fleet made a 'goodwill' courtesy visit. For weeks before their arrival station orders had promulgated (what a fine bureaucratic word that is) the news that the Americans were coming. 'The Americans are our friends and Allies,' declared Part Two Orders, '... they are coming on a GOODWILL visit. Do not go downtown - do not fight the Americans!' That is not literally what was said, but in no uncertain official terms, that was spelled out in orders.

Of course, that Saturday night the bars and dance halls were thronged with British soldiers, sailors and airmen (all wearing 'civvies' being off-duty) in an atmosphere of charged expectation, parties of white-suited American sailors on shore-leave jostled and drank with their Limey allies. At midnight, as at a given signal, spontaneous and general mayhem erupted into violence in the streets and bars. In the dance halls all dancing ceased when wild fist fights broke out, furniture flew through the air, bottles were smashed (Hollywood films of the era set the pattern for bar-room brawling) the girls and the taxi-dancers shrieked and fled, the bands stood up and played *God Save The King*. The American Navy Shore Patrols, the British Military Police and the Civil Police who were waiting in reserve, outnumbered as they were, waded in and broke heads indiscriminately. The American sailors formed into groups and made a fighting retreat back to their ships flanked and guarded by their own baton-wielding shore patrols, all pretence at 'good will' now abandoned and all shore leave cancelled until they sailed away again. The British servicemen, honour satisfied, returned to their barracks, licking their wounds - and smiling.

It was in Penang that I experienced my only personal brush with violence of that description. Half a dozen of us had walked off in the late afternoon to a roadside bar near Tanjong Bungah for a few cooling beers before going back to supper. We sat drinking and smoking companionably. We were interrupted when a half-platoon of soldiers, armed, dirty and sweaty in their jungle greens, pulled up outside, jumped down from their truck and piled into the bar, stacking their rifles in the corner and shouting noisily for beer to the Chinese proprietor. It was soon apparent that they had spent a day or two on patrol in the jungle-clad hills that rose in the centre of the island a mile or two away (there were rumoured to be 'bandit' camps up there for local weekend 'training'). Not to put too fine a point on it, the soldiers smelled pretty ripe - they were sweaty, unwashed and dirty. Among our company we had an erk older than most of us, a former Palestine Policeman, who had as he said, '... joined the RAF for a quiet life.' I presume that what happened next could perhaps be construed in his terms as 'quiet' when compared with being shot at and blown up by the Stern Gang. This man, ignoring the fact that our group was heavily outnumbered, said in a loud and meant-to-be heard voice, something like, 'Cor! Those squaddies don't half pong. They smell like a Chinese pig-sty.'

The reaction was almost instantaneous. The soldiers made some gratuitous remarks about, 'Poncey Brylcreem boys.' Our principal protagonist stood up menacingly while the rest of us hastily checked the location of the nearest exits. Part of the trouble was that in those distant times people had seen too many B-movies and John Wayne Westerns and modelled their bar-room aggression on the brawls they had seen when balsawood prop furniture and paper-thin sugar-glass bottles are splintered into matchwood and harmless shards over the actors' heads. Reality is not like that. Hastily emptied beer bottles were heaved at us by the squaddies, (they were not so foolish as to waste full ones). Heavy wooden chairs were picked up and brandished menacingly and our own table was upset with a crash, spilling bottles and glasses as we, including our companion who had provoked the confrontation now clearly perceived discretion as the better part of whatever valour we possessed, made fast for the exits. As I made for the bar counter and a door that led into the kitchen - and thence presumably into the open air, I could see the Chinese proprietor furiously cranking the wind-up handle of the telephone while casting anxious glances at the mayhem that engulfed his bar. A bottle crashed into the mirror, starring it into a spider web of radiating cracks. Just as I nearly reached safety and the back exit a soldier's fist made stunning contact with the side of my head and I fell to the floor at the feet of the owner who was still shouting into the telephone.

Fortunately the nearest Military Police Post was only a short distance away. When their jeep roared up they swiftly rounded up most of those who still remained on the premises - including myself, still seeing stars -

names and units were taken, threats of dire retribution made and the Chinese barman was promised compensation. Reports did later follow me back to Seletar, but while no pay was docked for the damage - for I strongly denied any personal liability for the fracas - I fear the incident was held against me when I later hoped, vainly as it turned out, for promotion to corporal. In retrospect, it was all for the best as my period of service was fast approaching completion and the additional responsibility would not have been welcome.

Another day at the Kek-Lok-Si Pagoda outside Georgetown a group of us ascending the long stairway above the turtle-filled pools were severely ticked-off by an elegant Chinese lady, tripping daintily down the steps in her silk *cheong-sam* with her oiled-paper and bamboo *wan-chai* umbrella to shield her from the sun. After she had passed, a caged mynah bird that we were encouraging to talk, let out the most realistic - more real than real - deep-throated wolf whistle, of the sort that brings to mind a tattooed and bare-chested builder's labourer (complete with 'brickie's cleavage') and a passing floozy on a hot summer's day. The Chinese lady turned and stormed back. Furiously she laid into us, giving us a handsome tongue-lashing and ignoring our protestations that it had been the mynah bird that had produced the vulgar whistle. She accused us of being, '...a disgrace, ill-mannered liars - your mothers would be ashamed of you and if I knew your unit, I would report you!'

On another occasion one of our small party was guilty of provoking a scene when a few of us, including a young Rhodesian SAS trooper (see Note 9: Appendix) who understandably preferred convalescing with the RAF at Tanjong Bungah rather than at the Army's much more basic leave centre down the road, having broken both his legs in a jungle parachute drop a few months earlier, and our jovial former ex-Palestine Policeman, were eating and drinking one evening in a downtown restaurant. One of our number, a very funny Cockney - but renowned neither for his refinement, nor for his IQ - became convinced that a pretty Chinese girl supping alone at a nearby table was, to use the delicate phraseology of a modern-day sociologist - a 'part-time worker in the local sex industry.'

The Chinese girl picked daintily at her food with her chopsticks and was fussed over by the waiters. She wore the then popular (and I for one deeply regret the passing of this fashion), stylish *cheong-sam*, a high-collared, tight-fitting sleeveless dress, usually silk, calf-length and sexily slit to the thigh to reveal an often pretty leg. Combined with the raven-black hair and the small-breasted but otherwise slim and shapely silhouette of many Chinese - it was a vision, in the immortal words of Dashiell Hammett (or was it Raymond Chandler?) - 'Enough to make a Bishop kick out a stained-glass window!'

The girl made up her face with powder and lipstick in the mirror by the door. As she got up to leave she had glanced across at our table. At this our uncouth would-be Romeo became fired-up with passion and he determined to make his move. He sidled across to the girl as she prepared to leave, flicking back his Brylcreemed-down hair as he went. Making his well-practised approach, he said ingratiatingly, 'Ow much for a short-time then Miss?'

The response was both immediate and surprising. Swinging her handbag with astonishing strength for one so petite, she caught our Lothario a heavy blow across the side of his head which sent him staggering back, tripping over a chair and falling to the floor. 'You some silly bugger, you!' she shouted over her shoulder as she stormed out and clattered down the stairs to the street. 'You think I look likee Chinese tart? Next time I teach you ploper manners!'

As we fell about laughing, the waiters picked up our friend from the floor, unable to restrain their own giggles as they dusted him down. One saying, 'She not plostitute - she taxi-dancer - next time you must buy ticket before you speak!'

At the end of my second fourteen days leave in Penang (July 1952) I was in a bad way. The day before departure I had dozed off on the beach in the shade of a palm tree. A few days before that I had already been painfully sunburned across my shoulders. As I slept, the sun had shifted and I was cooked again over my already bad, but just about bearable sunburn. The second overdose of sun created a large area of blisters across my back and shoulders. By the afternoon when Steve and I took the ferry back to the mainland to catch the night mail-train south to KL, the blisters were becoming much worse and I was in a lot of pain. During the night as the train slowly trundled southwards my individual blisters combined into one large fluid-filled sac. Something had to be done - I was virtually immobilised. Steve went off and found one of the army medical orderlies forming part of the train's regular escort. He took a look at my back, rummaging about in his medical pack and said comfortingly, 'Blimey mate! I dunno wot to do about this. I could fix you up if you'd bin shot... but I dunno...'

Eventually we went out onto the open observation platform at the end of the carriage, where having removed my bush shirt I leaned backwards over the handrail whereupon by the dim light of the moon the obliging soldier slit and drained my huge blister onto the slowly passing rail-track. He then took the largest field dressing he had and bound it in place, tying the knots around my chest. The relief was instantaneous and I put my shirt back on, sitting bolt upright and dozing fitfully until we arrived at KL in the early morning. By then of course the dressing had soaked through and my shirt was firmly glued to my back.

At KL further disaster struck. The railway line between KL and Singapore was out of action, (see Note 10 - Appendix). The 'up' night-mail had been derailed and ambushed (yet again) and there were no trains south until further notice. Steve was nothing if not resourceful. We were due back on duty at Seletar the following day, but by now, more importantly, I also needed proper medical attention. Steve managed to telephone his opposite number in the Movements Section (knowing each other already by name) at KL's RAF airstrip. He explained our dilemma and asked, 'Was there any chance of hitching a lift in any aircraft bound for Singapore?'

Within the hour, the two of us were clambering into a Dakota, (see Note 11 Appendix) bound for Seletar to undergo urgent repair. The snag was that it was a supply-dropping transport. There were no seats and no doors, just large windswept gaps where the air-despatchers normally threw out the cargo into the void. Apart from the pilot and flight engineer, Steve and I were the only people on board. We stowed our rifles and packs behind the crew compartment and clung on to the overhead rails to which the parachute static lines were normally attached.

'Hold tight, lads!' shouted the engineer back through the open door to the cockpit. The acceleration was such that our rifles and kit started to slide back down the deck towards the wide-open doorways. We scrabbled about and managed to recover them before they - and us, disappeared into the blue - while trying to retain our own footing. As we lifted above the end of the runway, airborne at last, there was a violent explosion below us where a battery of 25 pounders served by bare-chested gunners let go a salvo directly beneath our wings. They were shelling the wooded hills of the Ulu Gombok Forest Reserve off to the north-east, which many years later I found out was then harbouring Chin Peng's No 2 'Yeung Kwo' unit, two of whom in 1953 managed to penetrate the town to within two hundred yards of the military headquarters before being killed. I always welcome the mention of Kuala Lumpur as it permits me to use the useful conversational gambit, 'The last time I flew out of KL there was a battery of 25 pounders in action below us as we lifted off the end of the runway.'

We flew under thick cloud cover all the way south to Singapore, weaving just above the thickly forested hills through heavy rain and occasional thunder until we dropped down over the Johore Straits and rolled to a stop some few hundred yards from my quarters.

I reported sick, was 'torn off a strip' by the MO and told that I was lucky not to be charged with the crime of 'self-inflicted' injury. I had to pay for a new bush jacket from the stores, the old one having to be soaked off and cut away from my back. It would have been embarrassing to have come up before the Squadron CO, 'Tug' Wilson, being marched in by Mister Pugh. Normally it was my own function as the squadron clerk to act as 'escort' for airmen brought before the CO. That and the other 'incident' probably ruined my immediate chances of promotion to Acting Corporal's rank - for which I had been angling, knowing that there was a vacancy on the unit's establishment.

12
COURSES FOR HORSES

'Anyone 'ere play the piano or any other musical instrument?' 'Yes, I do Sarge.' 'OK! You'll do, 'op along at the double now and clean out them h'ablutions for CO's inspection. Spotless mind - or I'll 'ave your guts for bleedin' garters!'

Old Sweat's advice to sprog airman, 'Never volunteer for anything.'

In September 1951 I 'volunteered' myself for a ground combat course being held at the hill station of Diyatalawa in Ceylon. It seemed like a halfway decent sort of jolly, as indeed it turned out to be, and I was away for nearly three weeks. I had barely taken up my duties in the Radio Repair Squadron Office with Warrant Officer Pugh, but he didn't raise any objections, those came later. I was hoping that a change of climate would clear up the various ongoing and aggravating fungal skin infections that I had brought over with me on transfer from the East to the West Camp. I was also concerned about the medical clearance I needed before going on the course. If the MO inspected any of my various nooks and crannies he was going to paint me bright purple and probably refuse to pass me as fit. In the event a very laid-back young MO asked me facetiously as I stood before his desk, 'Hives? Hernia? Haemorrhoids - or piles?' On my denial of these distressing conditions, he signed the form. I saluted and left before he could think of any more shattering witticisms.

About twenty airmen from all over Malaya, including an Australian from Tengah, assembled on Changi airstrip before dawn, together with two or three WRAF from Seletar going on leave to Kandy in Ceylon. Our Australian Air Force DC3 took off an hour or so before sunrise and after twenty minutes gaining height up the Malacca Straits we had just unbuckled our seat belts when, without warning, we flew slam-bang into the solid wall of a Sumatra squall. The Dakota bucked, kicked, fell like a stone, and was whirled upwards and thrown sideways like a fragile ship in a storm, while lightning fizzled and slashed through the chaos outside like a maniacal fireworks display. Blue crackling static outlined the wings. The now unrestrained passengers floated and vomited their early breakfasts into free-fall weightlessness while trying to grab some part of the aircraft and fasten themselves in whatever fashion to some fixed part of the cabin. How we escaped injury I do not know but after some further ten minutes corkscrewing and vaulting through the storm we broke clear and managed to sort ourselves out, as we came through into the dawn sunshine amid the puffy monsoon clouds of the Andaman Sea.

By late morning, some half-hour after our scheduled ETA for a re-fuelling stop (and *tiffin*) at the RAF staging post on the coral atoll of Car Nicobar*, away south of the Andamans in the Nicobar Channel, we were still looking for our landfall. We were lost, the Australian crew cheerfully informed us. I was unsurprised at this. The crew had spent most of the past hours crammed up in the cockpit, smoking cigarettes and drinking coffee with the Seletar WRAFs, paying (in my opinion) scant attention to the more pressing needs of flying our Dakota in the right direction. We zoomed low over several promising islands, spectacularly beautiful with their white beaches, densely wooded interiors and surrounding coral reefs in dark blue crystal-clear waters - every one obviously uninhabited. All was eventually well and an hour late we landed safely on a steel-planked airstrip, whizzing past the suitably decrepit, palm-thatched control tower perched up on stout coco-palm timbers, parking at last in front of a flagpole flanked by captured Japanese field guns and a notice which declared, 'Welcome to RAF Car Nicobar - on the Dakota Trail.'

Car Nicobar lies to the south of the Indian province of the Andaman Islands in the Bay of Bengal and in 1942 had been the furthest west that the Japanese had managed to expand their vaunted Asian co-prosperity sphere. After a few early raids mounted by the Japs on shipping and on Ceylon, the Allies had simply ignored it, bombing the airstrip from time to time and effectively isolating the Japanese garrison. It would have been too costly to invade - and pointless. The RAF moved in when the war ended and established a staging post for the Far East Air Force. RAF airmen only did a six months tour of duty on the island where the living facilities were minimal. I was once told that the highlight of one's stay there was the invitation to the occasional local pig-roast held by the

---

* The remote island of Car Nicobar has been 'closed' off-shore territory of India for many years now and off-limits to foreigners, to protect the aboriginal Negrito inhabitants from exploitation (one hopes).

aboriginals when a live pig, trussed up with wire, was thrown into a large fire. When the squeals ceased, it was considered 'done', taken out and eaten. It was also said to be a great place to save money, for the men were not paid in cash, but used a 'chit' system in the NAAFI canteen - the only place on the island which offered anything at all (presumably apart from fish and coconuts) for sale. I have a photograph taken as we re-embarked. The shirtless Car Nicobar erks clustered around us, all their attention concentrated with searchlight intensity on the three WRAF girls.

On our next leg to Negombo, we were again late - not because we were lost this time, but because the Aussie crew (smartly clad in white flying overalls) took us, for the benefit of the WRAF now permanently and firmly ensconced in the cockpit, on a low-flying jaunt over the north of Ceylon to see the ancient and impressive rock fortress of Sirigiya perched on its lonely mountain top.

On landing at Negombo in the late afternoon our party destined for Diyatalawa were fed and watered, driven in a three-ton truck to the railway station and decanted onto a small steam train which was to chug its way up into the mountains towards Kandy throughout the night. As 'other ranks' we travelled 'hard' class. Desperately uncomfortable slatted wooden seats in a cramped carriage were our lot. Three or four of us swiftly discovered a first class dining car with upholstered seats and an obliging attendant who raised no objection to our presence. The list of refreshments offered little that we could afford - except for shots of local gin at the equivalent of much less than a shilling. The obliging steward regaled us with more than adequate quantities of this firewater which he explained was, 'Arrack - distilled from palm-toddy.' It predisposed us to sleep as the small train chugged skywards through the night-time hills suffused with the scent of the ubiquitous tea gardens. The first class sleeping car attendant came by and made an offer we could not refuse. By 2am he said, there would be some vacated berths when a few passengers left the train. For a modest sum of rupees their empty berths could be ours. Rather than return to our 'hard' class wooden benches we attempted to sleep for the meantime on the relatively clean dining-car seats and floor.

I managed to sleep for a while on the hard floor of the dining-car, my sensibilities suitably dulled by several more shots of local gin. The train clacking and rattling in the dark, the compartment lights now extinguished, I was abruptly awoken by a tickling sensation on my left leg. Something quite large, with numerous legs had crawled inside my trousers, well past the knee and was now on its way up to my crutch.

In such circumstances I am not one to hang about idly conjecturing what might or might not be my next best move. As in Africa many years later, I knew of an occasion when someone had said quietly, 'Whatever you do, don't move, there's a snake under your chair.' The recipient of this well-intended information leapt convulsively into the air, upsetting his drink, his 'small chop', his fellow guests and the seat beneath which lurked the snake. He leapt for refuge onto the table which then collapsed beneath his weight, the room being simultaneously plunged into darkness as he clutched for support at the electric light over the table while the rest fled for safety.

My own immediate reaction was remarkably restrained. I let out a high screech of alarm, leapt to my feet while scrabbling at my trousers - trying to pin down whatever beast it was that had invaded my nether parts. My companions were suitably concerned. One found the light switch while all regarded my antics with alarm. Eventually I managed to confine the creature in a sort of constricted bag, pinching my fingers around a large fold in the material of my (fortunately) capacious and generously cut KD slacks. It took some time for the three of us, and some remarkable contortions on my part, to remove my trousers while I kept the 'beast' closely confined. At last the deed was done and we shook out the contents of my trouser leg onto the table.

It was nothing more than a very large cockroach, some three inches in length, which we then trapped beneath an empty glass. When the sleeping car attendant arrived shortly afterwards to say our berths were ready, we displayed our catch to him. 'That is being a mere nothing, sirs,' he said disparagingly, 'more plenty, much bigger are dwelling here. You should be seeing inside galley when I am switching on light!'

Diyatalawa was a small pleasant hill station, too high for tea to be grown, but situated in a ring of hills with patches of forest, dotted with tangled thickets, open heathland set about with shallow streams and grassy meadows dotted with encroaching bracken. The countryside bore a remarkable resemblance to parts of the English Lake District where I have now lived for the past thirty years - except for the Buddhist temple in the valley below our low-roofed quarters, whose bells and gongs tintinabulated gently from dawn to dusk. The rocky slopes in the far distance displayed the regimental badges, set out in whitewashed stone, of the many units of the Fourteenth Army who had trained here during the war.

There was an RAF Regiment detachment, known to some airmen as 'rock apes' for reasons which escape me, but never referred to as such to their face (by the same logic one avoided calling soldiers of the more rustic county regiments, 'swede bashers'). The regiment's task was to advance the basic weapons training and simple infantry tactics that we were all supposed to be familiar with from our recruit days. Some of us were more familiar than others. We had no formal parades or drills, our days were taken up with stripping, cleaning, re-assembling and firing the standard .303 No. 4 service rifle, the Bren LMG plus the 'plumber's delight' - that loosely assembled jumble of coiled metal springs, cheap metal stampings, tubes, pins and pipework known as the Sten submachine gun. We stripped, cleaned and primed grenades. We were 'gassed' in the gas hut once more. It was obviously all lies as we were told as recruits that we would be gassed once only for training purposes during our service. We were issued with suits of jungle-green denim, with webbing pouches and gaiters, and chased up and down the low hills while thunderflashes banged and cracked around our heels, thrown with evident delight by the two sergeants and the Flight Lieutenant who ran our course. Also taking part were a group of ten or so Sinhalese airmen, founding members of the still newly-formed Royal Ceylon Air Force - all seemingly named Fernandes, Pereira or Bandanaraike - and undoubtedly destined for high ranking careers in the fledgling Dominion's service.

The climate in the hills was delightful. It was cool, summery and dry compared to the steam-bath of Malaya. Within a few days all my skin troubles had cleared up. The freshness of the air re-invigorated us and we thrived on the ample food and compulsory exercise. But as in all would-be Edens - there was a piece of grit lurking in the otherwise soothing ointment.

Haemadipsa zeylanica belongs to the family *Hirudinea*. It is more usually known as the common segmented ground leech. At Diyatalawa not only were they common, they were literally a bloody pest. We were swiftly introduced to them on our first exercise. Our training group were advancing in open order across a patch of ground when the two sergeant instructors, blowing whistles and tossing thunderflashes urged us to take cover. Ahead of us lay a shallow ditch which was the only obvious place for us to get our heads down. We lay prone for a few minutes, pressed against the damp vegetation (I hesitate to call it grass). Suddenly, the next man from me, a few yards down the ditch, let out a piercing, falsetto, 'Eeeekk!!' as he scrambled to his feet. Whereupon an instructor roared, 'GEDDOWN Laddie!!! 'Ooo gave you permission to stand up? GEDDOWN!!! The rest of you STAND FAST!!' As my neighbour lay down again overcome by *force majeur*, he attempted to suspend himself horizontally, supported only by his fingertips and booted toes, forming a rigid human plank from one bank of the ditch to the other.

'EeeekkKK!' he continued in the same vein. 'AAAaaarrGGGH!! F-----G bloodsucking LEECHES!'

By then of course it was too late for us all. Looking around I saw a moving carpet of matchstick sized, rubbery leeches, standing up stiffly at an angle on their hind suckers, gently swaying from side to side, looping and inching along as they sensed and scented the shortest route to their next meal. Which alas, was me.

Given the briefest window of opportunity, leeches will drop on you from fern fronds, from blades of grass, from leaves, from twigs. The moment you stop they are onto your boots, swiftly vanishing into the lace holes. They travel up trouser legs, inside collars, under watch straps, they end up in one's crutch, in the armpits, in the crease of the buttocks. A favoured spot is behind the ear - or worst of all, looking like some obscene hearing aid, inside the ear. They are quite painless, their movement on the skin undetectable. One relies on one's companions to point out the more visible ones. The hidden ones eventually make their presence felt, when gorged like a bloated slug they detach themselves. If in a boot they are then squashed, the wound continuing to bleed freely (leech saliva is both anaesthetic and anti-coagulant) until the whole boot becomes squidgy and sticky with blood. On one's back, when the leech falls to one's waist, a patch of blood mingles with the sweat blotches on your shirt.

To remove a leech before it has become engorged is difficult. To pluck it off with the fingers is virtually impossible. We used either a burning cigarette-end held close enough to make it release its hold, or a pinch of salt on its back had the same effect. It can then be flicked off with finger and thumb. The wound continues to bleed, eventually forming a clot, which when dislodged by washing or showering, leaves the bite to bleed all over again. For several weeks after, a small, dark, circular scar marks the skin. Back in Malaya the legs and arms of the jungle-bashing soldiers were often covered with a profusion of these scars.

We had no choice but to cope. We soon devised a system whereby each day we each put a 'chip' (one rupee) into the pot. At the day's end the chap with the most fresh leech bites scooped the pool. The highest number I remember anyone achieving in one day was thirty.

A few years ago I met Lt. Gen. Dennis Pereira, retired Commander-in-Chief of Sri Lanka's army. I mentioned Diyatalawa which he knew well as it is still a military base. 'The leeches,' he said, 'still remain an invaluable training aid!'

At the weekends we were whizzed around the mountainous winding roads in a three-tonner, visiting Diyaluma Falls where we swam in pools above the spectacular drop-off. We stopped to take tea in remote jungle rest-houses in steamy valleys. Half an hour later we would be swooping across open hill country above the clouds, gazing towards the 7,400 feet of Adam's Peak where the Lord Buddha left one of his many miraculous footprints in the rock near the summit.

There was a memorable evening in the NAAFI, shared with Royal Navy matelots on leave in another part of Diyatalawa, up from the naval base at Trincomalee. The airmen and the sailors vied with one another to recite and sing the hoary old service songs and a spectacular table-top soft-shoe 'clog' dance was performed by one of our number. *The Face on the Bar-Room Floor* and *The Killing of Dan McGrew* - were declaimed with classic gestures. An ancient naval stoker gave us *Eskimo Nell* to riotous applause. Our own RAF 'scouser' sang an over-emotional version of *The Wearing of the Green*, encoring with *They're Hanging Danny Deever in the Morning*. Turned out of the canteen at last we staggered back to our quarters, the road lined with trees sparkling with clouds of fire-flies.

It seemed that our course was liberally supplied with vast quantities of war-surplus small-arms ammunition destined for disposal. On the ranges we blazed away freely. The rifles and the Brens were fired until the barrels were smoking hot. During a sudden downpour of rain, the patched target faces peeled off in sodden strips, the field telephone gave up the ghost and in the middle of the storm one of our number let loose an entire Bren magazine on full automatic - rather than the officially approved 'short bursts' - aiming through clouds of steam and managing to dislodge a large lump of concrete from the parapet in the butts. It landed on the head of the sergeant in charge of the squad of markers, rendering him temporarily unconscious. I suspect that much of my own high-tone deafness in later life was in part due to these sessions on the range. Either behind or acting as Number Two on the Bren the repeated concussion of rapid fire at such close quarters (ear protectors were then unknown) wreaked a cumulative effect on my sensitive ear drums. I could still hear bats squeak in those far-off days.

Our final assault course was memorable. Pounding on foot across rough country we 'attacked' a hill top on which was an empty trench system we were supposed to occupy. I was by this stage labouring heavily, cross-country running then as now, never my chosen sport, and I was one of the last to reach the summit. The others were already disappearing into the relatively shallow trenches ahead of me. Seeing a spoil heap and a 'hole' immediately to my front, I jumped in, promptly regretting my hasty decision and finding myself several feet down a deep pit, amid thick vegetation, and with little chance of extricating myself. I was petrified by the thought that this pitfall was ideal habitat for a nest of Ceylon's notorious and famously venomous 'tipfalongas' - a local version of the Russell's pit-viper. I raised my voice, shouting feebly for help. I also raised my rifle and bayonet on which I had spiked my off-white handkerchief, waving it, I hoped above the parapet, to attract my comrades' attention.

'Wot the bleedin' hell are you doing down there? Stop poncing about like a pox-doctor's clerk!' shouted the sergeant. Adding to my already considerable alarm he said, 'If I were you I'd get out of there in double-quick time. You never know whatever else might be in there as well!'

In the end two or three fellow erks had to remove their rifle slings, and by dint of linking them together lowered them down to my level and hauled me out, safely and in one piece but severely shaken, if not stirred by my experience.

I did however redeem myself before the day was out. On the final exercise of the assault course we doubled up to the twenty five yard range, our rifles discarded, our chests heaving with effort. Lined up on the firing point, a Sten gun and loaded magazine at our feet, within the space of one minute, we had to fire ten single aimed rounds from the shoulder, the remaining twenty-two shots to be fired in short bursts from the hip. Amazingly every single shot of mine had registered on the target. With exactly the correct number of holes I had achieved a 'possible' maximum score! I was congratulated all round and the sergeant said, 'Blimey, I never seen that before. Well done lad!'

Later that day handing in our kit to the stores, my immediate neighbour to my right on the firing point, Dick, the Australian airman from Tengah, took me quietly off on one side. 'Blue,' he always called me by this curious Aussie nickname because in those far off days I then had reddish hair, 'Blue - you know how many hits I scored with the Sten today?' I shook my head.

'Bloody zero, not a single bloody hit! And you know how come?' I shook my head again. 'Blue, when we finished I realised I had been shooting at your bloody target all the time! Bloody marvellous innit? Between us we got exactly the right bloody number!'

~ ~ ~ ~ ~ ~ ~ ~ ~ ~

Back in Singapore again in late October, two disasters had occurred during my absence in Ceylon. On 6 October 1951, the British High Commissioner, Sir Henry Gurney, who was responsible for the overall strategy of conducting the Emergency against the Communist terrorists, had been ambushed and murdered, or killed, depending on one's viewpoint, on the road to Fraser's Hill to the north of Kuala Lumpur. Sir Henry's Chinese butler, subsequently questioned by the Special Branch confessed to being a member of the Min Yuen, the Malayan Communist Party who maintained civilian cells across the country. Effectively, although Sir Henry's assassination was a great propaganda coup on the part of the CTs, it was nevertheless an own goal for it greatly concentrated the official British mind. General Sir Gerald Templer was swiftly appointed as successor and from then on the CTs' collective goose was cooked. Templer's grasp of the serious state of affairs, his drive and energy and his greatly increased powers began to reverse the rapidly deteriorating situation.

By August 1951 the Emergency was already in its third year and beginning to run away out of hand. During that month alone the toll included a hundred houses burnt by CTs in Malacca (then under direct British administration), thirteen policemen killed in Perak, a rubber planter killed in Negri Sembilan and another five members of the Security Forces killed, again in Malacca. A British policeman and two constables were killed near KL, another British police officer was murdered near Tampin, a

The ambush site where Sir Henry Gurney, High Commissioner, died in the ditch on the left. He was en route to play golf at Fraser's Hill, 6 October 1951.

garage, petrol pumps and many vehicles were gutted at Tanjong Malim - all this apart from the many Malay and Chinese civilians who were also killed. The carnage continued into September and October when the High Commissioner, although escorted, was ambushed and killed as he took cover in a ditch alongside his Rolls-Royce on his way up to Fraser's Hill to play golf.

The second disaster affected me much more directly. The day before my departure from Seletar to Ceylon I had fired my annual musketry practice on the rifle range. I had cleaned my rifle as thoroughly as I could in the circumstances. On my return I was horrified to discover that in the intervening three weeks while it lay in the barrack-room rack, the inside of the barrel had choked up with thick rust. Only with difficulty could I force a pull-through from breech to muzzle. Flannelette 'four-by-two' patches simply shredded on the rust. Desperate remedies were required or I would soon find myself on a fizzer - a charge! Discreet enquiries among my fellows produced a small square of illicit wire gauze - mere possession of which, far less use - was strictly restricted to the armourers. By surreptitious and highly illegal use of this on my pull-through I finally managed to restore the rifle's bore to gleaming normality, although to the practised eye, it must have appeared suspiciously smooth, the rifling grooves having virtually disappeared.

~ ~ ~ ~ ~ ~ ~ ~ ~

King George VI died on the 9 February 1952. As the first sovereign to expire for sixteen years he caused a flurry of hastily improvised ceremonial parades all over Singapore and a rash of black ties and black armbands erupted throughout Malaya. Two days later a plane landed at KL and there occurred another event of even greater significance. General Sir Gerald Templer set foot on Malayan soil for the first time as the new High Commissioner and his driving energy and determination became immediately apparent. In short order everyone became far more terrified of him than of the enemy. His first pithy memorandum to government officials set the tone. 'The idea that the business of the Emergency and that of normal civilian government are two separate entities must be killed for good and all.'

The *Singapore Free Press* and the *Straits Times* then headlined his barbed side-swipe at the colonial mentality, 'Bandits Don't Play Golf' and thereby gave the Asian population unlimited pleasure. The pace of the Emergency hotted-up. The floodgates of supplies and support were now opened wide. The unwieldy chains of command were loosened, administration was rationalised and up-country operational areas at last became clearly defined with the establishment of jealously guarded 'shooting rights.' Clashes when soldiers or Malay police, Gurkha 'specials' and auxiliary jungle companies not answerable to the Army, many operating independently in the same areas had fired on one another, now became less common. Friendly fire up until now had accounted for nearly twenty five per cent of the security forces' own casualties. Now a jungle patrol could be certain that on their patch there was no-one else but the enemy. In such situations, who shoots first in a 'bump,' more often survives. No-one needed to shout, 'Halt! Friend or foe?' The future of the British colony that provided more hard currency exports from tin and rubber than the rest of the Empire combined, began to look a little less insecure.

In March 1952 at Tanjong Malim in Selangor State, the bandits had cut a water pipeline. The repair party that was sent out included the local PWD engineer and the district officer plus twelve men of the accompanying escort - most of whom were killed in the ensuing ambush, another eight of the party being wounded. General Templer stormed through the nearby villages two days later and in a mood of blazing anger confronted the Chinese inhabitants. Drastic measures were at once imposed. Strict curfews, wire fences, searches and regulations were introduced and a 'home guard' was set up. 'At last,' said everyone, 'action!' Someone who was finally prepared to take responsibility, to overrule the bureaucrats and administrators, had arrived on the scene.

Until now, what with British servicemen being off-duty on Wednesday afternoons and the Malay administration closed down from midday on Thursdays until Saturday, plus civil and commercial offices closing on Saturday afternoons and Sunday, mix-ups and delay had sometimes ruled in the conduct of military operations. Templer immediately set up District War Executive Committees who were now on call around the clock. From a two-and-a-half day week, it now became a seven days a week co-ordinated effort. Even among the Seletar erks I think that everyone realised that the whole pattern of the Emergency was now shifting.

~ ~ ~ ~ ~ ~ ~ ~ ~ ~

To celebrate these changing fortunes of war I put myself down for a Monday to Friday current affairs course. The ever patient Mr. Pugh agreed with amazingly good grace to my renewed absence. With hindsight of course it probably highlights how little effect my presence or absence had on the daily routines of the squadron office.

The dozen or so other members of the course dozed through what I found quite interesting lectures by the station education officer, on the political and military situation around us and on 'Operation FIREDOG' which was the RAF's main role in the Malayan campaign. We visited the High Court in downtown Singapore to see the measure of colonial justice. The numbered prisoners in the dock were the tail-end of the rioters still on trial for their part in the December 1950 political disorders when some nineteen Europeans (including an airman, a corporal, from Seletar) had been killed, dragged from their cars or from buses and beaten to death by the mob. The Paladian style courtroom was remarkably hot and airless, the proceedings being translated from the be-wigged and red-robed

> **BANDITS KILLED IN SELANGOR**
>
> **SUFFOLKS' ACTION IN A SWAMP**
>
> FROM OUR OWN CORRESPONDENT
>
> KUALA LUMPUR, FEB. 6
>
> Ten Communist terrorists have been killed in various parts of Malaya in the past 24 hours, including four killed by the Suffolk Regiment in Selangor to-day. Among these was the chairman of the party's branch committee, who had a price of 8,000 Straits dollars on his head. He was known to have murdered at least eight people, the last with a spade.
>
> The Suffolks fought two actions, and the main one, in which three terrorists and one national service man were killed, was a classic of its kind. Because of information given by a member of the public, who pin-pointed the hiding place of the terrorists, the action could be carefully planned and the determination of the national service men saw that it was thoroughly carried out.
>
> The terrorist camp was in a clump of rubber trees between a road and a railway embankment near Serdang, and two flights of the R.A.F. Regiment were deployed behind the embankment, while a police squad held the road. One platoon of the Suffolks (Lieut.-Colonel P. A. Morcombe) closed in on the flanks, and a second platoon was detailed to advance through the box and flush the terrorists. The front was about 700yds. wide, and included a swamp and thick bush, as well as rubber.
>
> **AS MIST LIFTED**
>
> At dawn, as the mist lifted, the Suffolks, led by Major Martin, moved in and almost immediately disappeared in the bush, but, because the terrorists were surrounded, the advancing troops shouted in chorus to drive them out. Then there was a burst of Bren-gun fire and spurts of flame from a flamethrower, and your Correspondent saw two terrorists start like rabbits and run for the embankment. For a moment they were silhouetted against the sky-line, and then the fire of the R.A.F. Regiment drove them back and down into the bushes.
>
> The next phase was extremely difficult; although the troops holding the flanks could occasionally see the terrorists, they had been ordered not to fire, for fear of hitting their comrades. Fire discipline was good, but the hunting troops were then at a disadvantage, as the terrorists, in thick cover, could fire the first shot. One of them did, with a double-barrelled shotgun, as a national service man nearly stepped on him. The second barrel misfired, and the Bren gun fired at a range of a few feet avenged the 20-year-old soldier.
>
> A second terrorist was encountered and killed soon after, but a third could not be found. It was thought that he was lying in the swamp under water, breathing through a length of bamboo. Again the tired troops, already drenched to the skin and mud splattered, moved into the swamp, and a grenade eventually found the third man, who was discovered face down in the water.
>
> To-day's fighting raised the record of The Suffolk Regiment to 144 terrorists killed, the highest among British regiments who have served in Malaya. Their own casualties in the same period are eight dead. It also showed how efficient British line regiments can be when they are well trained and led, and when they receive information from the public.

(undoubtedly superheated) Judge's carefully measured English into Malay and Chinese. We also visited the island's fledgling industrial estates where Chinese and Indian entrepreneurs were even now, so soon after the economic stagnation of the war, beginning to lay the foundations of Singapore's future prosperity. We marvelled at new-fangled gleaming steel presses into which a highly-trained operative poured a cupful of bakelite powder as we watched and from which, several minutes later, a single plastic ashtray emerged. This was indeed the white-hot cutting edge of the technology of the future.

The highlight of that week's current affairs was a pre-arranged tour of the Tiger Brewery - the fount and source of everybody's favourite tipple. It took place on the final day of the course, a Friday. Suitably forewarned we had looked forward eagerly to the event. I am sure that it was the sole reason that several airmen had signed-up for the course. I remember little of the occasion - the clinical, shining steel vats and pipework were not of primary interest to our party as we were shown around the brewery's production lines. Our guide's well meaning, 'Any questions?' as he finished explaining the complexities of the process were met with total silence - any delay in our progress towards the hospitality room would not be countenanced. Unlimited chilled Tiger beer on draught (which would have cost us fifty cents a pint in the NAAFI - about 1s-2d) and some unnecessary nibbles, all free of charge of course, were finally placed at our disposal. A few erks, eventually rendered comatose by the challenge, had to be dragged out and manhandled into our *gharry* for our return to Seletar. But with all the respect due to my contemporary servicemen, rowdy drunkenness of the sort that would be so hard to avoid today, was both rare and unpopular with one's fellow rankers - except at occasions such as Christmas and New Year when sobriety flew out of the window.

~ ~ ~ ~ ~ ~ ~ ~ ~

Unlike the UK when most servicemen would have gone on leave for the festive season, and Christmas would have been observed with only a few men remaining with their unit, overseas it was a different matter altogether. A degree of licence ruled during a traditional RAF Christmas. A considerable quantity of drink had been smuggled in through the main gate and stashed away in the barrack rooms. The Station Warrant Officer, Mr. Bollard, normally a powerful and perhaps feared figure as on any RAF station as he was responsible for discipline, kept a low profile during the celebrations. Christmas Eve passed in a haze of mixed drinks following on from the extended consumption of beer and carol singing in the NAAFI. 'Lights out' was ignored in the airmen's quarters, tin and china half-pint mugs were filled and re-filled with tawny port, brandy (mostly cheap South African), gin, whisky, sticky sweet liqueurs or whatever had taken anyone's particular fancy in the shops of Seletar Village. As supplies dwindled, the remaining bottles of whatever was to hand were poured into buckets and basins into which we dipped our mugs. Singing of generally bawdy or sentimental choruses continued through into the early hours until unconsciousness or exhaustion brought matters to a close.

It is perhaps remarkable that I cannot recall any barrack-room violence between airmen during my time in the RAF - it simply didn't happen. If a barrack-room fight started to threaten, invariably someone would step in and matters would cool off. Habitual drunkenness was fairly rare. Boozers were often solitary men, unpopular with their fellows and left to their own devices. Sometimes cruel practical jokes were played on them - I remember a dead snake being picked up off the airstrip or the road and coiled up on the torso of a habitual piss-artist who was lying in a drunken stupor. On one occasion on the West Camp square, Warrant Officer Bollard marched on with his daily colour-hoisting detail to raise the RAF Ensign only to find one of our barrack-room boozers, lying fast asleep, tucked up in his bed immediately in front of the flagstaff. His comrades, unable to sleep because of his drunken snores, had carried him out during the night. History does not relate what the SWO said to him.

Back to that Christmas Day in 1951. The sergeants brought us buckets of early morning tea from the cook house, themselves bleary-eyed from their own extended celebrations in their mess. I recall that on Christmas Eve, the verandah of the West Camp Sergeants' Mess was picturesquely garlanded with coloured fairy lights and strung with rows of inflated condoms. By midday the airmen had more or less sorted themselves out. The group captain and his lady had passed by, waving and shouting seasonal greetings from a discreet distance - for them to have come too close would have revealed the detritus of the night's celebrations and a few still unconscious erks lying where they had fallen. Those who had rolled into the storm drains around the ground floor had already been removed to safer havens and headaches were being attended to by copious draughts of Alka-Selzter - or in some cases by freshly opened bottles of warm Mackesons' milk-stout, kept on hand for such emergencies by the more seasoned topers. At some stage during the morning, one of our barrack's resident pipers started to drone a lament from a patch of grass outside, until forced to stop by the hail of missiles directed at him from all directions.

Christmas dinner was served in the Airmen's Mess Hall over in the East Camp. We were served traditional roast turkey and trimmings by the senior NCOs and the officers - many of whom I regret to say were the worse for drink. The beer flowed freely, the station warrant officer was present, standing near the main doorway, baring his teeth in a severely strained smile as he watched the proceedings. At one stage, to wild

NONE THE WISER

Christmas Day Menu
1951

ROYAL AIR FORCE BASE
SELETAR
FAR EAST AIR FORCE

BREAKFAST
Cornflakes and Stewed Fruits
Grilled Ham
Fried Eggs
Fried Bread — Grilled Tomatoes
Toast Butter Marmalade
Tea — Coffee

DINNER
Cream of Tomato Soup
Roast Turkey
Roast Pork
Hipolatas — Stuffing — Apple Sauce
Green Peas Cauliflower
Roast Potatoes Creamed Potatoes

Christmas Pudding
Brandy Sauce
Beer — Minerals — Coffee
Assorted Nuts — Fresh Fruit
Cigarettes

TEA
Cold Ham
Assorted Cold Meats
Tomatoes — Beetroot — Cucumber
Mince Pies
Christmas Cake
Jellies
Fruit Salad
Tea — Cordials
Fruit Juice

cheers, an airman in a borrowed uniform jacket and peaked warrant officer's cap, with gaudy paper medal ribbons plastered over his chest, jumped onto the table nearest to him and strutted up and down in an immediately recognisable and obviously rehearsed parody of the SWO Bollard, who was by now almost audibly grinding his teeth. I recall wondering how much more provocation Mr. Bollard could stand. The situation was saved when one of our pipers, in a kilt and highland bonnet, heavily disguised in a false ginger beard, jumped up onto the table and gave us a bravura performance of *The Campbells Are Coming*.

By the time the plum pudding and custard was served, matters were deteriorating further. Mr. Bollard had conceded temporary defeat and had silently crept off. The officers were fading away, no doubt creeping away to their own mess. The sergeants were coping badly with clearing the tables of the crockery and plates. Several NCOs, staggering under piles of stacked plates had decided that rather than take them off to the kitchens, they would tip the dirty crockery over the verandah railings onto the concrete paths outside - the crashing of shattered plates being greeted with wild cheers. Much more I cannot remember - apart from the fact that at our next pay parade we were informed that a not inconsiderable sum had been deducted from each man's pay for the resulting barrack damages.

At some stage during that Christmas period, one of the headquarter's sergeants held a party in his married quarters inviting the dozen or so clerks from the HQ Registry and the 390 MU's squadron offices. It was kind of him to do so and we repaid him by getting quietly - not rowdily - drunk, in his small bungalow on Seletar's married patch. That night, not being a habitual beer drinker by choice, I nearly destroyed my liver, drinking three-quarters of a bottle of rum mixed with the then new-fangled Coca-Cola - thinking what a delicious and refreshing combination they made. The lingering flavour of the rum that permeated my entire being for the next several days led to a violent dislike of the stuff - until I re-discovered the delights of the Cuba Libre some forty years later while briefly in Venezuela. I left the sergeant's bungalow in the early hours, thinking it best to stagger back to my own quarters, leaving my fellow pen-pushers either slumped in their chairs or snoring on the floor of the sergeant's house. On my way to the garden gate out on to the moonlit road I tripped headlong over the unconscious body of one of my colleagues where, failing to reach the gate, he had decided to pass the remainder of the night.

New Year's Eve was much the same as Christmas Eve in drinking terms, and then we were once again back to normality, our seasonal bacchanalia was but a memory, discipline and the station warrant officer ruled again.

I broke the unspoken rule that I was brought up with that says 'a gentleman is allowed to get drunk - but only once,' by getting properly plastered a second time (or perhaps third - if the truth be told) when Steve and I decided, in the interests of pure research, to see how many dry Martini cocktails we could drink and still remain sober. To do this necessitated a visit to one of the bars in Seletar Village where they served hard liquor - forbidden on the base itself for the ordinary erk. If you wanted to drink anything alcoholic other than beer one had to leave the station or reach the rank of sergeant.

The Chinese and Indian bars and grills all listed a few cocktails on their bills of fare - gin *pahits*, whisky *stengahs*, Tom Collins plus the ever popular rainbow in which half a dozen different liqueurs were poured into a glass in multi-coloured layers. The blue lagoon came second to the rainbow which, amongst us erks, was considered the height of sophistication.

We found a suitable bar - strategically not too far from the main gate, and settled in. To provide a reasonable foundation we started off with egg and chips which we washed down with our first dry Martini. A properly constructed dry Martini consists of nine-tenths chilled London Dry Gin plus the merest suspicion of dry vermouth - and a green olive on a stick. Whether shaken or stirred has always been immaterial to me, some aficionados will also dispense with the vermouth - perhaps waving the cork of the bottle in a symbolic gesture over the gin, many will also discard the olives as superfluous, piling them up uneaten by their empty glasses. It is a delicious and nourishing drink and in its natural habitat, New York or Chicago perhaps, it is (or was) the custom of the homeward bound banker or stockbroker to call in at the nearest bar, to down two (never three) dry Martinis in quick succession and then swiftly make his way home before their insidious effect caught up with him and he collapsed, like a puppet whose strings have been cut, on his home doorstep.

Neither Steve nor I then knew the most salient truth about drinking dry Martinis. This is, that by the time your mind and body begin to insinuate that perhaps you have had enough, it is in fact already far too late and you have probably had twice as many as any reasonable person might require. They exert a steadily cumulative influence over mind and body, reaching their climax about an hour after the last measure was taken.

Steve and I consumed in the space of an hour or so, six - or was it seven dry Martinis apiece? We managed to settle the bill, lurched to our feet realising that we were now much more than 'half-cut' and that it was time we pulled ourselves together before we passed the rapidly approaching point of no return. By dint of tremendous concentration and choosing our moment we staggered past the guard room on Bow Street undetected. We stumbled a little further down the road to Piccadilly Circus (all the Seletar roads carried London place names - Park Lane of course being reserved for senior officers) where we both fell over. Steve lived on East Camp whereas I was much further away in West Camp.

'G'night 'ol chap - hic!'

'Cheerio 'ol boy - don't get lost.'

Steve made his barrack room in one piece, eventually arriving long after lights-out crawling on his hands and knees as slowly and as single-mindedly as a snail.

I ricocheted and wobbled my way along the Edgware Road, barely conscious of crossing over the runway, (modesty forbids me to recall whether or not I threw up en route), kept upright by the last vestiges of a faltering determination to make it to my bed. Eventually I fell to my hands and knees for the last hundred yards or so, guided only by the blurred and gyrating lights of the barrack block that marked my destination. Had my bed-space been anywhere other than on the ground floor I would never have made it. I lay on my *charpoy* as the world heaved and swayed, spinning around me as if on some giant roller-coaster.

I have never consumed more than two dry Martinis in any significant sequence since that long-ago night. The memory of the hangover that ensued has never faded.

The last course I put myself on (I think Mr. Pugh was on leave and it was too late to back off by the time he came back) was a two week 'passive defence course' at Fraser's Hill, to the north of Kuala Lumpur. In pre-Emergency days it was a popular hill station in Malaya. The previous High Commissioner, Sir Henry Gurney, had been on his way there to play golf a few months earlier when he was ambushed and killed when separated from his military escort. It was now May 1952 and I only had a few months to go before being demobbed.

The course assembled at KL and I think we must have flown there

'Passive Defence' course, Fraser's Hill. Author second from left.

from Singapore for I recall being issued with a rifle and bandolier from KL's station armoury (had we travelled north by train I would have taken my own) prior to our road journey to Kuala Kubu Bahru where we were to join a convoy for the last fifty or sixty miles. This was solely a military convoy of a dozen trucks or so carrying supplies to up-country units, our twenty airmen in an RAF three-ton *gharry*, plus an armoured 'pig' containing Malay police and three scout cars of the 13/18 Hussars for a bit more muscle. Like most British soldiers in Malaya at that time, the troopers wore their standard jungle-green floppy headgear shaped into the ridiculous semblance of Robin Hood hats or Arthur Askey style 'titfers' - much to the irritation of senior officers - unlike the Malays or Gurkhas who wore them as intended.

The golden rule of road travel at that time was to demonstrate clearly to any would-be attacker that not only would you dish out a hard time but would positively welcome the chance to kill them. This is indeed a very fine sentiment if you are sitting inside a 'pig' mounting twin Brens or inside an armoured car with a Besa machine gun and a two pounder to hand. But, packed knee-to-knee in the back of a decidedly 'soft' three-ton lorry, trying to avoid poking out either your own or your neighbour's eye with the muzzle of your loaded rifle, this aggressive attitude was uncomfortably hard to maintain.

We were late arriving at the convoy assembly area. Our *gharry* had carelessly collided with a Chinese builder's lorry as we took a corner at the central cross-roads in the town of Rawang. A Sikh policeman was on the spot to sort matters out. A furious argument ensued until I saw our RAF driver take the Sikh on one side and pass over to him what I later learned was a five dollar note, whereupon the policeman waved us on our way, taking out his notebook and addressing his full attention to the Chinese driver who was now obviously solely responsible as the 'guilty' party.

Arriving at KKB we found the convoy sorting itself into some sort of order. Once under way our column would have extended over three or four hundred yards so that both head and tail would be beyond the limits of any ambush. We were briefed on ambush tactics. I was for some reason appointed to command the 'panic party' - possibly because I had managed to secure my place in our vehicle nearest to the tailboard - last in, first out, being the rule. If the truck stopped under fire it was my function to leap off, to decide where the best cover and least danger lay, and lead the ensuing rush for safety, ideally stopping in time to avoid getting separated and lost in the jungle. This was fine by me as it implied that the accompanying 'proper' soldiers of

The author i/c 'Panic Party' en route to Fraser's Hill, May 1952.

the escort would then afford all the firepower necessary for our defence.

We left the security of the convoy at the Gap police station, en route having had the roadside ditch where Sir Henry Gurney was shot and killed, pointed out to us as a salutary reminder. At the Gap I remember seeing the bullet-pocked walls of the burned-out and isolated police post at the road junction and feeling rather naked as our now unescorted vehicle meandered its way up through the forest on the narrow winding road the last few miles to our destination.

Fraser's Hill was a delight, set high in the thickly wooded hills, cool, often in the clouds or above the layers of mist in the valleys below. Our so-called 'passive defence' course was based in a large, formerly private, house with a tennis court on the edge of the village. We were lectured, drilled and practised in first aid, fire fighting and evacuating casualties which included lashing 'patients' into stretchers. I was a 'patient' on one session when the stretcher was turned upside-down and shaken to demonstrate the soundness of the knots and straps. These gave way from my waist up and when my shoulders fell free, my head was bashed quite severely on the hard ground of the tennis court where we exercised. We were driven round the nearby forested roads practising our ambush drills during which we fled our truck as soon as it stopped, bounding down the hillsides to supposedly re-group and return and attack the ambush site. It was an interesting - and in my opinion untried theory - that the enemy would always be sited on the upper slope above the road, never below.

We were of course 'gassed' once again, in my case making the third time I had been subjected to this ordeal. I remember little of what else we were taught, or learned, but I do recall on one occasion being lectured on self-protection methods while under attack from the air. One of our group addressed the RAF Regiment sergeant instructor thus, 'Ere Sarge, wot are we supposed to do if someone drops an atom bomb on us?'

'Interesting question that. H'mmm. It says here in my book, the very latest gen is that you turn your back to Ground Zero - whatever that might be. You don your waterproof ground sheet, or anti-gas cape if you have one. Keep your eyes firmly shut, your hands over your ears and you crouch down on the ground and put your head between your knees. Right, OK, any more questions?'

'And don't forget to kiss your arse goodbye!' muttered the erk who had asked the question.

May 24th was Empire Day. Originally to celebrate Queen Victoria's

Malay Police and Home Guard, Empire Day at Fraser's Hill, 1952.

birthday it later became designated Commonwealth Day and was later still dispatched to ignominy when it faded from any public notice whatsoever. It used to be widely celebrated wherever the British held sway - excluding of course England, where they may have flown the Union Jack on public buildings to general puzzlement and lack of interest (except perhaps for Roedean School where the girls had a day's extra holiday). In the colonies it was always a public holiday presumably serving to remind the locals who was really in charge. At Fraser's Hill the entire settlement was *en fete*. On the *padang*, the open space in the middle of the village, the local schoolchildren were parading in their crisp white shirts and blue shorts and skirts - mustered by their teachers while the Home Guard and the police wandered around genially with their rifles and carbines. A brass band thumped and brayed off-key traditional melodies such as *Land of Hope and Glory*.

Our group of airmen were roped in for tugs of war, egg and spoon races, sack races and obstacle races - that involved us getting flour plastered over our faces and hands - all to the delight of the onlookers and the giggles of the school children with whom we competed. Placards and streamers garlanded temporary triumphal arches that proclaimed 'God Save The Queen!' (King George having died a few months earlier) over and around the table for local dignitaries who beamed upon the proceedings. Having given out prizes to the children the district commissioner made a fine speech commending the loyalty of the citizenry and the band thumped and brayed once more the strains of the national anthem (British of course). Refreshments were distributed. The whole setting would have done credit to an English village church fete.

The occasion I felt had been somewhat marred by a disagreeable scene I observed early on during the afternoon when the district commissioner had berated, quite publicly, the Malay schoolmaster for allowing the Union Jack to be displayed upside-down on the arch above the dignitaries' table. The public loss of face incurred by the teacher and the intolerance displayed by the DC perhaps encapsulates in essence the inequity of the colonial situation.

On our days off we walked through the high forest on marked paths around the village, or attempted to play golf - totally unsuccessfully on my part - on the small nine-hole course set in amongst the *ulu*, the fairways lined with *lallang* grass and then thick jungle. We were advised not to play the green that lay up a narrow, thickly enclosed glen on a dogleg where we were told that two European golfers had recently been murdered. In my case that was enough to put me off whatever stroke I possessed. Teeing off from below the club house, our party's first ball flew high and wide down the fairway and to our combined horror struck a man who was cutting grass, swinging his hoop-iron blade round and round, hacking away at the coarse tufts of *lallang*. The ball took him fairly behind the ear and he fell heavily to the ground. To our great relief he rose unsteadily to his feet, looked around for the ball which he retrieved and brought back to us, muttering and rubbing the now rapidly rising bump on his shaven skull. We had a whip-round and mustered a few dollars which cheered him up and he went back to his grass cutting.

I drove off the second ball which I sliced handsomely off to the right with satisfying velocity. It made straight for the jungle where it struck the trunk of a tatty looking palm tree, some fifteen feet up. There it stuck, clearly visible, but firmly embedded in a patch of rotten wood, totally unplayable.

The next player drove off, straight down the centre of the fairway along the line of a soggy, water-filled ditch. We marked the fall. We

Convoy assembling at Kuala Kubu Bahru..

prodded and poked about as best we could, discovering nothing but several large frogs the size of dinner plates. By the third or fourth hole I think we gave up play, having nearly run out of our limited supply of golf balls and deciding that we could not really afford to pay for those we had lost, let alone buy more.

~ ~ ~ ~ ~ ~ ~ ~ ~ ~

Back in Singapore once more life resumed its normal routines. I still cannot recall in any detail what my particular duties involved - they could not have been onerous. The squadron orderly room where I performed whatever insignificant role I played in the workings of the RAF adjoined the office of our immediate CO, Squadron Leader W. F. J. 'Tug' Wilson, (see Note 12 - Appendix), a slight but impressive figure of an age with Warrant Officer Pugh, possibly both in their early forties (they might well have been younger, but to me then aged nineteen, they were definitely 'old'). Both were men of great experience as was the Wing Commander from Headquarters with whom Tug Wilson and Mr Pugh had served in the Desert Air Force during the North African campaign. I noted that the Wing Commander (when he dropped in from time to time) and Mr Pugh sparred warily with one another in their official exchanges. I had the impression that the paths of their service careers had meshed - or clashed - on several occasions during the war and that each perhaps knew too much about the other than was comfortable for either. Mr Pugh told me enough in his unguarded moments to suggest that some highly irregular incidents had occurred in Egypt and the Libyan Desert when both had been younger and perhaps less wise.

Armoured car escort in classic ambush country.

I knew little of Tug Wilson's distinguished personal history - my interest in him lay principally with his daughter Janet, who I remember well. She was a fair and lovely girl of sixteen or seventeen who on her visits to the squadron office reduced Mr. Pugh, myself and others to paroxysms of wistful lusting after her young, fresh innocence. I remember she occasionally did some typing for us during the absence of our Eurasian civilian clerk. If I said I was hopelessly in love with her, I am sure half the erks of the squadron also were. Alas, all unexpressed and unrequited in those far off days of innocent passion (at least on my part) and the restrictions of our semi-monastic barrack room life.

My own frequent absences from Seletar were matched by many airmen in the Radio Repair Squadron who flew on frequent detachments all over the Far East. In those days LORAN/SHORAN - long range/short range radar - relied on fixed beacons, both in short supply in the region, hence the frequency of the fitting and calibration parties who departed for weeks on end to destinations as far apart as Iwakuni in Japan, Borneo and Pakistan. As a by-product of their far-flung travels several airmen managed to pick up the two Korean War medals issued, including the United Nations medal, by flying over operational waters in the RAF Sunderland flying boats (known as The Kipper Fleet. See note 13 - Appendix). They received these medals while calibrating the Japanese beacons and some had a further medal awarded by the Pakistani government, which they were permitted to wear, in recognition of the assistance given by the RAF. One of our squadron's airmen thus managed to sport no less than four medal ribbons after less than two years' service - reducing a long serving (or suffering) sergeant to sputtering rage - himself only entitled to three, after years of war-time service on UK mainland airfields. He had received the Defence medal, the Victory medal - and the General Service medal for being in Malaya.

~ ~ ~ ~ ~ ~ ~ ~ ~ ~

In my own case, off-duty entertainment and visiting my mates on other parts of the station - for having earlier worked in 390 MU's HQ I had oppos scattered around Seletar - was made much easier by the acquisition of an ancient bicycle. A friend once said to me that no autobiography can ever be considered complete until it includes the phrase, '... and thus I became the proud owner of a bicycle.' Well, so I did. It was 'gash' - ie. although obviously an RAF bicycle, properly painted blue - it was not officially on strength and therefore fair game. I think I bought it off some departing airman for five dollars, (about 60p) and it was well worth its weight in scrap metal. The Astra Cinema, the Malcolm Club, the swimming pool, the shoreline of the Johore Straits beyond the flying boat sheds, the East Camp and Seletar Village were all within easy cycle range instead of being a long, hot trudge on foot.

The Astra Cinema showed popular films and musicals such as *Words and Music* and *The Jolson Story* (how I loathed that film!) plus the swim-suited epics of the ever damp and dripping Esther Williams and Westerns such as the always popular *Winchester '73*, the 'road' films of Bob Hope and Bing Crosby and on one glorious remembered occasion the first ever film of Marilyn Monroe in which she played a bit part, *Ladies of the Chorus*.

The sub-plot involving Marilyn Monroe concerns her being wooed by a shy, and embarrassingly wealthy, young suitor, who sends her extravagant but anonymous bouquets to the stage door. When she finally confronts him, she enquires breathlessly and disarmingly, 'Who are you?' To which the bashful young man replies in adoring tones, 'I'm Randy.'

At this unequivocal example of an unintentional trans-Atlantic *double entendre* the cinema's audience of mainly literal minded erks fell out of their seats with unrestrained laughter for several minutes, rolling on the floor with tears running down their cheeks. All subsequent dialogue was lost in the uproar - every time the unfortunate actor re-appeared on the screen the audience lost control again, baying and shouting, 'RANDY!! RANDY!!! We want RANDYYYY!!!!!'

For a brief interlude I joined the Seletar Theatre group - in the hallowed tradition of *Privates on Parade* - as a stagehand and scenery painter. I also joined several mates and oppos in off-duty drinking and smoking sessions backstage at the Astra Cinema where we idled away the evenings yarning and consuming warm Tiger beer instead of painting the scenery flats for whatever show was planned. The storage room where we worked was dark and stuffy. In the corners among the stacked scenery lurked huge spiders and on more than one occasion we disturbed long, poisonous centipedes which scuttled menacingly at high speed around the floor while we jumped for safety onto the tables and chairs.

Another interest which lasted for a few months was evening classes in Malay run by a civilian. However, apart from a smattering of what is at first sight a relatively simple language in which to learn the basics, including the necessary glottal stops which are not too difficult for the average English speaker, to progress further than a basic vocabulary and grammar is difficult. If our teacher was to be believed, the subtleties of spoken Malay relied heavily on obscure references to both traditional proverbs and *pantuns* - classical rhyming couplets. If I said that tropical inertia and indolence eventually led to the classes being abandoned, on my part that would at least be partially correct.

At least once or twice a month, Steve and I would make up a group of airmen, invariably fellow national servicemen, four being the ideal number, to go downtown into Singapore on a Saturday afternoon, usually after a fortnightly pay parade when we would be reasonably flush with cash. Typically we would take a bus for the fifteen miles into town, calling in at the Union Jack Club to take in a late afternoon tombola session, buying a couple of cards each to see if we could augment our funds with a lucky win, which was rarely realised. We would wander around the shops and sidewalks, along the narrow alleyways, eventually ending up in the early evening at some Chinese or Indian chophouse we knew, often ordering something like a mixed grill, or chicken with double chips rather than sampling the local cuisine, in keeping with the pervading air of incuriosity about local colour of the rank and file British serviceman serving overseas. Steve and I, if feeling flush and sophisticated, would share a bottle of wine with our meal, typically a nice little sweet Palestinian-type hock or similar, perhaps even Blue Nun, while the others drank their customary Tiger beer or Tuborg if feeling rich.

If there was a juke-box or record player we selected endless records of Guy Mitchell and the 'gang' belting out popular ballads such as *There's a Pawnshop on the Corner in Pittsburgh Pennsylvania!* or perhaps Spike Jones and his noisy novelty number *Cocktails for Two.* Jimmy Young (later of *Housewife's Choice* fame) would croon the romantic *Moon over Malaya* for us, or perhaps *Far Away Places with Strange Sounding Names* or the strains of *The Tennessee Waltz* would tickle our sentimental fancy. Was our taste in music better in the late forties and the fifties? Yes, in my opinion unequivocally so, for one could both hear and understand the lyrics, banal enough as they may have been and the accompaniment was played by competent musicians.

Neither were we entirely immune to Asian music at that time. *Flower of Malaya* (later bowdlerised into *Rose, Rose I Love You* to be belted out at Force Ten gale strength by Frankie Laine) was first heard and loved by many servicemen in the Far East as a haunting Chinese melody, sung in Mandarin in a woman's pure, high-pitched and almost (to Western ears) toneless voice. Europeans were fascinated by its elusive phrases, humming and whistling inaccurate snatches trying to catch its subtle, off-key melodies. The name Hwe Lee lurks somewhere in the dim recesses of my mind - perhaps she was the singer? There was another popular song, called *China Nights* which was Japanese I think and transported to Seletar via the flying boats, whose tune is now so elusive that it has entirely vanished from memory, but whose words were heard by us as 'Me ain't got my yo-yo.' (The 'yo-yo' being the flying boat squadrons' term for the starter cord for the auxiliary generator stowed behind a wing panel - used when afloat and in the absence of starter batteries.)

To go down town we wore smart shirts and slacks, occasionally with the jazzy ties then in fashion. We were generally smarter than the rude soldiery - with bad haircuts - who by 1952 were beginning to flaunt flowered Hawaiian shirt-tails hanging outside their pants. Unlike the present day there were both dress codes as well as standards of behaviour within which it was possible to find amusement. Today it seems to me that only 'style' remains, otherwise anything goes.

After eating we would sometimes go on to the Cathay Cinema if there was a new American film showing where we enjoyed ice-creams, Chinese sub-titles and the best air-conditioning available to us. The last time I saw the Cathay, in 1995, it was still just recognisable, though dwarfed beneath the towering steel and glass skyscrapers of modern Singapore and almost certainly scheduled for demolition. Often we would take ourselves off to the Happy World amusement park (the other one, the New World, being more frequented by officers). Here were infinite diversions - dodg'em cars, a Western-style cabaret, fortune tellers who would cast your horoscope in a sand-tray for a few dollars, letter-writers, shooting galleries and Chinese opera with its violent posturing, clashing gongs and cymbals whose cacophonies would drive us out again after a few minutes. There were open-air tea shops, food stalls and dance floors where the taxi-dancers were for hire at fifty cents a ticket. We would watch the Malays dancing the 'joget modern' - the women in sarongs and white high-collar tight-waisted jackets, their glossy black hair drawn back tightly into a bun, the men in tight-cuffed trousers and flowered shirts with the compulsory *songkok* pill-box hat, facing each other but not touching, as they danced to the wailing music. Here also was the Wayang theatre, where Javanese shadow puppets pranced and clashed across the flickering lamp-lit screen, behind which one could see the stage-hands adjusting their props and manipulating the jerky, jointed, silhouetted demons and heroic sword-wielding gods and goddesses.

With gold teeth flashing in brilliant smiles, white teeth stained with betel-nut, all human life was here among the side-shows and the acetylene flares. Malays, Chinese, Indians, scattered Europeans of a dozen nationalities, French sailors with red pom-poms on their caps, smartly uniformed French soldiers wearing *kèpis*, ashore for the last time on their way to their own messy war in Indo-China (no Foreign Legionnaires - they were battened down under hatches in port - with an armed guard to prevent desertion). Here were our own Army's Iban and Dyak trackers from the long houses of Borneo and Sarawak, their elaborate swirling tattoos clearly visible on their necks above their new shirt collars, and on their hands. They were dressed in western clothes, the loops of their ear lobes dangling as they gazed in wonderment at the scene around them.

As often as not we went there for the great central arena where the aptly named King Kong, Singapore's celebrated heavyweight all-in wrestling champion, held sway. The twenty-six stone King Kong - biting and gouging, 'Boston-crabbing' and forearm-smashing - bludgeoned his way to victory in a grudge-match against the equally famous masked Swedish Angel. The audience booed or cheered according to their mood. I remember King Kong jumping out of the ring when some puny spectator taunted him with unspeakable insults. The spectator fled in panic through the scattering audience as the gargantuan figure of the wrestler waded inexorably in pursuit, crashing through the tiers of seats like some unstoppable tank.

When we had enough of the Happy World we would find our way to the louche environs of Bugis Street, long since sanitised and concreted over in Singapore's quest for social order and modern conformity, where the late night food stalls and hawkers held sway and the deceptively beautiful 'boy-girl' transvestites would flaunt themselves, winking at the gawping sailors and sinuously swaying in their *cheong-sams*, slit to the thigh, between the tables and stalls that choked the whole street. We gawped at such delights and would have a late supper and a beer here, a bowl of chicken rice or something or other *fu-yung* stirred with egg that by now we knew we could either scoop up with chopsticks or a soup spoon - *mee* or sloppy noodle dishes were beyond our skills. Even chicken rice could be tricky as it could easily contain the odd chicken head complete with eyes and beak, as well as the feet.

Soon the four of us would share a taxi, and we would be driven back across the island to Seletar, as my permanent pass stated, along with the others, that by 01.00 hours we had to be back in our quarters.

That was our life. Compared with our fellow conscripts in the jungle, or those unfortunate enough to be in Korea facing the Chinese army, or even with those that most of us perhaps still envied, the national servicemen serving back home, we were indeed a favoured minority. I am sure that looking back, many of my contemporaries will recall the happier memories of those days as a time when youth held the helm, when we knew we were going to live for ever, and all the future still lay before us.

13
TRAINS AND PLANES AND THINGS

...The whistles blow forlorn,
And trains all night groan on the rail...
A E Houseman, from *A Shropshire Lad*.

My habit of squirreling away scraps of paper over the years occasionally pays off. Much of it now is brittle, brown, tatty and unintelligible dross beyond interpretation or recall, justifying the recrimination and accusations this practice attracts to me like flies to stinking fish. Shaking out my old RAF pay book has revealed a faded green and orange Malayan Railway ticket from Singapore to Prai. It is designated 'Third Class Military,' its price 14 Straits dollars and 67 cents and the faint date stamp on the reverse says, '7 MAR 1952' above a declaration that, 'The Railway Administration shall not be liable for the holder's death or injury however caused.' In view of what was going on at the time, this was a sensible standpoint for them to adopt. Yet another roneo'd shred of paper in the paybook is a temporary storage receipt from the station armoury, RAF Butterworth for my No. 4 Mk 1 rifle Serial No. R37908 and fifty rounds of ammunition. This is dated 14 July 1951, the previous

Travelling on leave.

year, a footnote shows the ammunition as 'BOC (Brought on Charge) Seletar' three days later, 17 July.

Were I to be put in the dock and pressed on oath to say where I was and what I was doing, for example, on any of those dates (and others) some forty-five years ago as I write, I could both state - and produce irrefutable evidence in substantiation. 'And what? Pray,' probes a snootily supercilious counsel, thumbs hooked in the armpits of his gown, 'What, pray, was the serial number of your rifle in July 1951?' 'R37908!' I answer triumphantly. The jury gasp in admiration, the prosecutor wilts. My defence counsel leaps to his feet, 'I demand that this case be dismissed without a stain on my client's character!' 'Granted!' cries the judge, leaning over to shake my hand as he says, 'Well done!' 'Clear the court!' shouts the usher, as I am carried out shoulder high by my supporters.

By July 1951 I had been a 'Clk/Org.' in the 390 Maintenance Unit Headquarters at RAF Seletar for nearly four months. Boredom was rapidly setting in. My pay book shows that no sooner had I completed my trade training on 5 May 1951 and became an Aircraftman First Class, then less than three weeks later on 25 May I was promoted again, to Leading Aircraftman (LAC). Such rapid promotion, even with hindsight, seems totally excessive and unwarranted. I find it difficult to recall at all, let alone in any detail, what it was that I did exactly. My sole remaining impression is that it was very little. Shuffling a few pieces of paper from point A to point B and then perhaps filing them, or playing battleships with Steve and LACs Sid Kydd and 'Gil' Gilhooly, in coded signs across the HQ Registry office under the ever watchful eye of Sergeant 'Smudger' Smith. The office was no hot-bed of industry, nor of zeal, as I recall.

Otherwise it was always hot, ceiling fans slowly stirred the damp air. Zul the young Malay messenger boy, brought us mugs of hot but weak sweet tea which made us sweat all the more. From time to time Steve and I would repair to the typing pool supposedly to practise our touch typing but really to chat with the delightful WRAF corporal, Pat - who was everything a WRAF corporal should be, smart, efficient and pretty - and who reigned in her office over two or three meek Eurasian ladies. In the office itself someone had to remain alert to watch out for the Adjutant, Flight Lieutenant Watkins. If he appeared we sat to attention at our desks until he responded, 'At ease.' Then we relaxed again, heads down but now busily shuffling papers. If, as occasionally happened, either the wing commander or, God forbid, the group captain made an unannounced entrance, we sprang to our feet, rigidly at attention until released, whereupon we sat down again, scribbling furiously. As a vignette of the tedious military life it remains vivid in memory.

One hot morning in the HQ Registry Smudger Smith looked up from his desk brandishing a chit and said, 'Before I detail one of you lot, I'll ask for a volunteer. One body needed to make up an escort detachment for a wagon load of bombs up to Butterworth.' The other three erks in the office averted their eyes downwards and fidgeted in silence. 'I'll go Sarge,' I said, foolishly ignoring the generally sage advice passed down by my elders and betters in the ranks, 'Never volunteer!' But it would make for a change.

'You must be f-----g round the bend!' chorused LACs Kydd and Gilhooly who were both three year regulars en route to becoming old sweats. 'Keep your f-----g head down mate. They f-----g well shoot people up-country if you're not f-----g careful! You'll get your f-----g bollocks shot off!' (See note 14 - Appendix)

I simply report this response both as a yardstick of the level of our everyday conversational exchanges - when as a general rule I exclude such expletives from this narrative - and also as an indication of the customary reluctance on the part of the regular rank and file to put themselves forward for anything out of the ordinary that might upset the familiar routine of their everyday lives. It is not unfair to say that compared with the longer serving career regulars the average national serviceman was often more enterprising and adventurous, but in their terms too green to know any better.

I certainly did two, if not three detachments escorting ammunition wagons by train up-country from Singapore to Butterworth in 1951 and 1952. The vexed question of how many trips is compounded by snapshots which seem to indicate three separate groups of companions at different times. The incidents (with the notable exception of what follows) that have stayed with me I cannot relate to any particular trip. The Butterworth Armoury receipt certainly indicates one trip in July 1951, the rail ticket another in March 1952, but there was one journey - certainly my last trip up into Malaya - which must have come much later, not more than several weeks before I was demobbed. This trip carried with it the seeds of potential disaster. Should the Ministry of Defence or the RAF Special Investigation Branch still retain any unsolved mystery files from that time, which I doubt, then what I am about to reveal will both breach my signing of the Official Secrets Act and enable the file to be finally stamped 'CLOSED' and laid to rest!

RAF Seletar contained a vast bomb dump of assorted ordnance, much of it left over from the war, stored above ground in snake-haunted bunkers amid a rubber plantation inside the East Camp perimeter wire.' When I saw the area again in 1995 it had somehow metamorphosed into a golf driving range and no trace remained that I could see of the rubber trees or the concrete blast walls where thousands of tons of high explosives had once resided. From here the ammunition, bombs and rockets were shipped out to the airfields up and down the peninsular to supply the tactical RAF squadrons who bombed and strafed the jungle, generally to little effect. Most of this was sent up north to KL and Butterworth by goods train rather than by sea, with maybe a hundred tons a time in two or three wagons with a small armed guard as escort. At this period of the Emergency, trains (particularly the night mail trains that trundled between Singapore and Penang) were being frequently derailed and sometimes ambushed and attacked by the CTs.

Travelling on duty - train escort.

With hindsight, considering that the mostly single-track main line running the length of Malaya then passed through jungle for much of its way it is strange that the 'bandits' did not go for such a soft target more often and more successfully than they did. But then the so-called Emergency was a low-intensity war fought savagely by both sides mainly with lightly armed foot soldiers operating as guerrillas. Hit-and-run, ambush, murder and subversion, retiring into deep jungle hide outs, were the tactics of the CTs, supplied and informed by their (mainly Chinese) supporters in the towns and villages. Over the years of the Emergency the CTs were harried and pursued with mixed success by British and Gurkha infantry, Malayan Police and the Malay Regiment employing similar tactics and were eventually starved of local support, implementing the Briggs Plan, by curfew and containment of the civilian population. But in 1951 the balance of the initiative still lay largely with the CTs.*

Depending on the number of wagons to be guarded, the train escort was composed of a corporal and two or three airmen. By slow goods train the journey from Singapore to Prai (on the mainland near Penang), via Kuala Lumpur, if uneventful - ie no derailments or other hitches - would take three days avoiding travel by night when the dangers were greatest. The return passenger service by the regular mail train then took a further thirty-six hours back to Singapore. These trains were more heavily escorted, particularly on the night stretches. To lessen the risk of derailment, the trains travelled slowly and were preceded by an armoured pilot train. Both locomotives also pushed 'crash wagons,' flat cars loaded with iron rails, so that in the event of the fish-plates being removed the 'crash wagon' would go off the tracks - not the locomotive. The pilot trains, and the mail train itself, also pushed another flat car on which was mounted either a *kubu* - a sort of steel pill-box mounting twin Bren guns, usually containing several sleeping Malay policemen - or a more alert and often trigger happy, half-platoon of British infantry, with a searchlight plus a two-inch mortar and a Bren gun or two, behind sandbags, or even an armoured scout car with a Besa machine gun and a two pounder gun. When the pilot engine was derailed or attacked - or as sometimes happened, allowed through and then a section of track ripped up behind it to de-rail the following mail train, either one could then come to the aid of the other, at night alerted by Verey lights or parachute flares fired from the mortar.

---

* Official casualty figures for the Malayan Emergency 1948-1960 were 719 British dead, of whom 520 were military. Malayan Police alone suffered 1,297 killed including British Officers. 2,473 civilians died, many were rural Chinese and Malay, mostly killed by the communist terrorists. Nearly 8,000 'bandits' were known to have been killed. The true 'freedom fighters' of the campaign were the majority of Malay, Indian and loyal Chinese citizens who fought and resisted the communists for so many years.

Reversing out of trouble was not a good idea as the track was often disrupted behind once the engine had passed, boxing it in. When this happened the trains were frequently shot up by the CTs with small-arms fire from prepared ambush positions. The attacks were rarely pressed home as many of the passengers were military personnel - all armed when travelling up-country and with a train commander and guard with a few automatic weapons and medical orderlies - all well capable of defending themselves. The drill, as posted on notices in each carriage, was that if the train was brought to a halt under fire, both military and civilian passengers were to descend to the track and take cover behind the iron wheels. The net result of these precautions meant that there were few military casualties, the civilians suffered most, particularly nuns and boy scouts as I recall, who driven by duty and their calling tended to over-expose themselves when succouring any wounded.

A Kubu, an armoured tin fort on a goods train. As usual no sign of the occupants.

The visible evidence of the mayhem caused by these incidents (which were so frequent at that time that they barely rated a short paragraph in the *Straits Times*) was indicated by the condition of most of the Malayan Railways' rolling stock, the fabric of the carriages and box-car wagons being pocked with crudely patched-up bullet holes, battered and dented by flying fragments of assorted projectiles and ordnance. Armoured as I was then in my ignorance, by innocence and extreme youth - I was merely interested - rather than alarmed by the information I gleaned before departure or by the evidence of my own eyes when I first travelled up-country by train.

I shall condense my experiences on these detachments up-country, both as they say 'to protect the guilty' and also to avoid inspiring a sense of tedium in the reader, through needless repetition.

The sequence was always the same. Find the corporal in charge of the detail, collect rifle and small kit from the barrack room, including water bottle, mess tin, mug and 'eating irons,' waterproof cape, belt and bayonet - and then go to the armoury to sign for a cotton bandolier of fifty .303 rounds. We were always admonished by the armoury sergeant, 'If you use any of these, bring back the empties or otherwise I'll 'ave you on a fizzer before you can say Jack Robinson!'

Escort detail, guarding bombs and ammo.

Usually the corporal would then go off to the cook house armed with a chit for three days' rations - wheedling and sweet-talking the grumpy cooks into giving us a few extras. We had loose tea (to be brewed-up with hot water from the locomotive) which was unfortunately for my taste already liberally mixed in with sugar. There were also tins of bully beef, jam, pilchards, liquefied butter, cheese, a sackful of loaves of bread, tins of Carnation milk, baked beans and peaches, hard biscuits and most important of all, small tubes of thick, sweet condensed milk, plus sugar and salt. In retrospect a highly constipating diet, but considering that any lavatories would be few and far between for the next few days, this was of no great disadvantage. We could always supplement these rations with fruit and any other goodies we might be able to buy from hawkers wherever we stopped.

Externally the Singapore Railway Station hasn't changed much since 1951 - inside it may have, but when I saw it last in 1995 it was instantly recognisable. It is an undistinguished series of low buildings with a few platforms and sidings, nothing else. The escort would arrive in a fifteen hundredweight truck from Seletar during the morning in time to see the last of the loading, for our corporal to check off all the crated bombs and rockets and to count the fat, stumpy 250 and 500 pounders being man-handled and stacked into the sealed wagons by sweating labourers.

I clearly recall a moment of stunned silence when a 500 pounder, being swung over from a lorry into a wagon on the boom of a hand cranked mobile lift, when the chain suddenly snapped with a sharp 'Twang!' The dumpy cigar-shaped bomb, still held fast at the rear, thudded nose first into the concrete platform, gouging out a saucepan-sized crater. 'Okay, okay, back to work, you lot. *Lekas-la*! Chop-chop! No fuses in these cookies thank Christ!' said the 'Chiefy' Flight Sergeant looking on. Our Corporal Plinge would sign the official receipts, having checked and re-checked the numbers. The formalities completed, from now on until we reached Butterworth we were on our own.

What I find extraordinary in retrospect, illustrating the mentality that ran the Empire so efficiently so long ago, was that there was I and my two companions - sent off to guard a train in the middle of a nasty little guerrilla war - and we still had to have the correct tickets! Our corporal, who I shall call 'Jonah' Plinge had to go up to the ticket window and hand over our official rail warrant in exchange for three 'Third Class Military' pasteboard tokens permitting us to occupy the laden box-cars we were taking off to war. It was Karl Marx who said of the Germans that they would make lousy revolutionaries, if for instance, they were required to storm the Berlin Railway Station, they would first feel obliged to queue up for platform tickets. Well, in those dying days of Empire, the British were just the same. I have read that in the Zulu War at the Battle of Isandlwana in 1879 the British army quartermasters were reluctant, almost to the last, to hand out reserve ammunition to the soldiers being massacred around the supply wagons. The soldiers fighting for their lives lacked the requisition forms signed by their company commanders. At the fall of Stalingrad in 1943 when the starving, ragged defenders surrendered to the Russians, the German stores were found to be crammed with food, clothing and un-issued supplies that their quartermasters had hung on to like their brethren in every Army throughout history. The very spirit of 'Jobsworth' lived on.

The long train of goods wagons drawn by the chugging steam locomotive pulled slowly out of Singapore station during the afternoon. Our three ammunition wagons placed smack in the middle - as far away from both the engine and the brake van as the driver on the footplate and the guard at the rear could devise. We ourselves were neatly sandwiched between the two locked box-cars of bombs, occupying a truck half filled with wooden cases of rocket heads and cannon shells, stacked at each end. Except at night we kept the steel sliding doors fully drawn back on both sides to allow as much air through as possible. The interior of the wagon was stiflingly hot, having been stewing in the sun all day. The train trundled northwards at about ten miles an hour across the island, steaming steadily towards the causeway across the Johore Strait and into Malaya.

Smoke and cinders drifted in through the open doors, illuminated in the narrow shafts of sunlight that pierced the interior through the jagged gashes and unpatched bullet holes in the wagon sides. We tried, without much success, to store our kit on the wooden boxes of rockets so that the three of us could sit or lie with some degree of comfort.

'No smoking, lads! Far too dangerous in 'ere,' said Jonah taking out a fag, passing over his issue tin of fifty Players to George - another young national serviceman - and myself. 'Have a light,' he said, deftly striking a match on the side of the box of high explosive which he had dragged over to the doorway and on which he now sat, shirtless, bare legs dangling in the open, wrinkled khaki hose sagging over his ankles, contentedly surveying the passing tropical scenery in the warm afternoon sun.

By dusk we were well up into Johore State. This was now definitive bandit country, where much of the terrorist activity was taking place at this time. Jonah had already told George and myself to charge our rifle magazines with ten rounds, but not to put 'one up the spout.' We had stopped once or twice at villages and settlements to allow faster trains travelling north and south on the single track to pass us on the short loop lines. We had contacted the Indian driver and his fireman, sweltering behind armoured steel shutters on the footplate of their huge, seething, black locomotive, hissing like a kettle. They had shown us how to make tea in our mess tins by releasing a thin stream of boiling water from a valve below their cab. Stephen, the cheerful Eurasian guard had wandered up to check that we were alright and to say that we would be pushing on until about 22.00 hours when we would stop for the night at a place that for the sake of argument I shall call Sungei Layang. Behind the locomotive there was the usual *kubu* containing two Malay policemen, but they had already changed into sarongs and showed signs that they had every intention of locking themselves inside their tin fort for a sound night's sleep.

I have failed to identify the settlement where the train drew up in Johore that bright moonlit night, alongside a deserted platform on the slope of a hill. I know it was on the stretch of line leading to Gemas, but whether or not it was north or south of Kluang, or it may have been somewhere between Sedenak and Layang-Layang or even Renggam, or Niyor, or Paloh or perhaps Beradin? After so many years, it no longer matters.

Below us to the right was an expanse of water-logged paddy, the moon glinting on the dark surface. Some fifty yards further off was the fringe of forest, black and impenetrable. On the slope that rose up to the left were a few darkened single-storey houses, without a sign of any life. The station was totally unlit and deserted. There was not a breath of wind and a sour reek of charred wood and recent burning lay over all. That scent still remains with me. Smell is perhaps the most evocative of our human senses and a whiff of a distant smouldering bonfire on a hot summer's night still has the power to occasionally transform me into a nineteen-year old boy alone on guard in the Malayan night. With the silence accentuated by the strident chirruping of frogs and insects, the seemingly total absence of other human life, made the time pass slowly.

Jonah, George and I had eaten when we stopped. Semi-liquid bully beef, the tin opened and hacked about with our jack-knives, bread and sweaty cheese, beans slopped into our mess tins in the dark - what splendid fare in retrospect! (See note 15 - Appendix) We had no light apart from the moon.

Stephen, the guard, had locked himself inside his caboose at the distant tail of the train where he lay fast asleep. The engine driver and his mate had closed up their bullet-proof steel shutters and slept safely enclosed within their cab with a wisp of smoke trailing vertically into the brilliant starlit sky from the funnel. The huge monster that was the locomotive emitted thin trails of steam, clicking and creaking as the hot metal cooled in the night air. There was not a sound from the two Malay policemen fastened snugly tight inside their armoured *kubu*.

Jonah had taken the first two-hour shift on guard, quietly smoking in a small wooden shelter on the otherwise deserted platform. He woke me at about 01.00 hours to take over. I had hardly slept at all, curled up in my poncho on top of the hard wooden rocket boxes, my head wrapped in a towel and pillowed on my pack. We had rolled down our sleeves and changed into KD slacks at dusk because of the swarming mosquitoes. The moon was still bright but casting longer shadows.

After about an hour I was desperately trying to keep awake, my mouth foul from too much smoking. I had walked up and down the length of the train a few times before settling, as had Jonah, in the open shelter near to our wagon. The setting moon glinted on my ridiculous eight inch 'pig-sticker' bayonet - fit for nothing but punching holes in milk tins - when off to the right, down across the paddy and along the dark edge of the jungle, a brief movement caught my eye.

Emotions are often difficult to recall. The finer feelings of remorse, guilt, embarrassment, shame and regret, are all very difficult to eradicate with passing years, but hunger, thirst, fatigue, heat and cold, lust, fear and excitement are creatures of the moment and not easily re-captured. As I strained to see what had attracted my attention, peering slightly sideways as one does in the dark to catch the detail on the fringes of one's vision, I feel sure my heart must have jumped into my mouth as I caught sight of a single file of figures moving slowly and cautiously through the shadows, in our direction. They were quite clearly armed and neither recognisably equipped nor uniformed!

With the wooden hut as cover behind me I scuttled across through the moonlight to the wagon and quickly woke Jonah and George who grabbed their rifles and came back to the shadows of the hut.

'Chee-bloody-rist!' whispered Jonah, 'who the f--k are they?' They were still in single file, about eight men, well spaced apart and moving cautiously towards us across the paddy. As quietly as possible the three of us each slipped a round up the spout. 'Safety catches off,' hissed Jonah, quite unnecessarily in my case, it was already off. We crouched in the shadow of the shelter, kneeling behind the flimsy uprights. The file of men were now scrambling swiftly and quietly up the embankment on to the platform; some had rifles and carbines, others shotguns. They still made no noise and started in our direction, silently on padded soles, keeping to the shadows, weapons at the ready.

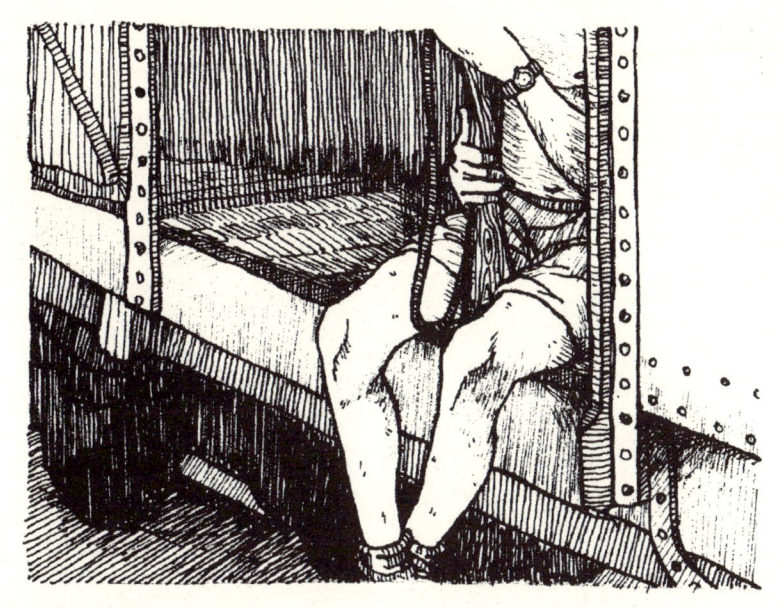

Jonah poked me in the side. He knew I had a smattering of Malay. 'Challenge them,' he muttered, 'we'll shoot if they don't seem right!' This was serious stuff. I had already taken up first pressure on the trigger when I called out as the first man was about twenty yards off.

'BERHINTI! - Jika'lau tidak, saya tembak!' was what I meant to say, the full challenge in Malay is quite a mouthful, (lit. 'Stop - if not, I shoot). All I got out was, 'Berhinti!' before the leader called out, 'Sah! Sah!! Don't shoot, we Home Guard!'

A diminutive Malay wearing a semblance of uniform between his beret and jungle boots and carrying a rifle as tall as himself came forward and gave me a salute and shook our hands. He and his men were a Home Guard patrol from the village up the hill to the left. The smell of burning that had stuck in our nostrils we now learned came from the settlement which had been attacked and partly torched by a group of CTs two nights before. The police and the army had already been and gone, leaving the local defences in the hands of the rather ragged Home Guards, some clad in sarongs and khaki shirts belted with bandoliers of shotgun cartridges. It was unlikely the CTs would return, but the Home Guard

Car Nicobar, September 1951, en route to Ceylon. Left to right, Alan, Jock, Dick (RAAF). Front row - Scouse, Terry and the 'CO's No. One Boy.'

were leaving nothing to chance. In our acute relief, our keyed-up anxiety relieved, Jonah, George and I pressed cigarettes upon our erstwhile 'enemies.'

The three of us slept as soundly as we could for the rest of the night. The diminutive Home Guard corporal assured us that he and his men would stay around the station until dawn. Jonah was not one to miss a trick, he should have stood the graveyard shift from 05.00 until dawn had the Home Guard not come to his rescue.

By first light we were alone again, our night visitors had long gone. The two sleepy occupants of the *kubu*, the engine driver and his fireman, Stephen the guard - had all heard nothing during the night. The locomotive provided us with mess tins of early morning tea. The taste of such tea, redolent of steam coal and cinders, tea leaves floating free, sweet and milky, drunk from a tin mug, is with me still.

~ ~ ~ ~ ~ ~ ~ ~ ~ ~

Another day, another time. We were south of Gemas where the branch line forks off up to the east coast of Malaya, still in Johore State. It was not Jonah this time but from the point of continuity I shall continue to call the commander of our humble guard by this name - in retrospect I suppose Jonah can serve for narrative purposes as the universal corporal. If Jonah is still around, as he may well be, and should he ever read this, then I can always assure him that it was someone else.

There were four of us this time, which probably contributed to the confusion. The train was steaming steadily northwards at a good fifteen miles an hour through a hot sunlit morning. We sat as usual, shirtless, bare legged with our socks sagging over our ankles hanging out in the breeze over the edge of the wagon. It was a long train of goods trucks and closed wagons with our ammunition wagons as always, playing 'pig in the middle.' The guard's van was a long way behind us and the *kubu*, being towed behind the locomotive, typically showed no signs of life. We were on a long curving bend, on the outside of which to the right, was steeply rising ground crowned by thick jungle. The twenty or thirty yards of cleared ground which continuously flanked the single track for most of its length was here foreshortened to fifteen or twenty yards because of the steep edge of a cutting rising above us.

I know now that in 1951 the region of Johore State which we were traversing was constantly under threat of terrorist action, perhaps here more often translated into reality than other regions. A few miles off to the east lay Mount Ophir among a range of forested rolling hills surrounded by thick jungle. There were probably several hundred CTs actively operating over the whole of Johore at that time. Today in south-west Malaysia, much of what was formerly jungle has been cleared of high timber and replaced with vast areas of oil palm and rubber, a repetitive and boring form of tropical monoculture. The undergrowth that in former times would have been cleared by gangs of labourers is now cleared by machinery or burned off by frequent dousings of herbicide. In 1951 the whole area had much more thick jungle, the edges of the roads and the railway being laboriously cut back by hand to reduce the ever present risk of ambush.

We were quite a long way from anywhere as the train trundled along up a rising gradient. Jonah was inside, perched on a box of grenades that formed part of our cargo and reading a tatty, dog-eared Hank Jansen. I was sitting on the edge of the wagon, my legs dangling over the track watching out for birds or wildlife. A few miles back we had caught glimpses of a troop of gibbons on the edge of the forest. Paddy, a saturnine and unusually quiet Irishman was telling his rosary which normally hung around his neck, his lips moving silently. Tony, another regular, dark and sun-tanned with a neat moustache, sat on a wooden box smoking and gazing out at the passing scene.

If you ask me what I was thinking of my immediate situation at that time, I would answer that I was probably quite content. It was better than sitting in the office, bored, back at Seletar. It was much better than being a bank clerk back in the City of London. I was nineteen years old and life was reasonably interesting as I surveyed my surroundings. I had no need to worry about my future for the next several months as the RAF would take care of that. I was happy enough to be there.

With no warning, there were at least two, perhaps three loud metallic 'Thumps!' Followed almost instantly by the loud and unmistakable 'Crrrack!' of rifle shots coming from the jungle edge above the cutting. The bullets had struck the wagon right behind us! Our reaction was both immediate and startling.

'JAYSUS!!!' shouted Paddy, dropping his rosary, jumping to his feet and trying to push closed the sliding steel door of the wagon.

Jonah also started to his feet, knocking over his mess tin full of cold tea and spilling it over the book he had dropped. 'F--k me! Where's my f-----g rifle gone?' he yelled, sounding severely alarmed.

Tony and I were both scrabbling in amongst the wooden ammo boxes and our kit looking for our own rifles and bandoliers. Jonah tripped again just as I found my rifle, knocking it down between a stack of boxes and the edge of the wagon where it lay firmly wedged and for the moment looking irretrievable. 'Sorry mate!' said Jonah, unhooking a pocket in his bandolier and stuffing a clip into his magazine, having found his own weapon.

Paddy peered out cautiously through the narrow gap left in the wagon doorway, the rosary held in his left hand that also clutched the stock of his rifle. Tony and I pushed and heaved the heavy ammo boxes aside, furiously trying to retrieve my rifle. I suppose it took our minds off what we otherwise might have half-expected to hear - the rending and tearing of metal as the train ahead of us started to come off the rails.

Fortunately for all of us, that was it. Nothing more happened. By the time we had sorted ourselves out a few minutes later, the train was out of the cutting and into safer territory a few hundred yards on as if nothing had ever happened. I remember we were quite shaken by what had occurred. No-one mentioned the fact that had we been derailed and attacked, other than simply being subjected to a little random target practice, the only cover immediately available to us consisted of thin steel wagon sheeting and stacked boxes of high explosive. I was also more than a little upset when I examined my rifle a while later to find that either someone's foot or the battering received behind the ammo boxes had sheared off the battle sight on the bottom of the slide. This by no means rendered it useless but meant that only the adjustable target sight could be used. I never reported the damage to the armoury back at Seletar knowing full well that I would almost certainly have to pay for the replacement - and luckily for me it was not noticed when I finally handed it in many months later.

Jonah as our leader I think was more disconcerted by the incident than we were. He felt aggrieved and was determined that, 'Something ought to be done about it!' Quite what this should be, we were not sure. In the event he decided that it must be reported, and preferably to the authorities. An hour or two later the train halted. I think it must have been at Segamat, a small town in the north of Johore State

Jonah jumped down from our wagon and went off to see the driver and the guard. None of the train crew had heard anything at all and were surprised when Jonah told them what had happened. They all came back and inspected the wagon behind us. There were bullet holes certainly. But were they old or were they new? In the end Jonah found a European ASP (Assistant Superintendent of Police) sitting on a platform bench. He was smartly dressed in grey flannel shirt, crisp khaki shorts, blue topped hose above gleaming shoes, cane and peaked cap on the seat beside him. We wandered up as Jonah voiced his complaint. The policeman heard him out patiently. 'You are telling me,' he said, 'that you were fired on approximately fifteen miles south of here, back down the line?'

'That's right Sir!' said Jonah now patently relieved of his burden by having reported the incident to the authorities.

'Well, if I were you,' continued the ASP, 'I wouldn't say any more about it. We know they're there. Now you know they're there - all over the place at the moment actually. Probably just some junior bandit having a bit of target practice! No harm done. You haven't expended any ammunition. But if you keep cracking on about it we'll all have to fill in a whole lot of reports and waste everybody's time. Bags and bags of bumf! Wouldn't want that, would we?'

Jonah, still only partly mollified, reluctantly agreed and we all sloped off in turn to find a stand pipe so that we could sluice ourselves down with the dirty white 'crash' towels we all carried - emblazoned with the red Chinese characters that said, 'Good Morning' and to re-fill our water bottles. Then for a few cents we had our mugs filled with coffee, thick and sweet with condensed milk from a hawker in the road outside the station. The locomotive whistle tooted, we ran back to the wagon and hauled ourselves back aboard as the train pulled away.

~ ~ ~ ~ ~ ~ ~ ~ ~ ~

The last escort detachment I volunteered for was I think, in late August 1952 which was about three months before I was due for demob. Warrant Officer Pugh in the Radio Repair Squadron office was beginning to chunter on a bit by now about my repeated absences on various courses and detachments. 'Skiving off,' as he said. I persuaded him that it didn't really matter all that much. We had a civilian clerk, a Eurasian who was really much more efficient than I was and in any case the squadron was undermanned and all the wireless and radar fitters were hard pressed. He would have had to detail one of them if I didn't go. I promised it would be for the last time. No more leave, no more courses, no more detachments. 'Three days at the most and I'll be back at the weekend!' I said, fingers crossed behind my back. Mr. Pugh reluctantly agreed to let me go. I should have kept my mouth shut.

Three days later we were still no further north than Kuala Lumpur, barely half-way to Penang. The train had been slower than ever. We had eaten all our rations and now we were tucked away in a siding some distance from the centre of the town and its magnificent main railway station which is a crenellated dream of Imperial ice-cream splendour crowned with Mogul towers like the Brighton Pavilion. We could see its outline in the distance. We were hot, dirty and hungry. We were also short of cash. We had missed a pay day back at Seletar because of our absence.

Our journey had been painfully slow. Trains had been derailed ahead of and behind us and the traffic had been more disrupted than usual - exacerbated by heavy rains washing away sections of track. Near to our trucks was another wagon guarded by three Gurkhas bringing up supplies for their unit outside KL. We had been glad to have them with us. They lent us extra security and we gratefully accepted their offer to stand sentry whenever the train stopped at night. They were cheerful and keen soldiers and although their English was minimal we had no trouble communicating with them. If the train stopped long enough they would swiftly light a fire at the edge of the track, cook rice and curry and offer the three of us fragrant portions of these in our mess-tins in exchange for tea and cigarettes. They would have a half-gallon tin of water and rice, stirred with a bayonet - a proper bayonet with a blade, unlike our own silly pig-sticker spikes - cooked to perfection over a fire of twigs within fifteen minutes or so.

Author at Car Nicobar, 'hospital' and captured Japanese field gun in background. Trouser pockets stuffed like a chipmunk's cheeks with cigarette tins, etc.

Now in Kuala Lumpur, we were all shunted off into a siding. It was raining hard again, drumming noisily on the steel wagon roof. The cheerful Gurkhas had gone, leaving only one of their number behind to guard their stores. Corporal Jonah shuffled off glumly, to have a *shufti* - a recce, to take a *dekko* - sloshing through the puddles under his ground sheet cape, leaving my companion Stan (another conscript) and myself to mind the shop, as it were. Jonah returned after an hour as the rain died away. He was soaked to the skin and steaming gently in the watery afternoon sun. 'What's the 'gen'?' we asked him.

'The f-----g railway lines are all f-----g cut north of KL. To add to that the f-----g embankments are f-----g washed away all over the f-----g place,' Jonah said. 'When I asked for how f-----g long? They said they f-----g didn't know!! Two days, perhaps three, perhaps four!' He added, perhaps superfluously by now, 'F--k!' Jonah wasn't happy.

As Jonah continued his mounting tale of woe, the awful truth of what he was saying was beginning to sink in. He had also found a telephone and had got through eventually to the RAF at KL's airfield, explaining our predicament and asking for assistance in the form of a roof over our heads until the train was ready to go again, plus a relief guard and rations for the rest of our trip. All three requests had been turned down, flat. 'I got through to the f-----g station adjutant and he told me, 'Hard cheese! You're on you own, nothing to do with this unit. Get yourselves sorted out!' No messing, f-----g rude, right out loud, just like that!'

The three of us became increasingly despondent as Jonah's dire news sank in. We had almost no food left except some loose tea and sugar with a little mouldy stale bread. We had hardly any cash. We were just about out of fags and the nearest water tap was several hundred yards away. We were dirty and no doubt smelly (but had reached the stage where

We could be as smart as the Guards when necessary. Preparing for a VIP visit in October 1951. Author is sixth from left in front rank. The Station Warrant Officer 'Joe' Bollard extreme right.

one's own effluvium coursing through the grime no longer offended our own nostrils). What was worse - we no longer had a locomotive to supply us with boiling water for our tea! There is a very sensible military maxim that states 'no situation is so bad that it cannot get worse.' Small knots of Indian and Malay *chicos* appeared and began to pester us, like irritating flies. We constantly had to be on the alert to stop them creeping up and harassing us for anything they could wheedle out of us - what little we had left, we wanted to keep. We had also been warned to keep an eye open for possible saboteurs who might try to put stones in the axle boxes.

By the late afternoon (it was a Saturday and the chances of any succour or relief before the weekend was out seemed to be lessening with each hour) our immediate prospects were fast deteriorating. But we had forgotten our good friends the Gurkhas. An army lorry appeared with a handful of labourers, another two or three small brown soldiers and a British sergeant in clean, well-pressed jungle green. As the labourers started to unload more stores from the truck into the wagon, the sergeant, a genial Welshman, came over to chat to us. The Gurkhas' wagon was eventually going on further north and he had come down both to post a relief guard and to add to the wagon's cargo. We explained our harrowing situation to the kindly Taff who listened sympathetically to our troubles. We exclaimed at the Army's manifest efficiency in such matters as looking after their own welfare - unlike the mean-spirited attitude of the RAF in our hour of need.

Sergeant Taff was charming. He immediately proposed a happy solution to the problem. Why not go with him out a few miles north of KL to Sungei Bisi (or was it Sungei Buloh?) where the 'N'th Gurkhas were based? (Jock Nicol, ex-Special Branch Malayan Police, to who I recounted this tale only recently, says they were almost certainly the 'N'th, adding, 'They were a very dubious lot of 'specials' - some of whom were nearly six foot tall, wore turbans and spoke no Urdu!') We could spend a day or two in the British Sergeants' Mess. We could clean up, eat, have our *dhobi* done, rest and charp it off a bit until the train was ready to leave. The Gurkhas would be happy to post an extra man or two to guard our bombs and rockets - and they would bring us back again as soon as the train was due - after all they had to catch the train as well. What a splendid chap was our Sergeant Taff, so practical and generous. A welcome comrade in our adversity.

201

I doubt if Corporal Jonah gave it more than a few moments thought before accepting on our behalf. Jonah, Stan and myself were three innocent flies stumbling into the honey-trap baited by the cunning, and as we were to discover, probably devious as well as genial Taff.

The Gurkhas looked after us in style. Their British Sergeants' Mess was clean and comfortable. The food was good and we were plied with beer. Our *dhobying* was done swiftly and we had clean uniforms again. For two nights we slept on comfortable *charpoys*, undisturbed in an *attap* roofed *basha*. Sergeant Taff was a good host. The Gurkha unit he was attached to was not a regular formation, they were 'specials' recruited to assist the police and the Army in jungle operations. As always in the east, the camp swarmed with hangers-on. Soldiers' families - wives and children, *dhobis*, cooks, *char-wallahs*, bearers, labourers (and their families too.) It all seemed very jolly to us. Taff told us that they operated an excellent intelligence system with all these camp followers, some of whom were informers and had direct contact with the 'bandits.' Taff told us that the Chinese camp barber was a double-agent acting for both the CTs and the Special Branch. We were very young and gullible. Instead of our suspicions being aroused by all these tales and confidences we simply lay back and enjoyed ourselves for forty-eight hours. Such sweet innocents were we - lambs for the slaughter.

Taff told us the train was at last ready to go. We were given a whole lot of buckshee Gurkha rations, which were much better than we would have got from the RAF at KL had they bothered to give us any. We were driven back through downtown KL to our railway siding, with Taff and his Gurkhas who were going back to guard their own stores once more. Everything seemed as we had left it and there was a smart sentry standing by our truck with his carbine and fixed bayonet. As the train drew out, heading north once more, we waved our grateful thanks to Taff and his merry, smiling Gurkha crew.

14
THE GREAT TRAIN ROBBERY

Oh wretched fools! That liv'st to make thine honesty a vice.
O monstrous world! Take note, take note, O world!
To be direct and honest is not safe.
William Shakespeare, *Othello*.

The remaining eighteen hours of our long and disrupted haul to Prai was uneventful. Once past the towns of Tanjong Malim and Ipoh the railway skirts the heavily wooded hills and limestone cliffs of the central mountain ranges of Malaya. It is spectacular country with vertical rock faces and soaring dome-headed bluffs showing the many entrances of unreachable caves - no doubt swarming with fruit bats and tropical swifts. To see all this for free, to have travelled half-way around the world, to be young, knowing that in a few short months one would be out of the RAF and a civilian again - was a great adventure. We had no responsibilities and all the future to look forward to - life was exciting and full of new experiences. Sometimes I can still recapture those feelings and slip off the weight of all the intervening years that have clouded the freshness and energy of youth.

We arrived at Prai. Our wagons were shunted off into a siding where a flight sergeant with a crew of labourers accompanied by several three-ton trucks guarded by local Malay Levies now appeared on the scene from Butterworth to unload our cargo. We hung around in the shade while the 'chiefy' armourer counted and checked the wagon contents. After a prolonged second check, 'chiefy' called our corporal over and their two heads bent over the sheaf of forms on a clipboard. Jonah and the flight sergeant were now grim and unsmiling as they re-checked and re-counted the piles of wooden boxes that held the sixty pound rocket heads now cleared out of our wagon and stacked on the ground. Jonah was looking glumly at the sheaf of forms as he counted the boxes a third, and then again a fourth time. At long last, the flight sergeant told the labourers to start loading the trucks.

Jonah trudged despondently over to Stan and myself where we sat under a shade tree with our kit, puffing away at our buckshee cigarettes from the Gurkha sergeants' mess - keeping a respectable distance from the highly explosive cargo, now that we were under the watchful eye of the Butterworth 'chiefy.'

Our forlorn corporal swiftly shattered the afternoon calm. Stan and I had quickly sunk into that torpid 'switched-off' condition, akin to that Buddhist state of mind which is either the cellar or attic of existence - or perhaps neither, but some remote plane in between - that all servicemen in the ranks learn to adopt once they know that no NCO is going to tread on their shirt-tails for the next half-hour.

What Jonah had to say swiftly jolted us back to the present. 'For Christ's sake, don't say a word about us leaving the wagons back in KL. We're short of three f-----g boxes!! Chiefy's refused to sign for the full load. He's made me sign a deficiency chit! Effing Nora! (See note 16 - Appendix) There's going to be all hell to pay if we don't watch out.'

The three of us, out of the hearing of the flight sergeant, roundly cursed the memory of our jovial Welsh host back in KL on whom our suspicions immediately fell. It now seemed to us that Taffy was indeed a Welshman and in the words of the old nursery rhyme, 'Taffy was a thief!' as well. I don't think it then occurred to either Stan or myself that it was principally Jonah who was now effectively mired up to the eyeballs and standing on tiptoe.

I can no longer recall clearly what happened next. I remember there was no transport laid on for the three of us to get into Butterworth. We managed to hitch a ride in a passing army ambulance which drove by. It was full of very young Gurkha riflemen slumped shoulder to shoulder on stretchers or lying on the floor, some obviously feverish and sick and one or two others in bandages and slings, as if they had been in an accident. In spite of the affinity that normally existed between British and Gurkhas we could get nothing out of them as to what they were doing, or what had happened to reduce them to the sad state they were in. Their almost trance-like silence crammed up together in the close-packed vehicle allowed the three of us hanging on at the rear by the skin of our teeth to discuss our predicament without any risk of being overheard or understood. 'Leave me to do the talking. Say nothing. Say we never left them wagons unguarded,' ordered Jonah.

With hindsight I think we must have hitched a lift with the sick parade of some Gurkha unit being shuttled off to the nearest military hospital at

Butterworth or Georgetown.

Stan and I were not questioned by the Butterworth RAF Police or anyone else there. In the mess hall where we were fed, I sat down opposite a young airman. To our mutual surprise we instantly recognised each other. Back in Civvy Street we had been fellow clerks in the same city bank. He explained to our considerable amusement why so many of the tin issue mugs from which our fellow diners were sipping their tea were stylishly hand painted and garlanded with a steamy and somewhat florid slogan which read 'Blobber's Club' (See note 17) in the rustic fashion now known to country craftswomen as 'tole' painting.

We spent the night in a flimsy *attap*-roofed *basha* with torrential rain pouring off and through the thatch, before catching the next morning's mail train back down to KL again. Without any further incident and another night mail train's journey from KL to Singapore we were back at Seletar once more. In the squadron office Warrant Officer Pugh was fuming. I had been away over a week. The Eurasian clerk had been off sick. 'Not my fault Mr. Pugh,' I said, 'blame the weather and the bandits!' I was due for another twenty-four hours off duty for my extended absence which in deference to Mr. Pugh's feelings I gave up.

During the next few days, Jonah kept in touch with Stan and myself in our respective sections on the base. By now he had been thoroughly grilled on the rack by the SIB (Special Investigations Branch of the RAF Police) and was continuing to maintain his total innocence of any circumstances that could have led to the loss of the rocket boxes and their contents.

Stan and I met up to discuss our dilemma. 'We were only obeying orders!' has been the time-honoured excuse down throughout the ages of military disasters. Well, so had we. It was obvious that Jonah had dug himself into a deep hole and was continuing to ignore the first and most important rule of 'holesmanship' - 'When in a hole - stop digging!' Stan and I had so far not been questioned by the SIB. If we confessed that in KL we had left our post for nearly forty-eight hours, admittedly having made arrangements for a relief guard with the Gurkhas, then Stan and I would probably be in the clear. Jonah as the guard commander on the other hand, having already consistently lied, would be buried so deep in the shit that his whole RAF career as a regular would be in jeopardy. He would certainly lose his corporal's stripes. He would most likely be court-martialled and he could well serve a stretch in the glasshouse. I didn't think Jonah was sleeping very well for several weeks at that time.

A few days later the telephone rang in the squadron office. Mr Pugh put the receiver down and looked over his desk at me. 'What have you been up to that rates the attentions of the SIB?' he asked quizzically. 'You're wanted over in the PR (photo reconnaissance) Section office now. Watch your step!' he added kindly, but not jokingly.

I remember that the two SIB sergeants were in civilian clothes. After being questioned for a while, sticking to the story that at all times the wagons had never been left unguarded, with always at least one of us present, I was asked for a written statement to this effect. To support my evidence I also offered a photograph I had snapped during the journey which showed how the rocket boxes had been stowed in relation to the sliding doors of the wagon we occupied. I was trying to imply that they might have been taken when our backs were turned, or had perhaps fallen out of their own volition. I signed the statement and was dismissed.

Stan made a similar statement later the same day. I don't think the SIB believed us. We were called back and questioned again. By this time neither Stan nor I were sleeping at night any more than Jonah. The photograph that I gave the SIB that showed the arrangement of the cargo also showed our gallant guard commander, perched cross-legged on top of a pile of ammo boxes. Jonah was quite clearly smoking a fag!

We later learned that at least two of the missing rocket heads turned up in the next several weeks. One was used to demolish a railway culvert in an attempted derailment of a train north of Kuala Lumpur, another was used in a similar incident involving a night attack on a passenger train. In neither instance was anyone injured, but Jethro Plinge, a quiet and cautious man from my barrack room, another of those former Palestine Policemen who had joined the RAF 'for the quiet life' and who at last had felt secure enough to venture off the camp and north to Penang for a spot of leave was blown up while on that mail-train. During the subsequent attack on the immobilised train his carefully packed suitcase with all his new civvies purchased especially for his holiday, received a bullet plumb through the middle which penetrated layer after layer, fold upon fold of his pristine, brand new clothes (far beyond the skills of any 'sew-sew' to repair).

Jethro had taken refuge on the floor of the lavatory compartment where another random bullet shattered the large clay water pot *chattie* or *tong* provided for the varied multicultural ablutions practiced by the passengers. Jethro was soaked by the cascading water while his ears were blistered by the oaths of the train's escort who were sheltering below the compartment and were caught in the run-off through the drain in the lavatory floor. When Jethro finally returned to our barrack room he vowed never to set foot off the base again until his return to the UK. I said nothing, keeping quiet about any possible involvement in his mishap. After all, I had only been obeying orders.

Jonah was subsequently reprimanded and nearly lost his stripes for smoking in direct contravention of safety procedures. By the time I left Seletar in early September to sail for the UK and demob on the *Dilwara* the SIB's investigations were still proceeding. I have often wondered what conclusions were finally reached. (* see note page 208).

It was a moral question then as it still is now. I was just twenty years old and ill-equipped for such complex issues. Both Stan and I were shortly due for demob. Jonah was OK in our book. Should we tell the truth and ruin him? Should we lie and protect his cover? What about the Taffy sergeant, his merry Gurkha 'specials' and their informer friends from Sungei Bisi? They had almost certainly 'lifted' the boxes of rocket-heads for their own nefarious purposes. Should they get off scot free? The latter would simply swear blind they also never left the wagons unguarded. I have often (but rarely in recent years) asked myself since those far-off days what the correct answer to that moral question should have been. I hope that at least Jonah came to realise that by lying on his behalf both Stan and I had put our necks on the block for what was after all his own error of judgement.

---

　　* There is a final postscript to this episode. In 2003 in a brief article I wrote for *Searchlight,* the journal of the RAF Seletar Association about these detachments, I made no mention of the 'loss' or part of our cargo and the nefarious circumstances surrounding this episode. Subsequently in corresponding with and comparing experiences with a contemporary whose service was later but overlapped with mine at Seletar, it transpired that he did several up-country ammunition train escorts on which he stated that there were always at least six airmen, including a corporal. With hindsight it can be deduced that (a) perhaps the SIB (for want of evidence) did actually believe our fairy story, and (b) that to increase secuirty, future escorts were doubled. In passing, my informant noted that these later escorts were issued with comprehensive daily ration packs and portable cooking stoves!

15
HOMEWARD BOUND

The Working Class can kiss my arse,
I'm on the demob list at last.'
(trad. air *The Red Flag*)

An RAF Trooping Song:

'We're leaving Khartoum by the light of the moon,
We're sailing by night and by day.
We've passed Kasfareet and we've f--k all to eat,
We've thrown all our rations away.'

Shire, Shire, Somersetshire*,
The Skipper looks on her with pride.
He'd have a blue fit
If he saw all the shit
On the side of the Somersetshire.'

(chorus) This is my story, this is my song,
I've been in this Air Force too f-----g long.
So roll on the Rodney, the Nelson, Renown,**
You can't have the Hood 'cos the bugger's gone down.

'Chocks away! Chocks awaaaay!
We'll f--k all the SPs*** who come down our way.'
(See note 18 - Appendix)

~ ~ ~ ~ ~ ~ ~ ~ ~ ~

If I do have any besetting sins, one of them as my family will testify, is that I can never easily throw anything away. Occasionally I will do so when hard pressed, but then only with a strong sense of regret and in the certain knowledge that I would find use for it in the near future - usually the next day as it happens. I have been known to root through dustbins, panic-stricken to recover some item or other, kept safe for years - discarded in haste and then found to be essential. (There are those who might say this is the result of too early potty-training.)

I have an ancient lizard-skin wallet which I bought in the hill village of Diyatalawa in Ceylon in September 1951 when I was there on a ground combat course. Among the miscellaneous items this wallet still contains is a small, faded square of buff coloured card. There is also my 'permanent pass' to RAF Seletar, dated March 1951, signed by the adjutant, allowing me to be absent from my quarters, to wear plain clothes when off duty, until 01.00 hrs. I could have presented this, had I had it with me, to the main gate guard room of Seletar to which I reported in November 1995, some forty-three years later, for permission to enter what is still a Singaporean military base.

This slip of buff card is army form W 5218D, my boarding card for HM Troopship *Dilwara*, 'Deck F, Section 2, Berth No. 63C, Draft No. 94.' It is undated, but I know that it was sometime in early September 1952. I can check this by back-dating from a postcard I still have, written to my mother in the Red Sea, posted at Suez and forecasting our arrival at Southampton on 2 or 3 October. Whenever it was, the four-week voyage plus the home leave due to us would extend both Steve's and my service over its two year period by some weeks. Again I can check this by referring to my final discharge certificate in my old paybook. The section headed 'CO's remarks,' signed by Group Captain Seymour describes me, I am pleased to see as 'smart, ...steadfast and reliable.' I was called to see this gentleman prior to leaving Seletar. I had not spoken to him in the preceding eighteen months, neither until then had he acknowledged my presence under his command. He asked if I would care to sign on as a regular, assuring me of a fine future career in the RAF. I declined and he thanked me for my service, then I saluted and left.

This was totally unlike my late friend G., who served for two years in an infantry battalion, mostly in Egypt in the Canal Zone. G had fought the Army every inch of the way, determined not to be broken - to be a 'King's bad bargain.' He never referred to his rifle as anything but his 'gun,' and resented every minute he served. As a result he spent considerable time in detention barracks and on 'defaulters' or near permanent fatigue duty. When his service was completed, standing before the CO, the Colonel said, weighing up the thickish pile of 'crime' reports that represented G's service record, 'Well, G. - it's been a fair fight. I've taken it as read that you don't want to sign on. Let's shake hands on it and call it quits. Good luck!' This remark was patently untrue as the odds had always been heavily on the side of the Army.

By this stage of our existence both Steve and I were quite happy to soldier on for a few extra weeks for the sake of the long sea voyage home, half way around the world. We were now on a regular's rate of Air Force pay, let it be said, for our final six months of service which, with the overseas allowance, had made us quite flush with cash for once. We must have been earning all of £4 per week by this time. I believe that although Steve was entitled to keep his 'acting' corporal's tapes up, he probably reverted to his substantive rank of SAC for his last pay periods. It was I suppose one final military experience to tuck under our respective belts. The only misgiving I experienced about any delay in my exit from the RAF was the knowledge that the Special Investigations Branch almost certainly had not closed their files or their enquiries into the incident of the missing boxes of rocket heads. Without the shadow of a doubt my name and various statements would still be lying somewhere on someone's desk. Although I had heard nothing for the past few weeks, I knew that I was not in the clear until I was in Civvy Street once more - perhaps not even then.

The *Dilwara* was due to sail from the Empire Dock on the old Singapore waterfront by 14.00 hrs. With half a dozen other airmen, Steve and I passed through the impressive main gate of RAF Seletar for the last time, in a three ton-truck, at 07.30 hrs, having had our long awaited early breakfast. (It was not quite the last time for me - I did check in at the guard room again in November 1995). Together with our full webbing kit, big and small packs, water bottle, mess tins, plus the bulky kit bag with all our home uniforms and equipment, we were each allowed an extra suitcase to take home our 'loot' to the cold, still half-starved, dingy Britain of 1952. This was full 'christmas tree' marching order with a vengeance. We were already soaked in sweat. Excited to be going home at last, but tinged with regret at leaving our mates, the friendly faces and familiar routines that had become second nature for so long. We also knew that our departure would not raise even the smallest ripple on the base. The main emotion evinced by the oppos we were leaving behind was that of envy.

We gazed out from the open sides of the *gharry* as we were driven through the friendly streets of down town Singapore. We drove down Orchard Road, past Collyer Quay, over Cavanagh Bridge and the river, past the 'go-downs' and warehouses with their teeming labourers. Bales of raw rubber bouncing out of laden trucks like giant tennis balls were being manhandled into a hundred *sampans*. The smells of China Town - of cooking and richly perfumed drains, the strains of what was now familiar Chinese and Indian music, the noisy crowds of people in the narrow streets - we were seeing it for the last time. A mixture of nostalgia and a desire to board our ship consumed us. We cheered happily as we rolled in through the dock gates.

To embark several hundred troops with all their kit onto a 12,000 ton ship in the space of a few hours is a major enterprise. It was all done as a matter of routine. The upper decks of the *Dilwara* towered above the quayside, lined with jeering and cat-calling soldiers already loaded at previous ports of call in Korea and Hong Kong. We, the embarking drafts were now drawn up on the dockside in our various untidy ranks, marshalled by fiercely shouting, pompously strutting, stiffly starched Army redcaps into some semblance of order. Trussed up with webbing and canvas packs, kit bags balanced across our shoulders, now we were totally sodden with sweat, our own faded and starched KD wilting like soggy blotting paper in the full blaze of the morning sun. We dragged our extra suitcases behind us as we approached the gangway. That half-hour spent boarding ship was I think one of the most unpleasant experiences of my time with the RAF.

We were a small draft of only twenty-eight airmen on the dockside, assembled from the airstrips of up-country Malaya and of Singapore, a small knot of khaki-clad men with blue berets adrift in a sea of jungle-green soldiers. We looked at each other in horror as we saw the Army drafts, even more laden than ourselves, being doubled up the steep gangway into the side of the ship, amid screaming redcaps! With ever increasing alarm our language became more obscene than its normal effing and blinding. We were f-----g bloody Airmen! Not f-----g bloody squaddies to be doubled around by f-----g bloody redcap baboons, etc., etc.

But alas, we were. Corporals, time-expired regulars, senior men with rows of war-time ribbons, national servicemen en route to demob - we were all chased and hounded up the near vertical (or so it seemed) gangway like the common soldiery. The ordeal still remains vivid in my memory. We were doubled along companionways, down steep ladders, laden like broken-backed pack camels, guided and abused by military policemen far down into the bowels of the ship. I remember stopping exhausted by a ventilator that was belching foul fumes into a passageway, unable to move further, retching with dry heaves, dribbling saliva. A sailor looked out of the galley doorway and said kindly, 'Not far now, mate. F Deck? Only another three decks to go - all downhill!' By the time we finally reached F Deck we were all in the same state, slumping white-faced and shaking on our piles of kit.

Our berths were up forward, near the bows of the ship, on the waterline. The scuttles were screwed up fast, letting in a little green daylight through the thick glass. The cramped space was taken up almost entirely by tiers of metal framed laced-canvas bunks in sixes, allowing some eighteen inches of head space. The narrow gangway between each tier was no more than two feet wide. It all stank of stale sweat and overheated, damp humanity. A few puny ventilators hissed sweltering tropical air at us. Steve and I claimed our bunks, stowing our kit at the far end of the section where our 'excess' suitcases of personal gear and our kit bags made an untidy pile. We looked gloomily at each other. 'Jesus bloody well wept,' said Steve, 'and to think we could have f-----g flown home!'

The *Dilwara* (which means 'heart' in Hindi) was a regular on the Far East trooping run. She was a sister ship of the better known *Dunera*, which were both owned by the British India Steam Navigation Company. She had a long history of war service. As a former passenger liner she had been commandeered by the Admiralty in 1939. Amongst her exploits she had carried French troops in August 1944 - in the same conditions we now experienced - to the 'Second D Day' Operation Anvil landings in the south of France. She was crewed by a mix of Indian lascar deckhands, cooks and stewards, plus a few British merchant seamen and officers. The service families on passage, the officers and senior NCOs occupied the old first and second class accommodation on the upper decks. The troop decks down to below the waterline were crammed to bursting point with the hapless other ranks plus a few sergeants travelling unaccompanied.

I don't know now how many passengers the old *Dilwara* carried below deck - perhaps two thousand? With the exception of our draft of twenty-eight airmen, the rest were soldiers of a score and more regiments and Corps from all over the Far East. We were tour-expired, time-expired, national servicemen due for demob. and old sweats together, from Korea, Malaya and Hong Kong. There were Green Howards, Gloucesters, SAS (Malayan Scouts), Royal Signals, RASC, 13/18 Hussars, Royal Artillery, Devons, East Yorkshires, the Middlesex, Royal Ulster Rifles, King's Shropshire Light Infantry, the West Kents, Royal Engineers, Argyll and Sutherland Highlanders and half a dozen more of the old county regiments. Many of them were a tough bunch, battle-hardened veterans in not a few cases. Now they were on their way home and away from the discipline of their parent units. In the parlance of the time they 'didn't give a tit' (or some such phrase) for any NCO or officer foolish enough to try to tell them what they didn't want to do or know.

As was traditional on troopships of the time, the small RAF contingent were appointed to the role of ship's police. We were expected to keep this lot in order. When the senior RAF officer on board, a diffident wing commander who we never saw again, gave us our instructions there was a universal groan from the assembled knot of airmen on F Deck, Section C. 'Effing stroll on! Roll on bloody demob!! Roll on death!!!' Behind me an Irishman wailed, 'Mother darlin' - sell the pig and buy me out!'

The mammoth task of organising some sort of order on the ship continued as we pulled away from the dockside. Noisy cheering echoed from the troops thronging the main decks as the *Dilwara* made for the Malacca Straits, heading up past Sumatra to the Nicobar Channel en route to Colombo, first port of call on the month-long voyage to Blighty.

The ship's galleys cooked from dawn to dusk. Breakfast, dinner and supper being dished up almost throughout the day to shift after shift of hungry men, in numbered sittings. The food was poor compared with what we had been used to and one of our 'police' tasks was to occasionally check meal tickets to prevent men coming round a second time - a task tempered by a sensibly anxious desire not to antagonise our charges.

There were queues for everything, especially for the canteen where for a few hours a day, warm frothing beer was poured out from huge jugs after long delays - there seemed to be no cooling system for the kegs and in the tropical heat all that could be done was to draw off gallons of sudsy foam from the barrels and wait for it to settle. It was small consolation after the ice-cold Tiger beer of Singapore. There were queues for the small library, for the 'heads' and for the wash rooms with their salt-water showers. We queued to occupy chairs and tables in the recreational saloons where the card schools soon established themselves. In the evening there was sometimes a 'Housey-Housey' session, or a makeshift concert. During the day we had the occasional lifeboat drill - which usually spun itself out over an hour or two. The later emergency drills raised little enthusiasm among the ranks of the soldiery, many of whom had to be routed out from their bunks amid a shower of boots and abuse directed at the RAF 'police' who were sent below to chase them out. We were also assembled on deck, lying on our backs waving our bare feet in the air for foot inspection - who did they think we were - 'the f-----g infantry?' The final indignity was the FFI (Free From Infection) inspection conducted down below on the troop deck a few days after sailing. We were squashed shoulder-to-shoulder, shorts and trousers dropped round our ankles in the narrow gangway between the bunks while a bored Army MO avoided our eyes while passing a cursory glance over our nether parts.

After a few days at sea, as always, shipboard life soon fell into a humdrum routine. Ship time seems to have twice its terrestrial value as the pace of life slows to match the throb of the engines and all contact with the land vanishes. For the likes of us there were no communications, no wireless, no mail and no newspapers. One lazed on deck with a blanket and a book, yarning, smoking, playing cards, dozing in the wind and sun. After the first few days watching the flying fish we rarely looked at the sparkling deep blue of the Indian Ocean - unless schools of dolphins appeared - until even they became familiar and only a pod of whales would draw us to the ship's rail.

In spite of the long, heavy swells, accentuated by our position in the bows of the *Dilwara* - which alternately made our bodies as heavy as lead when ascending companionways, or tried to lift us off our feet propelling us to the deck above - I recall little sea-sickness among the troops. At night down below in our bunks on the waterline the phosphorescence glowed and flashed in the water that washed by the scuttles. Once or twice NCOs tried to organise compulsory PT sessions on deck, but only those who wished to do so took part. With such a complement of bolshie and potentially dissident time-expired soldiery it would not have been worth the risk to compel them to take part. There is an image which has remained with me over the years of a large tattooed soldier, bare-chested in the sun and resembling a six-foot-six gorilla in repose - stitching away on a small embroidery frame, delicately crafting in coloured silks the emblem of the Malayan Scouts, the winged dagger and the 'Who Dares Wins' motto of the SAS. No, compulsory PT was definitely out!

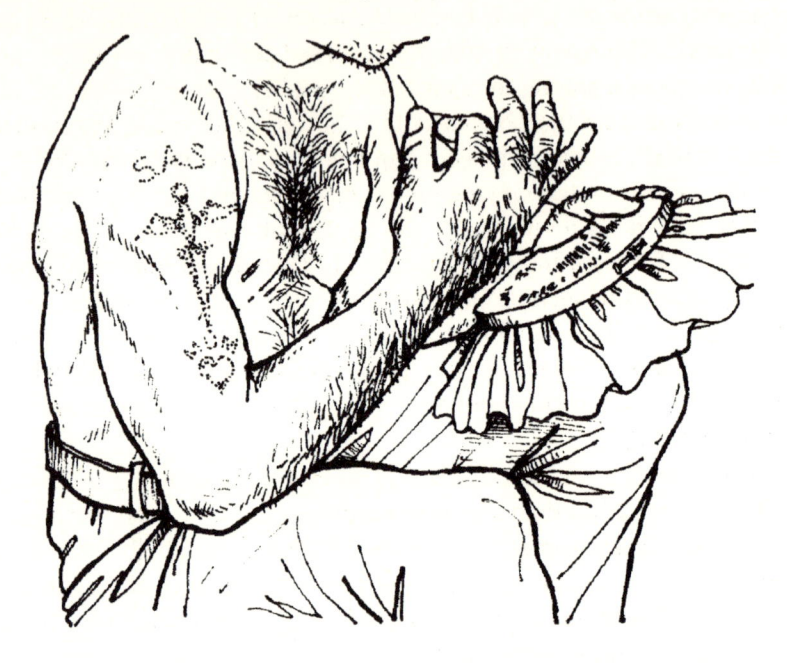

After a few days steaming across the Bay of Bengal we tied up along the quayside in Colombo. Our early morning arrival as we crept up the coast was spectacular. Steve and I had gone up on deck before breakfast to take the air as a relief from the overnight fug of F Deck. Everywhere one looked, from horizon to horizon - except for the distant loom of the shore - were schools, colleges, whole universities of dolphins. It seemed as if the entire world's population of dolphins were in our vicinity, splashing and blowing, porpoising in unison across the smooth waters off the coast of Ceylon. In among them were small native fishing boats with triangular sails making their way out to sea. It was a magic vision that I have never forgotten.

As it transpired, Colombo would be the only port of call we were allowed ashore. A small group of airmen including Steve and myself went into the town - most of the troops remained on board or ventured no further than the dockside. They had had enough of foreign travel after their years in the Far East. The shores of England beckoned far more strongly than any real or imagined 'happy discoveries' on the Isle of Serendib. The ground heaved and swayed beneath our feet with the remembered motion of the ship. Steve and I made our way through the centre of town to one of the large hotels (was it the Galle Face?) where we stuffed ourselves with ice-cream, pastries and cold beer - sheer luxury after troopship fare - before casting a critical eye over the wares of the street-merchants outside. They had tray after tray of jewellry made from cracked and flawed diamonds and sapphires, chipped rubies and seed pearls. It was not our scene. We made our way back to the docks, nobody was going to miss this ship. We sailed in the late afternoon, bound for Aden across the Arabian Sea.

~ ~ ~ ~ ~ ~ ~ ~ ~ ~

Day after day passed as before. One hot mid-morning the ship hesitated with a juddering shock. On deck we rushed to the rail to see a huge whale veering away, streaming trails of blood into the blue ocean. I wondered if the helmsman had seen it before we struck, or if he cared. It looked badly injured and we guessed the sharks would soon make short work of it.

I joined a small card-school of airmen playing solo whist. There were about eight of us who played this four-handed game, taking up an empty seat when someone else left to go on duty or to take the air on deck. For me, this was a big mistake. I didn't know then what I have known for many years since. I am not a good card player, games of chance such as pontoon, blackjack or even snap! pose no problems, But games of skill, or bluff - and particularly games where it is vital to note and remember the run of the cards are a disaster zone. In these categories I include all the many varieties of poker and the various forms of contract bridge and whist. Of these latter games solo whist is perhaps the most dangerous for the beginner.

On the face of it solo is easily learned. You can play it almost at once, but to play it well requires both cleverness and experience. It has an added risk that to make it really interesting it has to be played for money, however small the stakes. Open gambling, except for tombola or perhaps crown and anchor, in the Services was forbidden, so no cash changed hands with us. We simply kept a list between us to settle at the end of the voyage. We played for tuppence a point (the stake has to be divisible by four at 480 old half pence to £1 Sterling). Carrying forward accumulating losses, combined with incompetence, soon becomes a recipe for financial catastrophe. As my card playing skills improved with the passing weeks - so did that of the other players. Thus my position at the bottom of the pack was maintained - but buoyed up by the entirely false conviction on my part that with my improving skills I could thus, by continuing to throw good money after bad, reduce my growing debts.

If any young person should read this narrative and learn nothing from it but the two truths that I am about to reveal, then the cover price of this book will have been repaid a hundredfold.

Firstly, when a man with experience meets a man with money, it is usually the man with the experience who ends up with the money and the man who had the money is left with the experience. Secondly, if you find yourself playing cards for money and after the first half-hour you haven't worked out who the patsy is - it's you!

~ ~ ~ ~ ~ ~ ~ ~ ~ ~

Long sea-voyages are all very well, but I must confess I have never been on a holiday cruise ship. My later voyages on the old West African mail boats and trans-Atlantic liners has confirmed my experience that after a while, the sea palls, tedium and boredom set in and one longs for land. These feelings were in their most concentrated form on the homeward bound troopships of the 1950s.

We sailed past the distant bulk of the island of Socotra, its bare, mountainous cliffs shimmering in a haze of heat where it lay across the approaches to the Gulf of Aden and the sea lanes to the Red Sea. For strategic reasons in the days of sea power it had long been British. Who, we wondered, were the poor bastards who had been condemned to serve there? How many of them had been driven mad? Every drop of water had to be shipped in to that dusty, stony wilderness of a desert island. Was it still British? Who cared? We didn't, we were going home.

We called in briefly at Aden, the harbour encircled by bare, spare-ribbed mountains hanging over the commercial town of Crater with its low white dusty buildings crammed together like dirty cement shoe-boxes. Black scavenging kites circled lazily above us. We were not allowed ashore and nobody minded. I would have gone had the opportunity offered, if only

British India S.N.Co's M.S. Dilwara, the troopship on which we sailed for home.

to say I had been there. I knew that the Chartered Bank had a branch in Crater and that it was regarded as a hardship posting - the expatriate Bank staff served no more than eighteen-month tours compared with the more usual three or four years in the Far East at that time.

Our brief stay was enlivened only by the unedifying spectacle of a prisoner, 'banged up' in the ship's brig since we left Singapore, being frogmarched down the gangplank by a group of military police who had come on board to claim him. He shouted and raged and swore as they pushed and pulled him along the dockside. His was a sad story. He was an RAF airman who had foolishly and without sufficient consideration signed on to serve a twenty-two year engagement - the maximum at that time. On having second thoughts - he had tried to back out, only to find that as a skilled fitter the sum demanded by the Air Ministry to buy himself out was far beyond his means. He was a determined man and he hit on an alternative solution.

The prisoner knew that if he was dishonourably discharged from the service he would be absolved of the remaining twenty years or so he still had to serve. After due research he committed a carefully calculated military crime, sufficient to be sent down for twelve months in the 'glasshouse' which would automatically mean he would be discharged at the end of his sentence. Whatever it was that the unfortunate airman did I never found out, but the court martial had awarded him a year's detention in a military prison, to be followed by a dishonourable discharge. Military prisoners sentenced to more than six months in the Far East were sent back to the UK to serve their time in Colchester, the tropical prison regime being deemed too hard for any extended punishment.

Our man was on his way back to Britain to serve out his twelve months when his trial was reviewed. Out of the kindness of their hearts the Air Ministry had reduced his sentence to six months (to be served back in Singapore). The dishonourable discharge was withdrawn and he was to be allowed to serve out his twenty-two years regular engagement - plus of course the six months he was to serve in prison, which didn't count. No wonder he shouted and raged as he was taken ashore in irons to await the next ship sailing east. I wonder what became of him?

Aden was always a desolate outpost of the Empire - a coaling station for the Navy, a staging-post for excursions into the Horn of Africa or punitive expeditions against the warring tribesmen of South Arabia. The RAF manned several remote airstrips along the desert coasts of Oman and up into the Trucial Emirates that fringed the Persian Gulf. They were not popular postings. I believe that one of the remoter airfields had a glass display case on the wall of the mess in which were framed a pair of frilly lace knickers - donated at the men's request by the first Englishwoman ever to make a brief visit to the place.

More than a decade after the time of which I write, withdrawing altogether from East of Suez, the British were extricating themselves from Aden and the Protectorate. It became a nasty little war, at the end fought out in the narrow, dusty alleys of Crater itself. During the final stages of the withdrawal only the airfield at Khormaksar was still held, defended by 45 Marine Commando. A friend of mine many years later, had been one of the last Marines to leave. As they embarked for the ships of the Task Force lying off shore, he managed to drop his rifle in the water. The tensions ran so high, the Marines were determined to leave nothing of value behind, a team of Navy divers was called in to recover the weapon, delaying the final evacuation for hours. My friend said that although he remembered quite vividly what the Marine RSM said to him, even some ten years after the incident he was still unable to bring himself to repeat the words to me. As the British marched out at the bidding of Harold Wilson in 1967, the Russians marched in taking over mountains of abandoned kit and equipment, bulldozers, machinery and aircraft. The Yemen then became a client state of the USSR. Years of murder and tyranny followed during which the 'revolution' steadily devoured its children in time-honoured fashion.

HOMEWARD BOUND

In the lands they colonised the British always left behind them more lasting memories than mere street names (usually changed in any case after they left to 'Independence Avenue' or 'Martyrs of the Revolution Square') or well-constructed public buildings, or functioning sewage systems shortly destined to collapse. They left behind the graves of the fallen, soldiers and civilians who died in battle, of wounds or the climate and disease - the latter often the most numerous.

I have always found it a moving experience, wherever I have been in the world to visit the cemeteries that mark the bloody footprint of the British over the years. Most are well cared for, a few neglected and overgrown. The Americans, less practised in these matters, usually spare no expense in repatriating the remains of their fallen heroes to the soil of their native land for burial in the presence of their families. It is perhaps a cogent reason why the American public are so reluctant to commit their boys to foreign conflict. The British, short of land for the vast areas that would be required, have never seen in their own country such telling evidence of the carnage of war at first hand. But the British, I suspect for reasons not unconnected with official parsimony - and perhaps sheer logistics when one thinks of the numbers involved - have always chosen to bury their dead close to the field of strife.

An image remains with me from the sixties, a news photograph of the Royal Northumberland Fusiliers burying their dead comrades at the Happy Valley Cemetery, Aden. The expressions on the faces of the guard and of the firing party are of such intensity that one can feel and understand the ties that bond such soldiers together. Where are they now? The living, almost certainly either unemployed or prematurely retired, now approaching old age, how do they remember those times? With pride tempered by sorrow? Or with regret and perhaps anger? As for the dead, they still lie quiet far from home in the arid dust of Aden. Is it still called Happy Valley? There is a Highland lament played on the pipes on such military occasions as long drawn out inspections, or when 'beating the retreat.' It is rightly called *The Barren Rocks of Aden*.

The Red Sea was distinctly unpleasant, even in late September. The *Dilwara* ploughed steadily northwards towards Suez enveloped in a hot and choking fog of fumes spewing from the funnel. We endured a following wind that matched our speed so that the air scoops and the ventilators that normally fed fresh air to the troop decks now sluggishly filled the ship with eye and throat-scorching smog. I wrote an undated, unstamped postcard to my mother, obviously enclosed in an envelope for Forces' Mail and mailed at Suez, (even then I must have suspected that postcards mailed in foreign parts are piled in untidy heaps on post office floors before the stamps are steamed off and the cards dumped in garbage sacks for disposal at sea). The card reads: 'At the moment we are anchored in the Great Bitter Lake in the Suez Canal. The last four days in the Red Sea were a foretaste of Hell. I never want to be so hot again, it was terrible. Should be arriving Southampton on Oct. the 2nd. Will 'phone on 3rd.'

This is something of an exaggeration permitted to the young, but sanctioned in the true, 'It ain't 'alf 'ot out 'ere Mum' genre. With hindsight it was hot, but I have been both much hotter and more uncomfortable since. In the Red Sea we spent as little time as possible below deck, except to queue for the ever deteriorating and diminishing supply of beer in the canteen. The canteen stewards still drew off nothing but gallons of warm froth from the barrels and any bottled beer was long since exhausted. This froth settled so slowly and the queues were so long, that in the two hour sessions that the bar was open, you were lucky to be served even once. I remember quite clearly that the beer was a Tennants' brew that was so badly kept and overheated that I have remained prejudiced against the brand ever since.

At night, not many men slept below in the foetid atmosphere of the troop decks. We were allowed to sleep on the open deck, lying on blankets we brought up from our bunks. We dozed, smoked and chatted through the night, watching the brilliant stars with the mast and navigation lights describing lazy figures-of-eight against the blue-black sky. Shortly after dawn the deckhand lascars hosed down the decks and scuppers with blasts of salt water. The hardier souls among us, of which I was not one, stripped off and capered naked in the coolish salt water. We gathered up our traps and went down below. Those of us who were on duty put on uniform and went off to control the queues for breakfast.

As my postcard said, our convoy for the run through the canal assembled in the Great Bitter Lake. Our slow progress through the narrow channels livened up the further north we steamed. The decks became crowded with troops, perhaps relieved to see land, however dull and sandy it might be, after so long at sea. Occasional knots of Egyptians, mostly labouring gangs, watched our passage, some may even have waved. After a while, some of the wags on deck began to shout and jeer in comic slang at the white-nightshirted *fellahin*. The Egyptians responded in kind by shaking their fists, screaming back abuse, lifting up their *jellabas* to display their nether regions and heaving ill-directed clods of soil at the *Dilwara*. As our ship drew level with a group of Egyptian schoolgirls shepherded by several starched and wimpled nuns the ribaldry became more intense and personal.

I noticed that on the upper deck of the *Dilwara* above us, our own female passengers, wives and families, were retreating into the saloons and lounges, as their tender ears became sullied by the repartee. More and more troops appeared on deck, drawn by the increasing uproar. Soon the assembled flower of the British Army began to sing and chant, ever more loudly whenever any Egyptians were seen. What they sang was the time-honoured soldiers' version of the Egyptian national anthem, sung to the tune of *Salaam Malik* (Salute to the King). It goes something like this:-

> *(Verse) King Farouk, King Farouk,*
> *Hang your bollocks on a hook*
> *Staniswiya,* pull your wire,*
> *King Farouk Bardin!'*
> *(Chorus) He's the King of all the Wogs.*
> *He's the King of all the camels*
> *And the horses and the dogs.*
> *He's the King of the plains*
> *where it never f-----g rains.*
> *Sayida,* Queen Farida, Shufti bint,**
> *Kam Fuloose.*'*
> *(Verse) King Farouk, King Farouk,*
> *You're a dirty, rotten crook,*
> *As you walk down the street -*
> *In your fifty shilling suit.*
> *King Farouk Bardin.*
> *(Chorus) He's the King etc.*
> *(Verse) Queen Farida's bright and gay,*
> *'Cos she's in the family way.*
> *Staniswiya, pull your wire!*
> *King Farouk Bardin.*
> *(Chorus) Queen Farida, give us baksheesh,*
> *Queen Farida, give us baksheesh -*

*She's the Queen of all the Wogs,
Of all the jackals and the dogs,
Talla heena, quois ketere, mungaree bardin.**
*(Verse) Queen Farida, Queen Farida,
How the boys would like to ride her,
Talla heena, quois ketere, mungaree bardin.
(Verse) They're all brown bastards
and they dearly love their Queen!
Talla heena, quois ketere etc.**

In any case the Egyptians on the canal banks knew full well that they were being insulted and they responded in kind with volleys of stones and screams of Arabic abuse. The uproar continued into late afternoon. The upper deck passengers had retreated diplomatically out of sight unwilling to be associated with the unruly mob below. Almost all the troops ended up on deck attracted by the racket. The thousand-voice choruses rolled out across the desert with undiminished vigour as the afternoon progressed.

I remember it all as quite satisfying at the time, however dire and reprehensible it seems in retrospect. Any modern theories of political correctness, although they might have been current by then in the more rarefied and select of Hampstead circles, were totally foreign to the milieu in which I found myself. A modern sociologist would perhaps describe the proceedings as a 'male-bonding' ritual. This is an apt description for many of those present had undoubtedly put their lives at risk for their comrades-in-arms in the recent past and were probably still prepared for further 'bonding' should any future need arise.

When the troops started to bring up crates of empty bottles from the canteen below, to hurl at the Egyptians in retaliation for their stone throwing, the authorities attempted to regain control. A few brave NCOs were ordered (probably by the OC Troops) to quieten things down. We RAF sensibly kept our heads down in the throng, hats off, to avoid being involved in any futile attempt to restore order. Events in the end took their natural course and the NCOs withdrew defeated, probably recognising

---

* Notes: Translation of Arabic words, etc.: * *staniswiya* - wait a bit; *sayida* pidgin Arabic for good day; *shufti bint* - look at the girl!; *kam fuloose* - how much?; *bardin* - tomorrow; *talla heena* - come here!; *quois keterre* - very nice; *mungaree bardin* - oh well - we'll eat tomorrow then. (See note 19 - Appendix)

superior force. The supply of empty bottles dwindled, the troops grew hoarse and tired as late afternoon turned to dusk and went below for their supper, well pleased with their efforts.

The morning of the next day was spent at anchor in Port Said fuelling and victualling - sadly without any improvement in the beer supply. There was no question of anyone going ashore. Relations with the Egyptians, both people and government, were strained to breaking point. To be recognisably British away from the military occupied Canal Zone at Ismailia, at the worst risked violence, at the least, insult. (See note 20 - Appendix)

I was on duty that late September morning in Port Said, supposedly policing the main promenade deck, but also watching the *gully-gully* men - entertaining conjurors who were allowed on board along with a few favoured traders selling trinkets and curios. On the water surrounding the *Dilwara* at anchor, were swarms of bum-boats sculling and backing for position, the hawkers shouting their wares and throwing up lines to the passengers above, to haul up their baskets of fruit and souvenirs and to bargain for their contents. They were too trusting - probably more used to the big P&O liners and the Dutch cruise ships en route to the Far East. An RAF sergeant drew my attention to a little bit of theatre being acted out below us. A bum-boat trader was tugging violently on a line that ran tautly to a porthole on E Deck. Heads popping out of scuttles on either side were shouting and jeering at the irate Egyptian boatman.

The sergeant said, 'I bet I know who that lot are. They're in the butcher's shop on fatigues.' Looking at me he said, 'You'd better go below and sort them out.'

This was not the sort of situation I had ever been trained for. Still, orders were orders. At least I was wearing an armband that signified something or other and also one relied on the Army not to recognise RAF rank badges. They almost certainly didn't realise that my SAC badge meant nothing more than a glorified private in their terms. I found them eventually. The door from the companionway was thronged with onlookers encouraging the fatigue party inside who were busy sharing out the contents of the bum-boatman's basket. The line on which they had hauled up their loot was made fast to a stanchion. Even from the doorway I could hear the anguished howls of the Egyptian as he futilely tugged at his rope. As a language, Arabic's guttural consonants and harsh vowels lend themselves readily to what sounded to me like a litany of vitriolic abuse condemning the accursed dogs of unbelievers to a thousand years in the outer darkness, there to be tormented by fearsome *djinns* furnished with an endless supply of red-hot pincers for plucking at their private parts.

The members of the fatigue party I had come across before. They were a rowdy crowd of time-expired Green Howards going home for demob. after a tour jungle-bashing in Malaya. To keep them quiet the *Dilwara's* OC Troops kept them more or less on permanent fatigue duty. Judging from the buckets and mops and swill tubs of 'gash' lying around they were supposed to be scrubbing out and cleaning the ship's butchery. If I say at this point that they were essentially good-hearted lads, who at home in England would cheerfully help old ladies across roads, I would probably be telling the truth. The immediate problem was that they were in Port Said.

Many years later in West Africa I was given a sage piece of advice, for what it was worth, by an Englishman in the colonial police. What he said to me was this, 'If you find yourself faced with an unruly mob who also outnumber you fifty-to-one and you want them to knuckle under, this is what you do. First, identify the smallest and weakest and least offensive looking member of the mob, preferably wearing spectacles. Fix him firmly with your eyes, go in fast and grab him by whatever scruff you can. Give him a loud tongue lashing so that everyone can hear, then throw him to the ground, stamp on his glasses and beat him soundly with your swagger stick in front of the crowd. This has the effect of cowing the mob and then when you turn on them and order them to disperse, they usually do!'

'That's all very fine,' I said, 'but what if they don't?'

'No problem,' answered my policeman friend, 'you simply order your constables to open fire! Over their heads at first - of course.'

Down below on E Deck in Port Said, that useless but interesting piece of advice was still years ahead of me. What I did was this. I managed to elbow my way through the crowd at the door and into the butcher's shop where the soldiers were happily munching their pilfered bananas and pressing gaudy yellow embroidered leather slippers and trinkets on one another.

'Steady on, chaps,' I said, 'play fair. You can't do this. Let the man have his basket. Either give him his stuff back or give him some money!' At the age of twenty I suppose I had a middle class accent and the vestiges of public school speech. In a similar situation today faced with a bunch of Yorkshire squaddies I would probably have been trussed up and shoved head first out of the nearest porthole. It says something for the truly classless nature of the Army in those far away days of conscripts and national service that all that happened was that I was generously offered a stolen banana while a soldier grudgingly untied the bum boat's line and tossed it out of the open porthole. As a basis for further negotiation it surpassed my expectations, but at the same time fell somewhat short of my hopes of a favourable outcome.

Emboldened by this limited degree of success, I argued with the squaddies, trying to persuade them to return the bric-a-brac they had filched or to pay their proper owner something. I shoved my head out of the porthole and spoke soothingly to the irate Egyptian bum boat captain who was now banging on the side of the ship with an oar. He calmed down slightly as I urged him to throw the line back up again.

'Come on lads,' I said, tying the line to the handle of the now completely empty basket, 'give it all back to him.' A forlorn hope considering that the bananas had now been eaten, the last by myself.

One of the soldiers took the empty basket over to the brimming tub of 'gash' and with his mates tipped in a foul mixture of fish heads and discarded banana skins. He took it to the porthole and carefully lowered it down to the bum boat below, then threw the line down after it and with the others resumed their jeering and taunting of the once again screaming and raging boatman.

Back on deck again, I reported, 'I made them give the man back his basket, Sarge.' 'Well done, lad,' he said, 'rather you than me.'

There has always been a widely held and popular myth among the insular folk back in Little England that Tommy was Britain's best ambassador abroad - always kind to children and animals - an even-handed and cheerful dispenser of justice and fair play. People at home thought of the British soldier rather like a sort of global boy scout winning the admiration of the rest of the world, particularly in the Empire. Well, in my experience so they were - sometimes. The trouble lay with the British rank and file, they simply didn't like Egyptians and never had done. Since the days of Arabi Pasha's rebellion in the 1880s Anglo-Egyptian relations had always hovered on a narrow line between the catastrophic and the ridiculous. Equally the Egyptians didn't like the British. The long and unfortunate history of joint British-Egyptian non-co-operation finally reaching its climax in 1956 with Anthony Eden's statesmanlike declaration, 'We are not at war with Egypt. We are in a state of armed conflict.'

Personally I have always found the Egyptians I have known and worked with since, a charming and friendly people, but in late 1952 I was only a national serviceman, still nothing but a small cog, or sprocket, no longer perhaps a 'sprog' airman, but still a very junior servant of the Crown.

Before dusk that day our ship turned sharp left at the end of the mole at Port Said with its huge statue of de Lesseps (long since pulled down by Egypt), his arm outstretched pointing south. We now embarked on our final non-stop stretch to Southampton. By late September the sea-breezes of the Mediterranean were blowing noticeably cooler blasts up the legs of our khaki shorts. Those of us who had been used to the damp tropic heat of south east Asia began to feel distinctly chilly. Goose-pimples now replaced the prickly heat rashes many had recently endured.

As we sailed past the distant shores of Sicily, in my memory a hazy strip, painted a pale lemon-yellow colour along the horizon, the order was finally posted that allowed the RAF to discard our KD's and the soldiers their jungle-greens and to change into the mildewed serge of 'home' uniforms. For several days now I had noticed small groups of soldiers struggling with needle and thread, cross-eyed in the strong sunlight on deck, attempting to sew their medal ribbons onto tunics and battledress blouses. The Korean veterans had the bright blue and yellow bands of their British campaign medal, plus the narrow blue and white stripes of 'MacArthur's Pyjamas,' the United Nations medal. Both quite bright and showy against the khaki serge. The dark purple and green ribbon of the General Service Medal, issued for Malaya, we sadly came to realise was virtually invisible on the breasts of our RAF blues.

The general parsimony of the British government has always been embodied in the way that they reluctantly issue campaign medals. Had we been Americans, or even the French who we saw from time to time on shore leave in Singapore, by now we would have had rows of gaudy plastic-coated ribbons, plus a garnish of stars, oak-leaf and laurel clusters with which to plaster our chests. They would have been awarded for enlisting in the first place, for proficiency, for going overseas, for good conduct, for promotion, for being sick or wounded, for being a fourth class marksman, for regular attendance at the cook house, for being within a week's travelling distance of the least risk of enemy action - our left shoulders would have sagged with the weight of it all.

The British are an entirely different matter. Either they issue an all-purpose medal, like the General Service Medal - well-struck from solid silver - which attracts a separate clasp for each campaign (in theory, with all the clasps issued this century, the ribbon of this single medal would now hang below the waist). Should there be any risk of upsetting a former adversary, then to avoid political embarrassment nothing is awarded. Or sometimes en-masse, a medal will be struck which recognises two or three years of hard campaigning - to be awarded in arrears to the survivors who claim it. Those who outlasted the horrors of the 1914-1918 trenches received two cheap mass-produced medals, derisively named 'Mutt and Jeff' by the soldiers, to mark their sacrifice. After Waterloo in 1815 the British struck an officers only medal - sensibly holding on until 1848 before the final issue of an other ranks version - by which time of course most of the participants were dead. In general if you see a British veteran with a proper row of shiny medals, then salute him. They have been hard won.

Some of us had problems with our home uniforms. Ill fitting in the first instance, since being put aside and replaced with KD they had spent eighteen months on coathangers on the back of the open barrack doors. Exposure to sunshine and the elements had badly faded the RAF blue serge. Great coat, best blues and battledress were all now a pale shade of grey on the front while retaining their original Air Force blue behind. It produced a bizarre effect, combining the appearance of sunshine and shadow. The other problem was that of size. In a year and a half of a healthy diet in a sunny climate, an eighteen year old slip of a lad can easily put on a couple of inches in height and a stone in weight by the time he reaches twenty. There were some odd sights to be seen as we pulled and heaved at too tight waistbands and attempted to fit fourteen inch shirt collars around fifteen inch necks.

The weather changed rapidly. The Straits of Gibraltar were awash with white-capped seas as the cold Atlantic winds struck us. In the Straits there were shore-to-shore dolphins again - even more than we had seen off Ceylon - their breath blowing in steamy spray as the blue waters of the Mediterranean mingled in tumult with the grey Atlantic. The balmy days of lounging on deck were over.

A few days later we made our approaches to Southampton in the cold drizzle of an early autumn day - 2 October 1952. The sea was flat and dull green with seagulls mewing over the wake searching for the last of the 'gash' tossed over the stern from the galleys, the last leavings of our month long voyage. We had packed all our kit overnight in preparation for docking at about 10.00 hours. The troops thronged the decks, mostly in silence but with brief outbursts of cheering and whistling as the *Dilwara's* sirens signalled our arrival.

I don't know if anyone had half expected an official welcome on the dockside. A military band perhaps, some cheering spectators, a mayoral delegation at least. There was nobody, nothing but a greasy dockside with a few longshoremen making fast the hawsers that now bound us to the shore. I think I was disappointed at the time that our homeland that had so lightly and dismissively dispatched us overseas to defend their interest, could in like manner now pay such little attention to our return. After all, it could not have been a military secret that our ship was due. Perhaps it was because it was a week day, I remember thinking.

Someone, somewhere must have opened a dockyard gate, for now a squad of military police marched up the quayside to halt by the gangplank being raised. A collection of uniformed customs officers shambled up, bearing clipboards. A small group of civilians, maybe a half-dozen, ran up, waving and shouting greetings. A pretty young woman held up a small baby to the ship, provoking whistles and cheers and ribald shouts of, 'Ullo Darlin' - where's 'is father then pet?' Or, 'Ow long's 'is dad been overseas luv?' and 'Don't 'e look like me sweetheart?' It would have been out of keeping with the spirit of the returning heroes if someone had not bawled out, 'Ow much for a short time then?' This reduced the crowded decks to tears of howling laughter.

Disembarking was as swift and disciplined as one had come to expect, but cooler and mostly downhill this time - no repetition of the heart-stopping physical tortures of boarding in Singapore. The various drafts were drawn up in extended ranks on the dockside, in open order, kit bags and suitcases in front of us. The customs men, each accompanied by an NCO or an officer and a military policeman then proceeded to extract their dues. They literally decimated us. Every tenth man (fortunately not me) was numbered off and ordered to empty out all his kit on the greasy wet concrete. The customs men then extracted the full amount of duty payable on everything - all the new civilian clothing, gifts, cameras, that they could see. They gave the man a receipt on the spot if he paid, or an official claim for a later deduction against pay. There was now no doubt about it. We were Home.

Armed with rail warrants we were bussed in short order to the station, decanted with all our kit on the platform and packed off via London to the north of England to be demobbed. I remember there were about ten of us - the rest of the RAF contingent from the *Dilwara* were regulars and went off straight on leave. I have often wondered what happened to servicemen who had no homes or familial bosoms to return to. With hindsight I suppose they hied themselves off to the Union Jack Club in London's Waterloo Road or perhaps took up temporary residence in a cheap provincial boarding house, filling in time until they were able to return to their real 'home' in the regimental depot or an airfield, a new barrack room or a ship.

Late that evening we found ourselves at RAF Lytham St. Anne's, near Blackpool. I cannot remember whether or not I telephoned my mother in London, it doesn't matter now, but telephoning in 1952 - particularly 'trunk' calls were not undertaken lightly by the general public when a telegram would arrive by messenger boy on a bicycle a few hours after despatch, or a postcard was guaranteed to be delivered by the first post (of two or perhaps three postal deliveries daily) the following day.

Five days later we were free. My discharge certificate from RAF Lytham is dated 7 October but my final release from the RAF was not until 31 October, taking in our backlog of leave.

There were no demob suits by 1952. We could either travel home in what was left of our uniforms (still required for the three and a half years for which we were liable for part-time service with the RAF Reserve) or we could wear our new 'civvies' bought in Singapore. Most of our kit was handed in, leaving us with barely enough to fill a kit bag. Some of the tropical KD we were allowed to keep. We were told we could use it for seaside holidays! Mine later came in very handy in West Africa. We wondered what the authorities would do with all our worn out gear and faded khakis, bush shirts and underwear. It was certain that a stingy government would somehow make a vestige of a profit somewhere. The mean-spirited, small mindedness epitomised by the customs men at Southampton was the rule in post-war Britain in that long ago October.

The final pay parade at Lytham enabled me to clear the balance of my shipboard gambling debts leaving me virtually penniless. The last residue was spent on our final evening in the RAF, in Blackpool - the one and only time I have visited that legendary haunt of pleasure. We smoked the last of our duty frees, drank the weak English beer that resembled thin gravy browning which was a poor substitute for the Tiger lager that we had come to appreciate. We looked glumly at the famous lights swaying in an early autumn gale along the Blackpool Mile as we shivered in the piercing wind and drizzle. The town was almost deserted. There were no girls to be impressed with our bizarre two-toned faded uniforms and medal ribbons. We found a warm and cheerful bar run by an ex-RAF warrant officer who yarned with us and joined in some of our increasingly maudlin songs until closing time.

I remember it as being somewhat of a sad occasion. None of us would have wanted to do it all over again but I think we recognised that we had achieved something in personal terms. In later years I was able to understand why some national servicemen signed on and stayed in the services as regulars. Not a few young men without their own strong family ties discovered a replacement family in the Army or the Air Force, and the impersonal world outside became increasingly unfamiliar and even hostile. The classic case in fiction is Brigg, the conscript anti-hero created by Leslie Thomas in *The Virgin Soldiers*. At the time we thought they were crazy and would live to regret it.

As for us, from tomorrow we would be on our own, the surrogate family we had bonded to for the past two years was visibly disintegrating around us. That moment prophesied in the final verse of the Far Flung Airman's Credo was now near, 'And in the Fullness of Time it shall come to pass that thou art required to depart for the land that is known as Blighty and there thou shalt be arrayed in strange garments and from henceforth be known as a civilian, and thou shalt walk among strangers for the rest of thy natural days.'

The transient friends and oppos would soon all be gone along with the shared discomforts as well as the pleasures and the comradeship and,dare I say it, a degree of pride. The small certainties of everyday service life that had shielded us from the need to think of tomorrow would all be exchanged for the unpredictable new lives that now lay ahead of us. The survival kit of mutual help that had supported us for so long, of what the Australians, rightly I suppose, now call 'mateship,' was about to vanish into the past. We checked in at the guard room at Lytham and were back in our billets by 22.30 hours - tomorrow at the same time it would be half-past ten in the evening.

Once it was over I never had any regrets or doubts about national service. It filled in that awkward gap for young people between the ages of eighteen and twenty, particularly at a time when a university education was only for the minority when the Schools Certificate was usually sufficient qualification to ensure entry to most occupations. For the majority of conscripts I still think that national service was a valuable and eye-opening process. It was certainly democratic. At the time it probably quite often didn't seem so good. Many conscripts longed for their 'demob' date - ticking each day off their calendar charts on the back of their locker doors, '150 days and an early breakfast to go.' If overseas, the final day was marked with a crude drawing of a ship or a plane. If they had been confined to the shores of the UK, it was still valuable, many young men at that time had never travelled beyond the confines of their home town or far less their country. It made people physically and mentally harder and fitter, more independent. My own period of service was varied with opportunities to travel and see parts of the world that only the wealthiest of citizens would otherwise have been able to visit.

I wasn't the same person that enlisted in 1950 when I came out of the RAF two years later in 1952. I met and made friends with people who in the normal course of events would never have crossed my path. I was lucky. There were a small number who were wounded and killed either by accident or enemy action, or young soldiers taken and kept prisoner in Korea and China for years during (and after) their service. I was never in any great danger, or like some, came to any harm, but there had been those tingles of excitement that to a young man certain in the knowledge that he was going to live for ever, make life worth living.

Apart from Steve with whom I had shared much of my service, I never saw any of them again. Steve rejoined the civil service and came to work in London. We corresponded for a while and met up one evening for a drink in a pub in Kensington Church Street. We chatted about this and that, about jobs and new exams to pass, about girl friends, reminiscing about Malaya. But that was it. The common bonds of adversity, of being oppos, of being thrown in the deep end to sink or swim, were loosed. We said we would meet up again, but we never did. We had new threads to pick up, new lives to make for ourselves.

From time to time old photographs from the 1950s come to the surface and bring that long gone time of national service vividly back to life for me. They are perhaps pictures of a small group of young erks ready for 'jankers' parade at Seletar, smart as new paint, brasses bright on their scrubbed webbing, crisp, starched KD with knife-edge creases, broad grins on all their faces. Or a faded newspaper picture of a bunch of bone-weary but still smiling young infantrymen clinging to a Bren carrier coming out of the line in Korea, risking their lives for four shillings a day. Or three bare chested riflemen of no more than nineteen or twenty in Egypt cheerfully digging a slit trench on the banks of the Sweet Water Canal (a misnomer if ever there was one!) I knew them all once and what made them tick. Any young man of that time would have recognised them. They were our mates, with whom we served and marched together. We laughed and sang as if there were no tomorrow, we drank together, some fought together (or each other if the spirit moved them), a few died.

As the years have passed I think I have come to understand the motivation of the young post World War II servicemen. Particularly those who served overseas and the few who ended up in action, some suffering great hardship and fighting their battles with bravery and courage. It was not for love of King and Country or some far-fetched concept of the Empire which rightly had inspired so many in the war against Hitler and the Japanese. It was not for love of or fear for their own families or homeland who were no longer under threat. It was not some glorious notion of a righteous and noble cause proposed by their political leaders, or even the orders of some distant general. You can be sure that the young soldiers of the Ulster Rifles, the Duke of Wellingtons or the Gloucesters in Korea were not fighting for some inspired vision of the United Nations. Neither were the national servicemen of the old county regiments in Malaya, Kenya or Egypt driven by such notions. They fought for each other and because, not by their own choice, that was simply where they had landed up. They fought not for an ideal but mainly for their mates and oppos, sometimes even perhaps for a ship, or a regiment or their squadron, and they fought not to die, but in support of and for each other. I salute them and remember them with love and affection. Romantic tosh? I don't think so.

And I wonder what the Hell became of us all in the last fifty years? We didn't screw it up, but somebody surely has!

Above, 'Jankers' parade at Seletar, 1951. Below, coming out of the line, Korea, 1952.

None the Wiser

Suez, 1956 — a milestone in the Middle East: 'The overwhelming reason for failure was the active opposition of the United States'

POSTSCRIPT

I hope you have enjoyed reading *None The Wiser*. The second part of this personal memoir of the mid-20th century entitled *Still None The Wiser* is principally concerned with the colonial and post-colonial era in West Africa where the author spent thirteen years between 1952 and 1967. This is due to be published by Hayloft Publishing Ltd. in the near future.

Here is a short extract from *Still None The Wiser*.

THE CROCODILE

It is shaped, sir, like itself, and it is as broad
as it has breadth; it is just as high as it is,
and moves with its own organs:
it lives by that which nourisheth it;
and the elements once out of it, it transmigrates.
From *Antony and Cleopatra*, William Shakespeare

'Everything around me is pitch black except for a few stars among thickening clouds in a moonless African night. The only other light comes from a dim electric head-torch constricting my brow, strapped round my head above my ears. As I turn my head the furthest feeble rays of the torch illuminate a circle of twinkling ruby-red, fiery sparks on the surface of the water in which I find myself standing waist-deep. Some of these menacing sparks are set in pairs, slowly moving closer, some appear single - unwinking and unmoving. From somewhere close by in the darkness there erupts the blood-curdling, high pitched scream of a tree hyrax, which as it reaches its bubbling crescendo is suddenly cut short, as if a dagger had been plunged into its heart. The gun I am clutching to my chest in a vice like grip suddenly seems heavy and useless. The high pitched whine of mosquitoes sings in my ears - mingling with the cacophonic chirruping, croaking, whistling and groaning cries of a multitude of frogs. Am I truly mad? Was this some sort of waking nightmare I was trapped in forever?

'Psst!' hisses my companion, virtually invisible a few yards away except for his own dim head-torch - only his torso above the dark water. 'There's a big one over there to the right. Must be nearly an eight-footer at least! Look at the space between his eyes - Wow!'

'Psst' indeed! I thought to myself. I should be so lucky! It would help make more sense of the ludicrous - and perhaps dangerous situation in which I now found myself.'

Appendix

Note 1 - The trenches of the Great War wiped out vast numbers of the young, educated middle classes who furnished the infantry subalterns necessary to feed the bloody butcher's maw that ground them into so much mincemeat. So in World War Two, Bomber Command took the young airmen of Britain and the Empire to cast them into the empty winds of Eternity, dying in their thousands in a sudden blaze of fire sparkling briefly in the night skies over Europe or entombed in the dark, swirling waters of the North Sea and the English Channel. Some fifty-five thousand young men of Britain and the Empire died in this cruel and useless way, thirty thousand of whom have no known grave, simply disappearing into the cosmos. Their brave sacrifice is matched only by the endurance of the citizens of the cities they destroyed - or perhaps by the U-boat service who comprised the pick of the German Navy, of whose forty thousand submariners less than ten thousand survived the war and of these fewer than half were taken prisoner. I wonder, if given the choice, how many of the latter would have preferred sudden death in the fiery skies to slow suffocation in the cold darkness of an iron coffin (with all the handles on the inside - as a U-boat was once so aptly described) submerged in the ocean depths? Including the Americans and the combatants of both sides some two hundred thousand air crew died in the European conflict. It is hard not to believe that the world now would have been a better place without the wasted lives of the bravest and the fittest.

Note 2 - The recruiting of young officers in time of war (until 1939-45 and after) always tended to take those with a grammar or public school education, as in general they were the principal schools that offered a secondary education beyond the Three Rs. The fact that the public schools were fee paying was incidental. Since 1908, at Lord Roberts' instigation, these (mainly) boarding schools had amalgamated their various volunteer and militia units into the Officers' Training Corps, (later the Junior Training Corps, then the Army Cadet Force and the Air Training Corps, later still the CCF, the Combined Cadet Force). These units were originally formed with the aim of keeping the largest number of boys amused and getting them tired out (and thus perhaps forestalling an unhealthy interest in sex) with the least possible effort by the teaching staff. For the same reasons rugby football was often played in these schools as needing more boys to a team than soccer. The old calumny that soccer was a game for gentlemen played by hooligans and rugger a game for hooligans played by gentlemen is long since outdated - both so-called 'sports' have their fair share of thuggery today.

Since 1905 a common syllabus had been worked out and a subsidy paid by the War Office, an examination was set - War Certificate 'A'. In the First War the rule became that as of right, a holder of Certificate 'A' would be entitled to a commission provided he had a good report from his school and could find an officer of the rank of colonel or above to countersign his application.

From 1914 onwards the young gentlemen who flocked to claim their commissions may have been still wet behind the ears but, and it is a very big but, they knew how to wind on their puttees, how to march and drill. They could site and pitch a camp, they knew how to use their basic infantry weapons - and how to give and to receive orders. In this respect they were several steps ahead of their fellow recruits on enlistment.

This is an effective way of officering an army in a hurry. In the Great War possession of the Schools Certificate plus Cert. 'A' amounted almost to a death warrant for the young school leaver of military age. It is also a very effective way of killing off an entire generation of young men with a secondary education. The Germans did the same in one fell swoop by mobilising several divisions of senior secondary schoolboys, throwing them into what became known as 'The Slaughter of the Innocents' - 'Kindermord' - at Ypres in October 1914. The Roll of Honour at Epsom College for the First War lists 153 names. This pales almost into insignificance beside Charterhouse, whose 'Old Carthusians' Roll of Honour lists 686 names. Strangely, 151 former Epsom pupils also died in the 1939-45 conflict. Given the differing styles of warfare one might have expected many fewer than in the previous conflict but for the fact that many of them would not have been simple infantry subalterns but serving medical officers for whom the risks remained unchanged. The so-called Pals' Regiments raised in the early days of 1914 and 1915 also destroyed at a stroke large numbers of young men drawn from particular localities in the country.

Note 3 - *Health & Efficiency* - this historic treasure, a nudist magazine founded in the thirties introduced whole generations of prurient and curious schoolboys to 'artistic' images of bare flesh long before the days of page three and television nudity. It flourished in a more innocent age when carefully posed photos of fleshy matrons cavorting in a state of nature (painstakingly airbrushed) on English lawns were the ultimate in titillation. *Health & Efficiency* was all about what you could get away with. It sadly folded at the end of 1996, driven out of business by no-holds-barred nudity and porn magazines. The final straw for this dotty, naturist philosophising publication was alleged paedophilia projected by photographs of naked children frolicking in similarly naked family groups. *Sic transit gloria mundi.*

Note 4 - These Iraqi Levies were I believe mostly of Kurdish origin with a leavening of Assyrian Arabs and Christians, all with a long history of persecution by the Iraqi government. They were left badly in the lurch by the British who finally abandoned the Iraqi bases after the July 1958 Revolution, during the course of which both the pro-British Prime Minister Nuri Pasha and the young King Feisal - a cousin of Jordan's King Hussein - were assassinated, after their murder being dragged by the mob through the streets by their heels. The Kurds and the Christian minorities, not to mention the dissident Marsh Arabs of the south have since suffered badly under succeeding Iraqi regimes up to Saddam Hussein.

In 1941 RAF Habbaniyah had been an important bastion against the expected advance of the Axis powers through the Caucasus from the north. The pro-German Iraqi army under Rashid Ali attacked and laid siege to the base for three weeks during May of that year. The base was defended by a force of 1,000 RAF airmen aided by some 1,200 Iraqi Levies whose armoured car squadrons together with the RAF planes had maintained law and order in Mesopotamia between the wars. In 1941 the base was also a flying training school (No. 4) who with their twin-engined Oxford trainers, Hawker Audax biplane light bombers and a few other museum pieces crewed with instructors and trainees, dive-bombed and harried their besiegers with gusto. Eight Wellington bombers from Shaibah and Basra flew up from the Gulf to bomb the rebels. To add to the strength there were also 350 infantry of the Kings Own Royal Regiment who oiled and cleaned up two ancient howitzers left over from 1918 to add to their mortars and machine guns, assisting the fliers and the eighteen armoured cars of the RAF Levies. The siege was finally lifted and Rashid Ali seen off for good by a small mobile force under General George Clark who together with Glubb Pasha's Arab Legion swiftly crossed the 500 miles of desert from Palestine, with the added assistance of a few supporting Blenheims hastily withdrawn from Greece.

Note 5 - At the end of the European war in May 1945 there were 938,000 men serving in the Royal Air Force, many of them highly skilled technicians and mechanics - vital for the huge fleets of aircraft that had been needed to win the war. Some 122,000 airmen alone were in the Far East (this latter figure much greater than the whole strength of today's RAF). Within a few months of the Japanese defeat in August of that year most were clamouring for demobilisation and a return to the UK and Civvy Street. The delays in repatriation led to popular and widespread near-mutiny with a series of effective strikes by servicemen of both the Army and the RAF, in Egypt and the Far East. By 1947 when the government at last woke up and realised there were still little wars to be fought, the remains of the Empire to be policed and Europe to be garrisoned, all the British forces had been run down and effectively de-skilled. The Atlee government was forced to re-introduce national service to make up the shortfall in men.

In the case of the RAF it was almost too late. Post-war demobilisation had bled away enormous numbers of skilled men. It took years of training to provide the fitters and mechanics needed to keep the aircraft flying. Even air crew could be trained more quickly than a highly qualified engine fitter!

By 1948 out of every ten men serving in the RAF on VE Day nine had already left. Of those who chose to stay many were downgraded in rank, status and self-esteem. Former sergeant pilots with DFMs drove ration trucks or clerked in the stores. Many of the specialist tradesmen as well as air crew such as senior NCO Flight Engineers, AG/WOPs (Air Gunner/Wireless Operators) remustered as MT drivers or to admin/stores, provost and catering, frequently with reductions in rank and pay, simply to retain a place in the regular RAF. Many of course left. Typically, in the RAF, the recruiting figures and the rate at which men were extending their engagements fell to an unacceptable low. I can remember drivers and storemen in 1950, who were still corporals with their faded air crew wings with rows of wartime ribbons on their tunics. Matters were just as bad in the Army and the Navy. From 1947 on national service began to provide the men in the numbers needed, particularly when the period of conscription was extended to two years, but they were not highly skilled. The military needs of Korea and Malaya then started a revival in quality, equipment and morale but by 1951 this was still barely noticeable.

By April 1952 about three percent of the Navy, fifty-one percent of the Army and some thirty-three percent of the RAF were conscripts. But, with the exception of the army whose basic need was simply for quickly trained infantry, skilled conscripts and the time to train them were in short supply. In the Far East the numbers of RAF national servicemen were proportionately far fewer than at home. I was lucky (some might have said not) to find myself in such a posting. In the Army the situation was totally different and at times during the Malayan Emergency up to seventy-five per cent of the soldiers jungle bashing up at the sharp end were national servicemen, many of them having a very hard time of it.

In 1952 the RAF still operated about 6,400 aircraft, reaching a post-war peak but many of these were old propeller-driven war-time aircraft, obsolete in modern terms. Spares and servicing were maintained with difficulty to the high standards required. Those in high office charged with determining the way ahead now saw the future in terms of strategic missiles - the 'mis-guided' missile scheme that would be delivered by the brand-new 'V' bombers. It was likely that the serious shortfall in skills needed to keep the planes flying influenced their thinking. The long term results of these policies meant that by 1973 the RAF probably had fewer than 600 operational aircraft. In the late 1990s the RAF had to hire helicopters from civilian contractors for the Queen's Flight and for rescue work in the English Channel aircraft are at times called in from the Belgian Air Force. Maintenance and servicing is handed over to civilian operators - presumably working office hours and unable or unwilling to work away from home. As far as the Royal Navy is concerned the United States Navy now has more commissioned deck officers alone than the UK has sailors in its entire fleet.

Note 6 - By 1960 the old pay parades were made obsolete and the serviceman's monthly salary was then paid into a bank account. By then guard duties, fire pickets, the much-hated kit inspections and routine parades were all also either eliminated or much reduced. Kit bags were replaced with holdalls and the birds-nest tangle of blancoed webbing and straps little-changed since the 1920s was thrown out. The green waterproof gas-cape groundsheets were replaced by smart raglan raincoats. The 'best blue' uniforms were no longer made from rough, uncomfortable serge but from smooth barathea. Brass buttons and badges became anodised - button sticks were thrown away. The faded KD shorts and bush jackets with their bright red shoulder flashes that I wore were also withdrawn and replaced with SCP - stone coloured polyester. The 'old' RAF that I knew has long since vanished in the same way the Empire had dissolved before our eyes.

Note 7 - Seletar had been chosen in 1921 as the site of the first permanent airbase in Singapore in tandem with the nearby naval dock yards but it was not until 1929 that the Far East Flight of flying boats became the first permanent RAF unit in Singapore. In 1927 four Supermarine Southampton flying boats had taken off from Cattewater near Plymouth. Flying in formation with a cruising speed of 83 mph it was four long months before they finally landed in the Johore Straits off Seletar - this was the proving flight.

Seletar airfield itself took five years to complete - clearing the jungle, draining the swamps, oiling the surface water to control the malarial mosquitoes and removing the vast amounts of spoil that were created in building the one thousand yard runway. Seletar's main runway was left with a very noticeable hump in the middle. From either end the other extremity is concealed by this hump - and in 1951 much of the strip had been covered with the all-weather PSP (pierced steel planking) laid over coconut fibre matting that frequently caught fire when the first jet-powered Meteors and Vampires were starting to use the strip for training purposes. The magnificent officers' mess building and station sick quarters - as well as the immensely luxurious bungalow for the CO, all built on concrete piles - overlooked the open parkland and golf course leading on to the runway.

Note 8 - Seletar's Base main HQ building was probably built in 1933 for the overall RAF Far East command when the second Singapore RAF airfield was created at Sembawang to supplement the flying boats and torpedo bombers at Seletar with fighter bomber and spotter flights. By 1937 however the RAF command had come to realise there might be a danger from land attack (how right they were!) from the mainland across the Straits and moved their HQ into the city to be nearer their other service colleagues.

In 1940 Seletar had become the principal maintenance support unit for the Far East including the Fleet Air Arm. There were also four squadrons operating ageing Short Singapore flying boats. As well as a few modern Sunderlands, there were slow and lumbering Vickers Wildebeest biplanes plus a few naval Swordfish and Walrus amphibians. Not an impressive line-up to face the Japanese onslaught in December 1941.

On 7 December 1941 when the Japanese attacked there were only 181 serviceable aircraft in the whole of the Malayan theatre. The RAF's ineffective fighter force relied on seventy-nine American Lend-Lease Brewster Buffaloes (it was said of the Buffalo that a successful flight was one in which both aircraft and pilot managed to land undamaged in any way). They were easy meat for the Japanese Zero. The ineffective RAF radar stations gave at best only thirty minutes warning of Japanese raiders and it took the Buffalo at least twenty-five minutes to climb to the bombers' attacking height.

Within two short months of the Jap invasion the mainland had fallen and Singapore was on the point of collapse. Seletar's airfield had first been bombed on 8 December and was then under constant air attack, coming under direct shellfire from across the Straits by 5 February 1942. The few Lease Lend Catalina flying boats that were still operational were machine-gunned and sunk at their moorings. The RAF had been destroyed in the air and on the ground, ceasing to be an effective fighting force. The remaining airmen were ordered to make their way to Java and Sumatra to continue the fight from there with the handful of newly-arrived Hurricanes (worn out ex-Battle of Britain Mark 1s) and the few other aircraft that had already left. Most of them made it out via the chaos of the Singapore docks only to be captured later. Sadly many of these airmen were to die in the last ditch defence, together with the Army and the Dutch forces, of the airfields near Batavia.

The RAF marine launches from Seletar evacuated many senior officers of the various services at the last minute, attempting to thread their way past the islands and channels across the Sumba strait to Java. Some personnel got through, many others were stranded, drowned, died of starvation or were eventually captured.

From the end of February 1942 the Japanese had occupied Seletar. On 5 September 1945 (the final Jap surrender was not until 2 September although the British had earlier ceased hostilities in mid-August) the first RAF Spitfires and Mosquitoes landed on the airstrip, flying down from Burma via the north of Malaya. Within a few weeks the base was being employed as an assembly point for evacuating surviving Allied POWs to Ceylon by Sunderland flying boat. There are descriptions of the pitiable near skeletons lying on stretchers, many of whom who had barely survived the years of starvation and brutal captivity, awaiting embarkation.

This is only a part of Seletar's history and it is I think a telling indictment of the way in which the RAF of the time neglected to make this a matter of record - and of pride, for the many thousands of airmen who served there over the years. We who served there in the immediate post-war years knew almost nothing of this - it is all information gleaned in later years. Unlike the Army, whose regimental histories of battles fought, won and lost are a valuable tool in instilling pride and morale, the RAF's squadron system sadly failed to encourage any sense of historical continuity among the rank and file.

Note 9 - The Rhodesian SAS (Selous Scouts) had arrived in Malaya to become 'C' Squadron of the Malayan Scouts in March 1951 - just in time to salvage the much-tarnished image of the re-constituted post-war SAS under Brigadier Mike Calvert. 'A' Squadron had been an ill-disciplined bunch of trouble-makers, many 'recommended' by their units (simply to get rid of them) and included a group of French Foreign Legion deserters who had jumped ship enroute to Indo-China. 'B' Squadron however had later improved their image, being made up of volunteers from the old wartime SAS and from the TA intended for Korea, but in the end only forty went to Malaya. In Malaya the SAS spent most of their operational time in deep jungle, setting up air-supplied strongpoints and undertaking 'hearts and minds' activities with the Sakai aboriginals, thus denying the Communists the latter's support. There were virtually no helicopters then, and the SAS troopers often parachuted into thick jungle. This was difficult and dangerous with incidents such as our Rhodesian friend at Tanjong Bungah who had landed in the top of a massive dipterocarp whose lower branches terminated some eighty feet from the ground whereas he was carrying only fifty feet of rope.

Note 10 - On 3 March 1952, the 'up' passenger train from Singapore to Kuala Lumpur was derailed and a bridge blown up near Rompin, north of Gemas, an unexploded aerial bomb being used by the CTs as a demolition charge. The armed escort of soldiers and police suffered no casualties and fought off the subsequent attack (from underneath the train) but many passengers were killed and wounded during the bandits' assault. This was a typical and frequently recurring incident and something similar would have been the cause of our own delay in July.

Note 11 - The Douglas C-47 Skytrain known in the RAF as the DC3 Dakota. A 21/28 seater with twin Pratt and Whitney Double Wasp radial engines, a maximum speed of 227 mph and a range of 1600 miles at 7,500 feet. General Eisenhower said, 'The four major instruments of victory in World War Two were the DC3, the 'bazooka,' the Jeep and the atom bomb.' (Naturally he ignored any non-American inventions). More than 11,000 DC3s were built between 1935 and the end of the war when production ceased. Carrying up to three-and-a-half tons of cargo, with a landing speed of a mere 65 knots and fabulously reliable - hundreds are still flying world-wide fifty years on. Like the *cheong-sam* there has never been anything to adequately replace these two classics of twentieth century design.

Note 12 - 'Tug' Wilson's diffident manner and unassuming appearance I was to discover many years later belied both a distinguished past and future career. In May 1941 he had been in Crete, a corporal wireless operator with 33 Squadron during the critical defence of Maleme airfield where the German invasion 'Operation Mercury' spearheaded by parachute and airborne landings had fallen most heavily. He had played a vital part in repairing and cannibalising wrecks to keep the few remaining British aircraft flying. Later he fought on the ground against the 2,000 German paratroops who made four drops on the area in successive waves. It was estimated that two-thirds of the first drop died in the first minutes of battle. The bloody nose given to the Germans by the defenders meant that the German High Command never again employed parachute troops in any major assault role. The remaining RAF airmen, now without planes to service or fly, lightly armed with rifles and a few Lewis guns plus two Vickers 'K' aircraft guns on makeshift mountings took to their slit trenches and joined the British AA gunners and ANZAC soldiers in beating off the continuing air and ground attacks. The airfield's defence was dominated by a New Zealand brigade who held a vital ridge to the south. For some unexplained reason the NZ commander withdrew most of his force during the following night, (the reason why still remains a mystery today) leaving the airfield to be defended only by a handful of airmen and a few soldiers, 'Tug' Wilson being one of their number. Without the vital support of the troops on the ridge, the battle for the airfield was lost and with it the battle for Crete. Within a few hours German aircraft and troops were landing and the remaining handful of RAF survivors were forced to withdraw. Veterans later suggested that if a medal was ever issued for this catastrophic campaign, it should bear the legend 'Ex-Creta'.

Churchill angrily accused the RAF of lacking the will to fight on the ground in defence of their airfield and of being 'mere uniformed civilians in the prime of life protected by detachments of soldiers.' This was both unfair and patently untrue. Two airmen won Military Medals (MMs) during the battle and there were many acts of heroism before they withdrew. Tug Wilson escaped, leading a small group of men across the mountains before being evacuated to Egypt by the Royal Navy. The disastrous battle and defence of Maleme led directly to the founding of the RAF Regiment who were responsible for ground defences, vital in the case of forward airfields as was later proved in the desert, in Burma and in Europe when the army had other priorities.

Tug Wilson was later commissioned and served at RAF Negombo in Ceylon as Signals Officer. After the war he was sent to command the Radio Repair Squadron at Seletar, later being loaned to the Royal Malaysian Air Force as OC Electronics. Returning to Britain he then became Senior Trade Test Officer in Air Electronics at RAF Cosford. Back to Malaysia again after Independence in 1960 as OC Joint RAF/RMAF Communications and finally back to Cosford as OC Aircraft Servicing Training where he was mainly responsible for founding the Aerospace Museum. He retired from the RAF in 1971, becoming bursar to two schools and retaining a close involvement with the Air Training Corps.

Note 13 - It would not be right to end this account of Seletar without mentioning the mainspring of its existence, the aircraft that made its history. The keynote aircraft of Seletar had always been the flying boat and by my time it was the Short Sunderlands of 209 and 205 Squadrons comprising the Far East Flying Boat Wing. The graceful shapes of 'The Kipper Fleet' lay at anchor out in the Johore Straits beyond the airstrip. Although no more Sunderlands were built after 1945, once the United States took back their Catalina flying boats at the end of the war in late 1945, the Sunderlands carried on for another fourteen years, cannibalised and cobbled together until the last operational flight was made from Seletar in 1959, shortly before the twelve year Emergency ended and Independence arrived in 1960. They were used for maritime patrolling, flying out from their base at Iwakuni in Japan during the Korean War. They were engaged in anti-piracy patrols in the South China Sea and in the Malacca Straits - and not least in an operational role in 'Operation FIREDOG' sorties over mainland Malaya where 209 Squadron harried the bandits' deep jungle hideouts, often carrying a full load of up to 340 twenty-five pound bombs. Airmen were detailed for these flights almost as for fatigues. Strictly speaking the bombs were supposed to be unpacked from their crates while airborne, the underwing racks cranked laboriously inboard by hand, the bombs then attached and the carriers wound out again and released over their elusive targets. The erks found this to be heavy labour and soon devised a better system whereby a chain of airmen lined up inside the Sunderland, passed the bombs one to the other and simply chucked them overboard, sometimes without bothering to first remove the twenty-five pounders from the boxes, until a horrified armaments officer found out and put a stop to the practice. Nevertheless this peculiar method of bombing an area of jungle was considered much more effective than the heavy Lincoln bombers used by the RAAF. The flying boat sorties usually concluded with several low runs over the area letting fly with the aircraft's considerable armament of .303 and .50 calibre machine guns.

There was also the station flight with its ancient Avro Anson. I think the PR Flight of 81 Squadron had another, and a few twin-jet Meteors and Vampires for pilots on conversion courses. The fiery jet exhausts frequently caused the coconut matting under the steel planks of the runway to catch fire. There was a target-towing flight with the last Bristol Beaufighters (an ignoble end for the famous 'Whispering Death' of WW2) still in service - until the last ever RAF Beaufighter sortie was made from Seletar in May 1960. There were the Photographic Reconnaissance Spitfire 19s (the last operational Spitfire flight was from Seletar on 1 April 1954) and 'Little Wooden Wonder' Mosquitoes of 81 Squadron who daily mapped the jungles from 17,000 feet. The crackling roar of their Rolls-Royce Griffon and Merlin engines being run-up outside the PR Section on the West Camp is one of my lasting memories of Seletar. The last RAF operational Mosquito sortie was a PR flight from Seletar in 1956. 390 MU itself ran at least a couple of Dakotas for its servicing parties.

Aircraft from all over Malaya were always flying in for maintenance - De Havilland single-seater twin-engined Hornet fighters (made of plywood like the bigger Mosquito), Bristol Brigands, another fighter-bomber and Army co-operation Austers. Solitary aircraft would come in from time to time and make belly-landings - Seletar was the emergency airfield for the whole area - as often as not because the undercarriage had stuck. Once a flying boat made an emergency landing on the grass verges of the runway, its hull badly holed from a collision with a submerged tree trunk while taking off from the Johore Straits, grinding away its graceful boat-shaped hull as it slithered to a stop in a slather of foam from the fire tenders racing alongside. Another day I watched a lumbering 'Shagbat' trundle in, rolling to a gentle halt on the upward slope of the airfield - a 'Walrus'* biplane amphibian - it must have come from the naval base further down the Straits, and was probably one of the last in service. (*Note: During WW2 a 'Walrus' - a single-engined 'pusher' biplane amphibian used for naval spotting and Air Sea Rescue was reputedly credited on one occasion with three 'victories' without firing a shot. When attacked by three Me 109s, the pilot dropped to just above the waves, jinking and swerving at top speed - about 90 knots - at sea level one Me 109 dived into the water, unable to pull out in time, the other two Me 109s collided and crashed in flames while manoeuvring to attack the unarmed sitting-duck 'Shagbat.')

Scattered between the hangars in the East Camp were large numbers of cocooned and mothballed aircraft, mainly the RAF's last single-seater piston-engined fighters - the immensely powerful Hawker Tempests. There were De Havilland Mosquitoes, deliberately exposed in the open to the damp and muggy tropical climate, testing to their unsustainable limits the now fungus-ridden glues that held their laminated plywood wings and fuselages together. Most of the Tempests were eventually serviced and restored to flying condition - sold to the Pakistan Air Force - whose pilots turned up one day in an ungainly Bristol

Freighter, departing a few hours later in their unfamiliar single-seater Tempests. As we watched them take off one-by-one, each Tempest in turn being forced off the runway onto the grass strip before becoming airborne - from the immensely powerful torque of the huge radial engine. One Tempest faltered in flight at about two hundred feet, out above the water beyond the end of the runway when its engine failed. In the distance we saw the pilot as he baled out, plummeting down into the water, his unopened parachute trailing uselessly behind him. The pilot hit the water and was dead before his aircraft plunged into the murky Straits a half mile further on.

Note 14 - 'Language' as epitomised in LAC's Kydd and Gilhooly's response to my volunteering for escort duty - I use the 'F' word here and elsewhere - but solely in context. It was part of the common currency of everyday discourse between those of equal rank or status and seldom signified anything except minor stress or emphasis. It was not much used, in my experience, in exchanges between higher and lower ranks - excluding corporals and below. Most senior NCOs and officers generally managed to avoid it. It was far from being the only expletive, just the most common. Witty and vulgar swearing of the most (to me at any rate) startling coarseness was often at the same time both inventive and subtle, highly amusing and much appreciated by the less imaginative. These speech patterns were frequently enshrined in many memorable service songs and dramatic recitations. Nothing but modesty and chronic forgetfulness prevents me from repeating in these pages some of the more outrageous and original expressions.

Note 15 - Food, synonyms for:- bully beef - incidentally much better than the homogenised mush that passes for corned beef in modern times, was often known as 'jungle chicken.' It was much more popular than its reputation suggests. In those times past it contained palpable morsels of tasty fibrous meat and lent itself readily to stews and curries. Indian troops and Gurkhas, being Hindu, of course would not eat it. In the tropics its main disadvantage was that although still perfectly wholesome the fat liquefied in the heat and it had to be either spooned or poured from the tin. Opening a bully beef tin with an issue jack knife (blade, marlin spike, primitive tin-opener) was a hazardous task often resulting in emergency first aid procedures.

Beans - baked beans of course, often of inferior brands for service issue, known as 'desert strawberries.' Quite acceptable eaten cold with a spoon straight from the tin particularly if accompanied by tinned sausages.

Bread - familiarly known to servicemen in the Far East as *roti* - pronounced 'rooty' (as in 'rooty tooty'). *Roti* is the Malay word for bread. There is, or was, in Malaya and Singapore a tasty snack sold by street hawkers, called 'Roti John'

- which is a sort of deep fried bread sandwich with various fillings, which was believed originally of European or perhaps Glaswegian origin.

Note 16 - Effing Nora! - Nora's name with its customary prefix has been customarily invoked by British servicemen at moments of stress throughout much of the last century, particularly when expressing surprise or mild outrage. I have heard it suggested that the 'Blessed Nora' was a minor Christian saint from late Roman times who devoted her good works to the alleviation of lesser ailments, such as blains, warts and other discomforts suffered by the commoner sort of Roman soldiery, brought about perhaps by the anxieties and pressures of active service. Nora was allegedly martyred when she expired after having been subjected to a bout of prolonged and unrestrained effing and blinding by a group of North British auxiliary Legionnaires who had been called to Rome to march in a triumphal victory parade of the Emperor Diocletian (AD 284-305).

Note 17 - Blobbers' Club - One of the lesser known facts of the medical history of the post-war Royal Air Force is that in the entire field of its world-wide operations, RAF Butterworth in the 1950s allegedly had the highest VD rate of any unit serving at home or abroad. The reason for this was very simple. Butterworth was only a short ferry ride across the water to Georgetown, Penang. Being a seaport - but not necessarily a very busy one like Singapore or Hong Kong - Georgetown had quite a large number of part-time prostitutes, many of whom being of Chinese or mixed race were very attractive. Many of these ladies liked to forge longer-term, often heavily discounted relationships with the Butterworth airmen. It was all very friendly and semi-permanent - and the RAF chaps usually got their frequent 'jollies' either free or 'on tick.' The irritant - or fly in the ointment so to speak, was that whenever a ship came into port the ladies had to go back to work rather than simply pleasuring their sybaritic boy friends, plying their trade with the lusty (and frequently diseased) seamen of the maritime nations of the world. The natural result of this was that within a few days of a ship leaving port, there was a lengthy queue of patients lining up on sick parade 'presenting' I believe is the modern term, with all the richly varied and classic symptoms of 'Cupid's measles.' At one stage the situation was said to be so bad that the RAF Medical Officer at Butterworth was obliged to reserve an entire carriage on each Monday morning's mail train to KL - filled with his patients destined for the venereal ward of the British Military Hospital at Kinrara. Some wag had painted a large banner which was proudly strung along the side of the coach, with the wording 'Blobbers' Express' for all the world to admire. Hence Blobbers' Club - ie. fully paid-up member and proud of it. I am sorry if any readers are distressed by these revelations, but historical accuracy dictates that such facts are not glossed over and brushed under the carpet.

Subsequently RAF Butterworth was handed over to the Australians and one can be reasonably certain that the RAAF continued with the hallowed traditions laid down by their predecessors from the mother country.

Note 18 - The Somersetshire song is sung to a mixture of tunes ie, *Ivan Skavinski Skavar* plus the chorus which like many service songs is hymn based, in this case on the popular crusader tune *Blessed Assurance*. The final 'chocks away' is sung as a *View Halloo* foxhunters' call.

*TS Somersetshire was a troopship on the Far East run both pre and post-WW2.

**The *Rodney*, *Nelson* and *Renown* were all major battleships of the Royal Navy. *HMS Hood*, a battlecruiser and the pride of the fleet, was sunk in action against the *Bismarck* in 1940 when a plunging German shell exploded in the main magazine, taking down with her my godfather, Lieut. 'Teddy' Lewis RN and her entire ship's complement (less three survivors). Many of the old songs of all three services have a cruel, heartless content which should never be taken literally, for as well as expressing a wry humour, there is also a rather savage element of pride in adversity.

*** SPs are RAF Police.

Note 19 - There are innumerable verses to this quite catchy tune. Most British servicemen of my time knew this song well along with many others. At their worst they were profoundly insulting to people such as the Egyptians who deeply resented the British anyway. At their best they carried witty words and tuneful traditional airs. British troops had always sung their own words to the Egyptian anthem, frequently leading to brawls with the local populace in public places such as cinemas. Although in September 1952 King Farouk had already abdicated (at the end of July), sailing into exile with Narriman his new queen, the king nevertheless was still popular with the fellahin, who also revered the memory of the beautiful (and generous) Farida.

Illustrative of the British soldier's attitude at that time is the story recounted to me a few years later by a friend, who as the wife of a soldier serving in Egypt had obtained a job with the British Army Claims Commission that dealt with Egyptian civilian disputes with the occupying forces. A British sergeant had been driving a military truck involved in a collision with an Egyptian royal car. Being asked to give evidence before the commission's Court of Enquiry, the sergeant spoke thus, 'Well, it was like this, see. There was this big Rolls Royce wiv these three Gippo geezers in it...' The major listening to the case interrupted, 'Sergeant, please do not refer to His Majesty King Farouk as a 'Gippo geezer.' Please re-phrase your evidence.' 'Oh, orl right then. It was like this see. There was this big black car wiv old Farouk an' these two other Gippo geezers in it.'

Note 20 - In the early months of 1952, anticipating the revolution that was to bring Nasser into power and force Farouk's abdication in July, the Egyptian gendarmerie had mutinied. In Ismailia itself, lightly armed police and militia had bravely defied the British Army and were swiftly slaughtered in a tank-led assault on their barracks, some fifty militiamen being killed for the loss of one British soldier. (A friend, now sadly dead, who was a national serviceman with a Lancashire regiment, took part in this engagement and told me that some of his fellow soldiers took pictures of each other, 'to send home to Mum,' smiling and joking, posing with their rifles like big-game hunters, one foot on the corpses of the slain gendarmerie). The Egyptian press hysterically accused the British of desecrating mosques and cemeteries and of 'great numbers of killed or wounded crucified on trees.' Predictably the aftermath resulted in rioting and looting in Cairo. BOAC planes were forcibly detained, Barclays Bank, Thomas Cook's, Shepheard's Hotel, the Turf Club, the British Council offices and W. H. Smith's bookshop, were all burned and destroyed. Several Britons were violently murdered, being deliberately left unprotected by both the police and the authorities. No, the British were definitely not popular in Egypt in 1952. We were confined to our ship, shore leave forbidden. Nobody complained.